They Gave Me a Hurricane

Action involving my flight of three – Pilot Officer Palliser, Sergeant Sheppard, Sergeant Rex. The final victory was witnessed and confirmed. (*Courtesy of Tom Neil*)

THEY GAVE ME A
HURRICANE

FROM FIGHTING IN THE BATTLE OF BRITAIN
TO THE DEFENCE OF MALTA AND SABOTAGE
IN SOUTH AFRICA

CHARLES 'TICH' PALLISER
DFC, AE

FOREWORD BY

WING COMMANDER TOM NEIL DFC*, AFC, AE
BRONZE STAR (USA) (RAF RETD)

Published in 2012 by Fighting High Ltd,
23 Hitchin Road, Stotfold, Hitchin, Herts, SG5 4HP
www.fightinghigh.com

Copyright © Fighting High Ltd 2012
Copyright text © Charles Palliser 2012

British Library Cataloguing in Publication Data.
A CIP record for this title is available from the
British Library.

ISBN – 13: 978-0956269683

Designed and typeset in Monotype Baskerville
11/14pt by Michael Lindley www.truthstudio.co.uk

Printed and bound by Toppan Printing Co. (SZ) Ltd.
Front cover design by Michael Lindley

*The author Charles Palliser died in September 2011. Charles's
manuscript was based on the notes he kept during the war, his
logbook and the recollections he recorded in recent years.
Unfortunately, during the editing and proof-reading phases of
this book, inconsistencies were discovered with regard to the spelling
of some of the less-well-known people in Charles's story. In such
cases, the most likely spelling has been adopted, where further
research has failed to provide a conclusive answer. The publisher
would be pleased to receive any suggestions for corrections.*

To my beloved wife of 63 years, Ruth,
and to my daughters Gill and Marianne

Contents

Foreword

When I was invited to write a foreword to this book, I found myself recalling, with some amusement, the old adage alleging that great gifts often arrive in small parcels. For the nation at large and those of us privileged to know and serve with Charles Palliser, he was one such parcel.

I first met 'Tich' Palliser towards the end of September 1940, when he arrived as one of three or four replacement pilots joining No. 249 Fighter Squadron, based at RAF North Weald in Essex. A small fresh-faced NCO, he was not especially notable.

As a bright young pilot officer of 19, I had been with 249 since its inception five months earlier, and, having fought through much of the Battle of Britain, although barely 20 years old myself, had achieved some sort of specious seniority and reputation. To me the 'young and callow Sergeant Palliser' was merely an inexperienced novice, qualifying, in my eyes anyway, for the slightly ignominious title I then bestowed on him of 'Tich'. Little did I know at the time that he was actually some months older than me, or that he would fly with such distinction in the months to come. It was also many years later that I was informed that he never really forgave me for my less than flattering reference to his lack of inches.

From the outset, it became obvious to all – including most of the officers in 249 – that Sergeant Palliser was a person of strong opinions, most of which he aired without restraint, one of them being that the NCOs of the squadron, like second-class citizens, were obliged to sleep under canvas while the officers of the unit lived 'luxuriously' in First World War wooden huts. Experience and a measure of success in later months, however, tempered his ire to such an extent that he accepted a commission in the spring of 1941 – to become a less vocal member of the officer class.

After his promotion and frequently while wearing his officer's Service

Dress hat at a jaunty angle, he was renowned for his merry quips almost as much as for his successes in the air, his prowess continuing in England for weeks before the squadron left for Malta in May 1941.

In Malta, condemned to fly obsolete Mark 1 Hurricanes against both the Italians and the Germans, 249 Squadron suffered grievously, resulting in many casualties. Despite being in a unit lumbered with inferior aircraft and much unserviceability, 'Tich' Palliser continued to prosper. In our monastic stone Officers' Mess at Torri Combo, RAF Ta'Qali, he lived in the next bedroom to me for almost nine months, so that, obliged to share the miseries of the summer heat in mosquito-ridden Malta, we came to know each other very well indeed.

After my own departure from the island on 29 December 1941, he continued to serve in 249 for some weeks, but was promoted and moved across to No. 605 Squadron at Hal Far after being awarded the DFC. Hearing later that he had been sent to South Africa on instructional duties, I then lost track of him for many years, although I did subsequently learn that he had married a delightful South African-born lady before moving finally to Australia.

In 1990, the 50th anniversary of the Battle of Britain, I met 'Tich' Palliser and other veterans of 249 at RAF North Weald. Looking much as he had done in 1940, but a little sleeker and a trifle rounder, he was his old self, a little less provocative perhaps, but voicing definite views of his own. And for many years thereafter we kept in touch, with a letter now and then, always a Christmas card, and very often a surprise telephone call from Black Rock, Australia.

Finally there came the faltering admission that he was growing old and failing more than a little in health. After that, the telephone calls became less frequent, until finally there was only silence and the distraught voice of his delightful, well-loved daughter, Gill.

Charles 'Tich', Palliser, an honest-to-God Geordie, was a good squadron pilot and a firm friend. This is *his* story, in which he graphically describes life as a fighter pilot during the early part of the war, although some of his descriptions of situations and events are not exactly as I remember them. However, he was a sound man, God bless him, who made a distinctive contribution to the achievements of No. 249 Squadron.

Wing Commander Tom Neil DFC*, AFC, AE, Bronze Star (USA) (RAF Retd)

Introduction

I will begin my story by giving an introduction to my early life, and the beginning of my destiny. My maternal grandfather was a maritime captain named Charles Calder, who sailed around the world on cargo ships. My maternal grandmother was a retired headmistress. My father was in engineering. We lived in a reasonably nice house and did not want for much. But by the time I reached the age of 7 years, my mother was finding taking care of her family a rather heavy chore. My grandparents suggested I join them on a sea voyage. My grandmother, Nanna Calder, approached the education authorities and assured them my education would not be interfered with. So, with great excitement, I boarded my grandfather's ship and commenced a wonderful three-week voyage to Amsterdam, Holland.

In Amsterdam two of the crew, who had begun to teach me the use of mercantile instruments, had been given permission by Captain Calder to take one of the small rowing boats to see some of the sights along the canals. They asked if I could join them. My Nanna jumped into the conversation and refused to let me go. After much discussion between my grandparents, with my Nanna worried that I may fall overboard, my grandfather's comment was: 'This lad has commenced his future. Like all of us, he has a destiny, which the Lord has mapped out for him. Let him go.'

Over the next couple of years two more journeys furthered my education. Then, after my 10th birthday, both my grandparents passed away. One month before my 16th birthday, and just at the time I was to commence my apprenticeship with Richardsons Westgarth, a maritime engineering company, a note was left on the table at home one morning. It advised me that my mother had left home. I was to live with friends of hers, Mr and Mrs Young, and their 3-year-old son. I moved into their house and they took care of me, as I collapsed in shock over what had happened to my family. After a year and a half my mother's brother, who was a maritime captain working with the 'Shell' company, returned home. He moved me into his house, where he and his wife, Aunt Lena, took care of me until I joined the air force.

Charles 'Tich' Palliser, DFC, AE (2011)

1. 'This Was For Us'

Long before the 1938 initial scare of Hitler on the move, four pals from school and the teenage years, Victor Bruce (Vic), Sydney Dawes (Syd), David Bennett (Dave) and myself, lived for and talked about aeroplanes. Anytime one of those small planes – De Havilland Moths, 'Tiger', 'Puss', 'Leopard', and so on – flew near to our town, Hartlepool, to land on our local airstrip, we would drop everything and cycle out to have a look. In mid-1937 the great day arrived with much excitement when Alan Cobham's Flying Circus flew into our local airstrip. For days we went mad, watching the many types of aircraft on display. The demonstrations were way beyond anything we had seen or even read about. We were allowed to look over and actually to touch an Avro 504K, which was being used to give spectators fifteen-minute flights around the circuit – something that exceeded our pocket money availability; however, to walk around this amazing machine, touching the control surfaces, wings and tail, and even grasping the propeller – this was for us!

Vic Bruce, a newly found older friend, Bill (Sticks) Gregory, and myself were really hooked on this flying game; however, Syd Dawes was looking at the strongly advertised Territorial Army Reserve, and David Bennett decided he would stick with his local bank career. We all had different vocations – David as a clerk in the bank, Syd in the town office timber company, Vic in the office of a shipping company and myself as a junior draftsman in a maritime engineering company. Bill Gregory, who was some years older than us, was a plasterer in his father's building business. His real claim to fame, though, was being a drummer in our local dance band – hence the name 'Sticks'. Despite the small age differences, we had great fun in those pre-war years, and we were all members of the local cricket and tennis clubs, as well as enjoying swimming, boating and fishing when we were not on the lookout for aeroplanes.

The year 1937 went by quickly; we had to pay attention to work responsibilities, as well as attending technical college and spending lots of

time studying. The rumours of Hitler's shouting and raving that had
bubbled to the surface, causing us some excitement, seemed to have died
down somewhat, and we drifted into 1938 with little on our minds but
work, fun and games, and of course an interest in girls. As the year
progressed, the news from the Continent revealed that Germany and
Mr Hitler were really creating problems, and German armed forces,
particularly their air force, were helping Franco in Spain to fight his war
against the Spanish government. Our engineering work was increasing –
we heard of aircraft factories being replanned and dispersed throughout
the country, warships being completed and launched, and a new and
bigger class of submarines (T Class) being built for future services.

'The pace was hotting up', as my chief put it, and we would all have
to put our backs into the general effort. I was now classed as a student
engineer and had been made an assistant in a new department,
designing and developing exhaust gas pressure (super) chargers for all
types of heavy duty diesel engines – more about this later.

Towards the end of 1938 the government had decided to build
operational airfields all over the country. A suitable area of land was to
be developed outside the village of Greatham, about 5 miles from our
town and adjacent to the Cerebos Salt factory, which was known
worldwide. This development brought the newly formed countrywide
organisation called 'CAGS' (Civil Air Guard Service) to our north-east
Yorkshire location, and with it came the commencement of flying
training for men and women as pilots and/or air crew, should war be
declared.

By the end of 1938 thoughts and discussions about the possibility of
Germany attacking Britain – us youngsters arguing and debating
whether we would be attacked or not – had cooled somewhat. The idea
of Germany attacking Britain was really preposterous, as we all felt that
we would be fighting alongside the Germans against the great 'Bear' –
Russia. However, be that as it may, at the beginning of 1939 the
announcement was conveyed by the media that No. 32 Elementary &
Reserve Flying Training School (E&RFTS) was to be established without
delay at Greatham Airfield and volunteers would be interviewed
forthwith, subject to health and academic qualifications, for pilots,
navigators and wireless operators/air gunners. Well! Vic Bruce contacted
me, yelling blue murder as he ran down the path to my home: 'They've
done it, they've done it! Come on, get on your bike and let's go.' Bill
Gregory screamed to a halt at the house in his Ford 8, hooting and

shouting – one would have thought that war had actually been declared. So one Saturday morning in early February 1939, three of us joined a queue hundreds of yards long outside a wooden office structure, which housed the newly appointed representatives of the Royal Air Force Volunteer Reserve (RAFVR). This group, a mixture of air force and civilian people, would administer and operate No. 32 E&RFTS. The officers in charge were Wing Commander Joly-de-Lotbinière RAF, assisted by a Major Orde ex-RFC. Imagine, although there were now three friends out of the original five, here we were looking at a door through which we were going to be taught to fly, and believe it or not, we would be paid for it. It was a dream come true – or so I thought!

Eventually, after a lifetime of waiting, pushing, shoving, shouting, threatening and otherwise playing the fool, we three were at the desk, facing the office staff, who were issuing forms for application to join the RAFVR. We were nearly there – though there were many questions to answer, first on the form, and thereafter before the examiners. Proceedings seemed to go well; Vic and Bill were through and were advised they would be called for further discussion in a few days. My form, completed in all detail, accurately and carefully, had been sent through to Major Orde, and I waited for what seemed like a lifetime finally to be called to his office. I was invited to sit down, and this tubby and reasonable sort of person looked at me over the top of his half glasses and said, 'Now, young fella, why do you want to join the air force?' I explained in every way possible. It had always been my dream! I had thought, talked and dreamed about aircraft development and flying, and wanted nothing else! He then explained very gently that, according to the information I had so carefully detailed on my application, I could not be accepted because of my being in an exempt occupation – engineering! I stuttered and argued, complained, suggested war was imminent, but Major Orde smiled and said, 'Sorry, son, good try but they are the rules. Next!'

Walking out of the building, I was screaming inside. Bill and Vic had gone, after a long time. Someone asked me if I was all right, saying I looked ill. I mounted my bicycle and rode home in a complete daze. It was the first knock-back I had ever suffered in my short life, although I knew what adversity meant. But I was determined that I was not going to stop trying. I realised now that I must not tell my plans to my friends in the office where I worked, and certainly not the head of the department, who would probably kick my backside.

I had, before the RAF first air school had opened or even been mentioned, applied to the Royal Navy Volunteer Reserve (RNVR) for submarine service, as the small department I was then working in was responsible for the design and manufacture of gas turbine pressure chargers (superchargers) for the diesel engines in the huge T Class submarines being built at Greenock – *Triumph, Tribune* and *Trident* – and Liverpool – *Thetis*. These pressure chargers were manufactured under licence from the Swiss firm of Brown Boveri. As a junior, I was a technical 'gofer' to the three senior engineers in the department, but it did spark much interest at the time, as it was very exciting to step aboard the underwater giants. Our efforts came to an end when Commander Pennington RN, to whom we were accountable, was killed on HMS *Thetis*. The whole of Britain was shaken by the loss of this boat, and I suffered much 'leg-pulling' from the men in the office, who remarked on my proposed application to the Navy (Subs) at that time. However, this had been before there had been any sign of a flying school being opened in our vicinity. No mention was made of reserved occupation. I had received an acknowledgement of my application to join the RNVR but nothing more, and when the RAFVR was announced I simply forgot about the Navy.

Now in 1939, having been knocked back by the RAFVR, I was more than fed up listening to Vic Bruce's and Bill Gregory's excited talks and discussions as to what they were doing in regard to aviation lectures and very short flying trips – this crazy pair really deafened me with their talk of achievements and potential possibilities. I was sickened by my inability to succeed in my efforts to join up and at the same time I could not allow this disappointment to interfere with my work in the specialised department. I had been very fortunate in passing exams that had allowed me to become a junior draftsman, and I would subsequently attain student engineer status in the department in which I was employed. Mr Tom Hall, the chief, was very highly qualified and a member of the Royal Aeronautical Society, as well as maritime societies. Jackson, a young 21-year-old, had worked on the 'Mercury-Mayo' composite design flying boat development of this quite radical aircraft attempt. Bill Jones, my direct chief, was a well-qualified mechanical and marine engineer and a remarkable design draftsman. These two, Bill Jones and Jackson, as well as pulling my leg about submarine service, now changed their interest to flying. Jackson's experience enabled him to explain to me the mysteries of the new fighter aircraft that were to be supplied to the Royal Air

Force; he spoke in depth about the Hawker 'Hurricane' fighter, which was the first of the monoplane aircraft capable of incredible speeds and performance, and fitted with eight guns, which could blow an enemy aircraft apart.

On a balmy May day in 1939 I was working with some of the engine fitters on a trial run of a new submarine pressure charger. The talk was all about war, and I let loose with my anger at the authorities who barred my applying to join the RAF, when one of them, not associated with my office, suggested that I apply as a 'labourer', which had no exemption qualifications and must get me through. Back to the recruitment office I went and once more filled in the forms, only this time I wrote 'labourer' in the job position. There was another long wait and then that dreaded request as before: 'Please wait, Major Orde would like to see you.' I was trembling like a leaf, making much effort to be calm as I hauled my 5'7" body into the presence of Major Orde. 'Palliser,' he said, 'there couldn't be another one. I thought I had seen the last of you.' I commenced some stammering reply, by which time I felt that my head was barely level with the top of his desk, but Major Orde shuffled a number of folders on his desk and asked me to sit down. His first remark hit me like a stone. 'What the hell is all this about, young fella. I've received more than enough applications from you. But what's this? You're now a ruddy labourer, heh?' This time my frustration showed. I endeavoured to tell him how and why and what I was trying to do, but it must have sounded like Swahili or Hindustani for all the understanding I was able to give. Major Orde, an old First World War veteran, could see how disturbed I was and came around the desk, put his hand on my shoulder and calmed me down in a true fatherly manner. Eventually I was able to convince him that I was going to join the RAF, no matter what, and that I was sorry about the deception. The Major then advised me that he would discuss my case with Wing Commander Joly-de-Lotbinière, who was the school commandant and would advise me as to what might be done. A further interview was arranged, and I was advised that, if I signed a document that placed all the responsibility on me, my application would be accepted. However, as there had been such a time lapse, I could be admitted only as a wireless operator or air gunner. I was told, however, that, as war was imminent, I would – as the weeks passed, and if war was declared – immediately be re-mustered to sergeant pilot status.

On 1 September 1939 we had all received instructions to be at the town headquarters early on Sunday morning, 3 September, where we

would listen to an announcement by Neville Chamberlain, our Prime
Minister. The excitement was electric – Major Orde with his ear glued
to the small portable radio and most of us clowning around swapping
wisecracks as to what we would do to old Hitler. The Luftwaffe had no
chance – in those days we were like a bunch of kids ready for glory, and
totally invincible.

2. 'Then the Marching Started'

We did not know or even expect that many of us would never see our 21st birthdays, or, for that matter, the end of 1940. We were all sergeant pilots, albeit under training, but who could stop us now! There were many others destined for positions as navigators or wireless operator/air gunners, all kicking up one hell of a noise as the Prime Minister concluded his speech with those dreaded words, 'We are now at war with Germany.' The Major proceeded to address us all as to what to expect in the days ahead. We listened to grave and sincere words from someone who had been there before. Gone was the silly chatter, laughter and joking as we heard the Major explain what the forthcoming conflict would or should mean to us. Suddenly the sun had stopped shining; we were looking at each other as the Major's words penetrated. This was going to be ugly; some of us might fail to qualify in the various categories; would-be pilots might become navigators, wireless operators or air gunners, and some might fail altogether and be relegated to other forces. No matter what, some of us would suffer hurt and some would lose their young lives. We had, at least at this moment, entered a new dimension of life from what we all had known. It was some time before the sound of voices was heard discussing the important inferences of the Major's talk.

As the day moved on and after we had been offered beer, light drinks and sandwiches, we dispersed to our various homes, just a little different from what we had been before the radio announcement. We were ordered to take care of our work and home affairs and report each day for information regarding our air force movements, and to expect to commence what would be our first journey to what had been described as Initial Training Wing (ITW).

I had lived with an aunt for most of my teens and I proudly arrived home to tell her that the big day had arrived and I would soon be on my way to win the war. 'Win the war!' she said. 'Damn it, you just don't know what war is!' And then, to my horror, she broke down and cried. 'Charles,' she said, 'you are 20. Why must all you youngsters have to go once again?' Her worry was twofold, as her husband, my uncle, was a maritime captain commanding a Shell oil tanker and would also be subject to great danger. She talked about the wonderful period from 1935 to 1939 when industry had revived in our area, many ships had been built and prosperity was everywhere. She reminded me of the good times I had enjoyed in my teens, playing tennis and cricket, swimming and fishing, and joining our girlfriends at dances and parties. We had had wonderful times in those years. But this time we were going to straighten out the world – make it an even better place in which to live! Forgive me, as I write, if my smile is something of a grimace! So, with most of my family in the maritime and Navy world, I was the first to join the Royal Air Force.

After two or three weeks of waiting around, attending parades and on lectures, and being advised by friends and relatives how best to organise myself, I received the order to report for posting to ITW.

The worst period had been explaining my actions to my work friends and heads of departments. My ultimate period of concern was when, on Monday 14 September, I arrived at the office of Richardsons Westgarth, the huge firm of marine and mechanical engineering manufacturers where I worked, and reported to the head of the department. I arrived at the office to be greeted by Mr Hall, who, with a huge smile on his face, turned from talking to Jones and Jackson and said to me, 'Now you little devil, war has been declared and we'll have to work bloody hard from now on.' I gulped hard and said, 'I'm leaving. I have joined the RAF.' Amid loud guffaws and much prodding and pushing, Bill Jones said, 'Well well, we've made a lot of humorous remarks but yours takes the prize. You cannot join up – you're in an exempt occupation.' Suffice to say I explained my movements over the previous months, which I had managed to keep quiet, apart from talk of the submarine service. As I produced proof of my commitment, the laughter ceased. Somehow news of my decision reached the company Chairman, who had the Managing Director escort me to his office. He asked me to sit, and looking down from a dizzy height, said, 'Do you fully understand what you have done to your future at a time when you are commencing a fine profession?' I answered, 'No Sir. However, I really want to fly and join the Royal Air Force.' After a short but fatherly lecture, he advised me that the company would support me to the limit, and, if my flying studies failed, I was to return to the company under a regulation that catered for such problems as I had created. He shook my hand and quietly said, 'Son, not many of my friends know this, but in the First World War I did exactly what you have done today.' So all obstacles were removed and my conscience was clear.

My aunt had bid me a tearful farewell at home, as I had insisted I wished to minimise the sad goodbye, particularly on a cold wintry railway station platform. It really was a most emotional scene when I arrived at the then West Hartlepool railway station. The crowds were incredible. There had probably not been so many people on a platform since the First World War. Whistles were blowing and guard's flags were waving and an uncanny quiet crept over the crowded platform as the train slowly moved out, and all goodbyes were said. We sat for a moment very quietly, as for once we all seemed lost for words. After we had watched the various families saying goodbyes, the sadness struck home, as I sat there in my seat at the window. This was indeed a big moment. We were leaving a lifestyle behind and we were actually going to war. What was going to happen to us? A door had closed on our teen years. The final years of the 1930s had been marvellous.

We started our journey south to our ITW at Hastings on the south coast of England, right on the English Channel between Brighton and Dover. The last view of Hartlepool Bay and the cold wintry North Sea vanished, and there was a little excitement as we passed the Cerebos Salt factory. Just over the fields was the last we would see of our local airfield and No. 32 E&RFTS ,where it had all begun, only a few months before. We were shunted through London and on to the south coast.

By the beginning of November 1939 we were billeted in an eleven-storey block of new apartments, along with many lads from all parts of Britain. These apartments, called Marine Court, were on the foreshore of Bex Hill, and overlooked the main promenade and the English Channel. Days passed, and 16 November 1939 saw us kitted out in full uniform; most of us had arrived in civilian clothes. The photographers did well, as each group was photographed, proudly displaying sergeant's stripes. The final act was to advise us of our RAF identity number: mine was 751910.

At our first introduction to our future programme, we stood with open mouths, watching aircrew who had arrived before us go through their marching and drill routines. The marching and drill NCOs were sergeants and corporals generally from RAF Uxbridge, and we listened in horror as all kinds of incoherent remarks hissed and bellowed from their mouths. 'How in the hell are we going to understand that language?', someone pleaded. Heaven knows! We knew that with a mix of men from all over the British Isles, we could expect a polyglot of accents, but the drill instructions were something else! We were advised that the next day (in mid-November) we would be on parade. We had never marched or drilled in our lives, except at school, and that was baby stuff compared to this. So next morning, immediately after breakfast, we walked up eleven flights of stairs (there were no lifts), made sure we were dressed correctly, and then walked down the stairs to be assembled in squads among what looked like hundreds of young lads. Then the marching started.

We were in the care of a Corporal McTaggart, a bright, smartly turned out chap who, to our amazement, had a head with a permanent lean to 'port' and also quite a husky voice. The introduction can well be imagined: we turned and twisted, bumped and stumbled, until I thought we would all die of shame. Then, after an hour or so, 'Mac' must have had relatives in heaven, for things began to take shape, and we were marching, turning, wheeling, halting, standing to attention, standing at ease – it was a sheer miracle, we all agreed. We never looked back and could not have enough of this treatment; physical training was the same. After a week we all felt like supermen and we could understand every syllable, word and movement of our beloved NCO instructors. Life was terrific! Some three weeks were given to RAF education. Drill and physical training were very intensive. However, there was time for winter sports – swimming, football, even a game or two of water polo, during which time we were under the jurisdiction of such famous sportsmen as Wally Hammond, Victor McGlouglan, and Len Harvey. There never a dull moment.

This period naturally had its funny occasions as well as more serious episodes. One piece of fun was perpetrated on a chum from Hartlepool, one 'Bowen', who was something of a grump and a little reserved. Ryan, who had been elected as squad senior, suggested the prank after an evening of dancing and merriment towards the end of November, when Bowen had refused to join us. Remember that there were eleven flights of stairs, it was now 2.00 a.m., there were very few lights on and a complete blackout of windows. Six of us tiptoed into our room, where Bowen was fast asleep. We altered the alarm to 6.00 a.m. and, remaining dressed, we yelled and pushed Bowen, rudely awakening him. We had included the lads in a room on the floor below in this fun. Once we had our roommate awake and rubbing his eyes, we yelled, 'Look, for heaven's sake, we've overslept.' And, with him looking at us in horror, we dashed out, downstairs, and into the room below. We waited for what seemed an eternity, and then down the stairs, cursing and swearing, three at a time, went Bowen. Up the stairs we ran, pulled off our clothes, and jumped into our beds. The shout as our air force chum ran out of the building into a pitch black cold winter morning, devoid of people, could have been heard across the Channel. Then we waited. After an age we heard footsteps dragging back up the stairs. The mumbling, gurgling and threats were horrifying, to say the least – suddenly the joke did not seem such a good idea – and then into the room burst Bowen, yelling, 'Who thought of this flaming joke? Come on. Own up. It was you, wasn't it?' I could just about smell his breath as I turned my head on the pillow to see his unwashed, unshaven countenance glaring into mine. The next thing my bedclothes were ripped off and, before anyone could move, he had yanked me out of bed on to the cold concrete floor and was knocking the hell out of me – I happened to be the smallest one in our group. In no time Ryan and the others grabbed the wronged recruit, dragged him to his bed and calmed him down – no mean effort. He was terribly hurt psychologically and I was in a mess physically. Nevertheless we all somehow eventually had a short sleep and managed to hit the parade on time the next morning, with lots of threats hanging over me – threats that never materialised.

About the end of November, while I was at lectures, I was called to the adjutant's office. This was like someone saying 'there's a policeman outside'. What had I done? I was asked to sit down and the adjutant shuffled some papers and asked me if I was happy in the RAF. 'Yes, Sir,' I said, 'Why?' 'Well,' he said, 'here are papers sent to us from your home to advise you to report to HMS *Calliope* in Newcastle for an interview re submarine training.' I had completely forgotten my application of 1938! To say I stuttered and panicked under the glare of this Wing Commander, who had eyebrows like a thorn hedge, is putting things mildly. However, eventually I calmed down and explained what had happened in those earlier days. The result was a direct question: 'Do you wish to do anything about the naval request?' 'No, definitely not Sir,' was my answer. He assured me that the air force would handle the documents and I never did hear anything more.

On 1 December we received our posting to No. 11 Elementary Flying

Training School (EFTS) at Scone (Perth), in Scotland. Groups were now being posted to these schools all over Britain. One somewhat entertaining experience occurred a few days before we left for Perth. We were summoned individually to attend an interview, conducted by a panel of senior RAF officers of Squadron Leader rank and greater, to ascertain which of us might, in the future, obtain a commission and officer status. I was asked questions on my work background, where I lived, my academic qualifications, general knowledge and finally sport. I felt as though I was back in school. Finally, the Squadron Leader leant forward and asked, 'What position do you play in football?' I replied, 'Right wing or half back.' 'Good grief, that's soccer! Don't you play rugby?' I told him that I had played a game or two but did not like the idea of my face being rearranged and had therefore given the game up. In any case I played more tennis, cricket and swimming and had had a crack at golf, so there had not been much time to be interested in football. The interview was terminated with my thinking, 'No commission for you, Palliser' and, until 1941, I was correct.

So we travelled to Perth. This was finally 'it'. It was indeed a journey into the unknown. The train trip can be remembered for its sheer dis-comfort. Despite our new issue greatcoats and full uniform, we positively froze. There was no heating, we were crammed into carriages, and we had to rely on station stops for food and drinks. The journey through London, Edinburgh and finally to Perth seemed to take for ever. A very miserable, freezing, hungry group of those who would win a war finally poured out of the train and were bussed to Scone (Perth) Airfield. What an anti-climax. There was snow all over the land and the wind blew straight through you. After being assembled and paraded to be checked in, we were marched into a large lecture room for a preliminary briefing.

Scone was the original airfield for Perth and consisted of a civilian flying club and two rows of dormitory houses – accommodation for would-be civil flyers in peacetime. These were brick units with no fires, but they were cosy if you clapped your hands and stamped your feet long enough. However, an issue of sheets and blankets offered some comfort. Finally came our introduction to the mess, which was the well-used lounge of the peacetime club. This eased our woes, and we gradually thawed out and relaxed. Our course was to be the twenty-third course in EFTS.

3. 'What a Sensation'

By the beginning of December 1939 we had accepted that this was truly the start of the most questionable phase of a new 'life'. The school was adapted for pilot training only and a course was already under training. By now other chaps had arrived from different ITWs and had commenced their flying training. Meeting such a cross section of young lads from all parts of the British Isles, we had plenty to talk about. At a preliminary meeting we were allocated to 'flights'. For training we would have a number of instructors for both ground subjects and flying. We were allocated accommodation in the houses or units, six to a unit, and consequently we once again met new friends with whom to swap yarns, problems and interests.

The accommodation was soon sorted out, with few complaints. Each room had two beds and enough cupboard space to hold our clothing. We still had some civilian clothing, although it was understood this could not be used except on leave. Each unit would cater for our sleeping and studies. Food, relaxation and discussions would be in the civilian main building lounge, which was most acceptable and very comfortable.

There were now thirty-four sergeants on our course, which was classified as No. 23. Much to my regret I cannot remember the names of the chief instructor commanding the school nor the ground instructors, who changed from time to time, but never at any time could we complain that lectures were dull and boring. But I do remember the name of our instructor in navigation and theory of flight, Mr Dobell, a short, tubby, baldish gentleman, who had been an instructor for many years with the civil school – a man who was a master in navigation theory and could converse on other subjects taught. He was an expert in rhetoric, told a good joke or two about flying and pupils he had taught. He also had a 'degree' in sarcasm, which offered us no harm. Some of the course members thought they knew it all and were as cocky as hell. It must be understood that we were now thoroughly mixed – some of us, like myself, had only started in the Volunteer Reserve (VR) in mid-1939, whereas others had been in the VR for a number of years. In fact one pupil had actually reached 'wings' standard when he joined course No. 22, ahead of us. Regulations were that we all had to start from scratch, regardless of prior experience, and the course was of peacetime Royal Air Force standard.

The volume of merriment and high spirits that had been our lot since ITW had diminished somewhat, now that we faced the reality of what was ahead. The cold, uncharitable winter on this rather bleak airfield was introducing many different feelings among us. Some were questioning whether or not they had chosen the right service – what would happen if they failed the course? One or two wondered if the Navy or Army would have been better. Who would be chosen for fighter training? Who would prefer Bomber or Coastal Command? Could we actually learn to fly successfully? What about accidents? Now our young minds were unconsciously seeking guidance of some sort.

We sat through lectures by various high-ranking officers of the RAF and one or two from Army generals, all instilling in us the glory of war, Empire, Britain, King and Country. One particular general of First World War fame was General Carton-de-Wytte VC, who, throughout his bloodthirsty presentation, reiterated with regularity that 'the Germans were too damned militarised and subservient to their leaders'. Also, 'the only good German was a dead one'. However, thank God, we think differently today. He then proceeded to explain the bloodthirsty bayonet fighting in the trenches of the First World War. No wonder we thought that, after all, the RAF was a much cleaner and more acceptable operation.

On 4 December, the day commenced with an assembly, during which we were advised that our theory class allocations would be programmed to relate to our flying instruction periods. Weather would obviously play an important part in this respect. Lectures contained the following subjects: Aircraft Engines, Aircraft Rigging, Air Navigation, Armament, Airmanship, Theory of Flight, Administration, Morse Code (Aldis Lamp). One can imagine how this list would have taken our breath away, as, apart from some administration and engines, most of us lads had no experience other than office, clerical, maritime and some engineering work. Now we had no time to worry, as it was explained that our education qualifications had allowed us 'pilot under training' status and it was up to us to work hard and assimilate. The instructors now with the school were up to the job, and hours of work and study were unlimited and in our own hands.

Some of the Romeos had already ventured into Perth city and established their bona fides in the Salutation Hotel, which was to become our favourite watering hole. The attitude of some of our cleverer types was quite simple. We are in uniform – RAF pilots of the future! There is a war on! If we can fly, why study? We soon learned why, when our briefing concluded with these ominous words: 'The initial course will conclude on 23 April 1940. The theory marks for the course will be a pass at 60 per cent and there will be a mid-term examination with a pass of 50 per cent. However, there will also be a mid, mid-term exam, at which time you will be assessed as to whether you are trying or not.' If any person failed the course at any time – this included flying assessment – he would have the opportunity to re-muster to navigator or wireless operator/air gunner status. The next alternative would be for transfer to the Army or whatever the failed person could accept.

So, on 5 December 1939, we were paraded in a hangar and issued with Sidcott flying suits, helmets, goggles, and hearing tubes (Gosports), which had to be fitted to our headgear in order for us to communicate. We were led to the parachute section, where we were instructed in the fitting and operation of this life-saving equipment, and then issued with a numbered parachute for which we were responsible. Finally we were split into small groups and introduced to our various flying instructors. Flight Lieutenant Holmes was to be my first instructor, and it is impossible to express my inner feelings when we were introduced and he commenced his introductory talk. The thrill and internal emotion were such that I hardly understood the first few minutes of his talk. I was listening to the first genuine (with wings) flying officer of the Royal Air Force I had come across, and my mind was miles away. However, my stupid vacant expression or whatever else I exuded was blown away when I was asked, 'Any questions?' What a question! Raw civilian youths who were only a few years into whatever academic path they had chosen, here we were standing next to what looked to us like the 'Holy Grail' and we were about to fly! We were literally struck dumb in the presence of this knight of the air.

Once we had changed, out of the hangar we waddled, thankfully clothed in our flying clobber and on to the tarmac and over to the flying machines 'DH82A'. If you are American, you would be impressed at such a number. However, these aircraft were Tiger Moths – 'Hell's Angels here we come!' By now we were standing next to this magnificent aircraft, three or four to each machine, and the instructor was ready to launch us on our new career. Then we noticed the cold! It was mid-morning on 5 December and it was cold! There was light snow on the tarmac and a reasonable wind blowing over the surrounding hills and mountains straight from the North Pole. 'Stop stomping your ruddy feet and keep still while I'm explaining the introduction to flying,' said Flight Lieutenant Holmes. We huddled closer, eyes starting to stream, ear tips frozen, flying helmets in our hands, teeth chattering. North Yorkshire was not as cold as this, or was it? At least the snow here was crisp and clean. We walked round and round the Tiger Moth, climbed on to the wing with our instructor pointing, holding and moving parts of the aircraft and explaining where, why and how it all worked.

After an hour of discussion, Flight Lieutenant Holmes turned to me and told me to get ready for what he termed a familiarisation flight. The others were to return to the lecture rooms and would be recalled in turn. I stood there, my mind boggling at the thought of leaving the ground for the first time. Flight Lieutenant Holmes turned to me and explained, 'You will now get into the rear cockpit. I shall be in the front, which in this aircraft is for the instructor.' My shivering got to him. He said, 'Say, lad, are you scared. Haven't you experienced flying in the VR?' I explained to him that there had been too much red tape to get around before and after I had finally been accepted, so I had missed out. I also explained that I was shivering because I was damned cold, and elated that I was entering the realm of 'flight'. Holmes laughed and told me not to worry, then proceeded to show me how to buckle on my parachute and, once I was sitting in the cockpit, how to manipulate the harness to hold me in the aircraft. I just could not believe what was happening.

Then, having shown me and explained the controls of the Tiger Moth, Holmes started to teach me how these features moved by use of the control column or 'joy stick' – ailerons, elevators and rudder. I watched as the propeller was swinging and listened to the back and forth instructions between the mechanic swinging the propeller and Holmes positioning switches and throttle settings. Soon the propeller was rotating and the wind was blasting across our heads. Then through the speaking tubes between my flying helmet and the aircraft tubes I heard Holmes as he advised that we would now taxi out to the runway and take off on this, my first flight ever, for what was termed 'familiarisation'.

In no time at all we were on the runway facing into the wind and then ice cold wind was buffeting my head and shoulders – my goggles were already down and my eyes protected – and we were airborne. What a sensation: ground receding, aircraft bouncing about, and climbing towards the cloud layer. Holmes's voice boomed in my ears despite the racket, first telling me to look around and notice features on the ground and all around, and then drawing my attention to the instruments: engine revs, altimeter, oil pressure, the important 'turn and bank indicator', which shows the relationship of the aircraft to the horizon, then the compass for navigation, and finally the throttle and fuel mixture controls.

After a period of flying around at about 2,000 feet altitude, and when Holmes had flown over the city of Perth and pointed out various landmarks, he asked me to place my feet on the rudder bar and my hands on the 'stick' (the name for the control column). 'Now,' he said, 'I want you to look ahead to the horizon and follow me through various movements of throttle, stick and rudder.' For about 15 minutes we worked together, moving the controls to make the aircraft climb and dive, and then turn by controlled movement of the stick to left and right, with slight rudder movements to avoid 'slip' or 'skid'. Most of these rather gentle movements were achieved with the throttle at cruising revs. Manipulation concerning increased or decreased throttle (engine revolutions) would be explained in subsequent flights. By now I was in a great state of excitement. At the end of this initial lesson Holmes explained that, as I appeared to have a good light touch, he wanted me to take over and try the initial movement as he had shown me. Now he said, 'When I tell you that "you have got her", you must understand that you are now in control and I have relinquished my control altogether, and you must immediately say, "I've got her Sir". When you hand the control back to me I will say, "I've got her", and you will repeat, "you've got her Sir". This assures both of us who is flying the aircraft.' And this is how we finished my first flying lesson. Flight Lieutenant Holmes had gently corrected my hand and feet movements and throttle control as we turned, reduced and gained height, and I was able to understand and respond without difficulty. We returned to Scone and he landed and taxied in to enable the next pupil to commence.

I was in cloud cuckoo land. It was my first flight and it was absolutely fantastic. I was ten feet tall. I had fulfilled my dream. I had flown an aeroplane! Flight Lieutenant Holmes soon brought me to earth with a shout over the aircraft noise of 'Off to the lecture rooms now and return your parachute.' Other pupils waiting for their flights were asking how it felt. Was I sick? Was I scared? All kinds of questions. I could only grin like a Cheshire cat and repeat, 'marvellous'. I had experienced many sea voyages with my grandfather, Captain Calder, and had been allowed short stints at the helm of a steam ship. I had attended a number of engine tests on ships at sea, in my work in engineering before joining the service. These had brought thrills and feelings of achievement. However, this was something else! This was the greatest thrill of my life: I had been in control of an aircraft!

So back to lectures with Mr Dobell, our introductory teacher, who introduced us to the length and breadth of the theoretical subjects that I have already mentioned. We were advised that the course was a tough one, with various hours being allocated relative to the priority of the subjects. Our time for study was our total responsibility and, as at college, if we were stuck or uncertain, we had to ask questions and study the subjects in our own time.

There would be time for sport and time for visiting Perth. However, the exams would be set for a quarter-term, half-term and full-term sitting. Failure to pass the laid-down percentages in any of the three exams would mean relegation to other grades of flying or ground duties, or transfer to other services.. This information was taken seriously by most of us. However, there had to be some who would claim to know it all, and, indeed, two or three were quite loud in their feelings in regard to studies: what was required for pilots was to fly, not to be academics. But we had been warned! Air Navigation, Rigging, Armament, Theory of Flight, Aircraft Engines – these were tough and serious subjects.

Over the next couple of days, flying continued with the mornings cold, clear and crisp, and the covering of night snow was dry and hard. Flight Lieutenant Holmes was as ever his serious but pleasant self. There were more discussions on aspects of flying and also the strengths and weaknesses of this marvellous small aircraft, DH82A (Tiger Moth). To me it looked exactly like the First World War fighter aircraft. Once again we were taxiing out for take-off, and this time Holmes asked me to place my feet on the rudder bar and my hands on the stick very lightly, and follow and absorb the movements. However, at the same time I should notice the altitude of the aircraft.

By the time we had our third flight I was confidently relating to the controls and aircraft altitude, as Holmes allowed me more control. We did a number of runs across the field taxiing, stick back, feet firmly on the rudder bar, swinging the aircraft nose from right to left in order to see clearly where other aircraft were, as well as possible ground obstructions. The Tiger Moth did not have brakes. However, it was fitted with a tail skid, which dragged across the ground and performed as a brake once the engine throttle was decreased.

Straight and level controlled flight was the next lesson, after I had experienced the movements of the controls during take-off. It was amazing how delicate the reaction was to the flying controls. Stick to the left, and up would come the starboard wing. Stick to the right, and down would go the starboard wing and up would come the port wing. Stick forward, and down would go the nose. Stick back, and up would come the nose, and, if you were bloody minded and too ham-fisted, many things happened to your guts. Then came the coordinated movement of keeping the stick steady, holding the nose on the horizon and neither gaining nor losing altitude. Move the stick gently to the left using a light pressure on the left rudder to stop the nose swinging to the right and upward, and the aircraft would start to turn, smoothly.

My thoughts strayed to the days when I had taken my first lessons in driving a motor car –very exciting days as my confidence improved, until I was ticked off for attempting to speed. However, when I had received my licence in 1937, I was on top of the world. Now I was sitting in the cockpit of an aircraft, and I was actually flying and controlling the flight – the feeling was indescribable.

As we returned to the aerodrome, Holmes once again asked me to place my hands and feet on the controls and follow him through the landing. As we glided into the wind with the engine ticking over, he explained briefly the speed of approach and the necessity of keeping the speed constant and the aircraft straight. Most importantly, as we neared the ground, I should look over the nose to the left, looking past Holmes's shoulder to the ground ahead, and sense the proximity of the approaching ground, and feel the gentle levelling-out through the elevator controls until the final closing of the throttle. Then the stick was brought back into the tummy and a three-point landing was achieved. Holmes then suggested I taxi in, taking care. This was another thrill of control. Although only three days had passed, the intensity of attention necessary to understand all that was going on around me in respect to this new wonder of flying made me exhausted trying to absorb it all.

So, the daily routine developed, with flying in the mornings and lectures in the afternoons. We were very much at home in the school and had now met and conversed with those chaps on our Senior Course 22, who appeared to be veterans. Soon we were parading, marching to our various instructors for flying and reporting in controlled groups for lectures. Evenings were spent in the Flying Club lounge, which was very comfortable and spacious, so that one could study quietly without interference, or alternatively retire to the billet.

There were two courses under training at any one time and those on the Senior Course 22 were always as keen to communicate with us as we were with them. Soon we were enjoying some of our leisure time playing cards, darts, bridge, snooker, and so on, or exchanging personal interests with each other. Great interest centred around where we lived and what our civilian work was. One can imagine the representation from the many counties of England, Scotland, Wales and Ireland – sometimes the conversation was like bedlam. This communication development was dampened a little by warnings of interference with studies. We were requested to remember the importance of our service responsibilities and at least wait until we had passed our mid-term examinations, after which we might relax a little. The warning precipitated further assistance to us, as the senior course lads became more interested in discussing with us their experiences of exams and flying lessons. The response to this was very good, although one or two decided they knew better.

We could feel and notice the change in us. Subjects in lectures that had been strange to us were now discussed in depth and with great interest. The flying was always the most exciting topic, particularly with lessons in taking off, climbing, gliding, stalling and the various turns and manœuvres. Then came the day when we were all learning taking off – watch the wind direction. Then with the engine throttled back came the approach to landing. The discussions on progress sounded like a cage of parrots, so excited were we all. We were also thrilled with the way our ground lectures were dovetailing with our flying lessons. We were beginning to be different people. Civilian work and home activities were rarely mentioned, and nothing existed outside of flying. The second week of December saw us all as keen as mustard, our upper air flying like turns, gliding, climbing, stalls, spins and general manœuvring giving us confidence in handling the aircraft. We were not exactly on cloud nine, but we were close.

4. Solo

It was 16 December 1939. I had had three days of concentrated take-offs and landings, and now I found myself gritting my teeth with excitement, on a nice gliding approach to the airfield, Flight Lieutenant Holmes not saying a word to me. I levelled off nicely and succeeded in yet another good landing. I taxied back to where the aircraft were parked and was about to climb out of my aircraft when Holmes, who was already on the ground, laid his hand on my shoulder and said, 'Palliser, that was very good, just as the landings were yesterday. I suggest you now taxi to the take-off point and do one circuit and landing, and return here. I shall be watching you.' Yes! At last, after 6 hours and 35 minutes (not bad), this was to be my first solo flight.

Now I was taxiing out, no large body in the front cockpit, no voices of instruction. Swing the nose right to left, watch where you are going, look around carefully to be sure the area is clear, nobody on the landing approach, turn into wind and now, as all the checks have been doubly made, open the throttle slowly, feet firmly on the rudder bar, keep the aircraft straight. Stick back, full throttle now, stick slowly forward, speed increasing, position stick to raise the tail into flying position, not too far – the nose must not be down. The speed builds up and gently the aircraft leaves the ground – hold the throttle position and climb, stick slightly back, keep looking around to make sure you are straight – climb to 1,000 feet and level off. Turn left, medium turn, stick and rudder nicely balanced, throttle back to cruising revs – look at the airfield over your shoulder. Now in the position as taught, another turn to the left (port), now we are on the down wind leg.

Look around – be loose, watch for other aircraft. Now the airfield is sliding past your left shoulder. Watch your height – still 1,000 feet. Airfield is now behind you, so another turn to port of 90 degrees. You now pick your landing patch, reduce your airspeed and reduce your height to 500 feet – engine revs still reduced, airspeed 70 mph at 500 feet.

Keep up your speed and study your descent. Reduce speed to 60 mph, steady on the controls, stick and rudder, wings level. Watch the ground ahead and commence levelling out at 100 feet to 50 feet and now concentrate on the 'flair out', that curve that the aircraft must make from gliding angle to landing position. Level the aircraft as you see the ground very close, throttle back, hold the stick back and complete the landing. Hold the aircraft straight until the run ceases. Now turn off the landing path and proceed to the parking area, where Flight Lieutenant Holmes is waiting.

I wanted to scream, shout, sing – anything to release the 'pent-up' feeling that every 'first solo' lad must have. Yes!! I have gone solo!!

Great excitement in the mess that evening, as well as much leg pulling during lectures. It appeared I was the first solo in a time of 6 hours, 35 minutes. This cost me a few noggins at the bar. The atmosphere among the course was really exciting, as quite a number of the lads were obviously ready for solo, which really strengthened the latent character that was there.

By mid-December we had visited the city of Perth and done the rounds of the shops, cinemas and pubs. We found the ice rink at last, and this was to become our number two entertainment – most of us were good at roller skating but had no experience of ice skating, despite the fact that quite a few of us lived in the northern counties of Yorkshire, Lancashire, Durham and Cumberland, where we were quite used to snow and the slush that came with it. Our number one venue was the Salutation Hotel, which developed into the most popular place of fun and relaxation. The locals were great people, and their hospitality was wonderful. People were very friendly and were interested in what we were doing. Communication was good until the propaganda campaign advised us: 'Careless talk costs lives.' Yes, the war had started.

The weather was cold and the wind blustery. However, this added to our experience of flying, particularly in open cockpits. As we reached the middle of January there were some days when wind, snow and heavy clouds made flying impossible. The ground lecturers enjoyed this, as they could concentrate on important lectures, particularly Navigation, Theory of Flight, Engines, and Rigging of Biplanes. The latter was important, as most of the pre-war aircraft had two wings, which were held together by metal struts under the name of 'rigging'. This went right back to the First World War. The monoplane development had achieved recognition only in 1935, when the Hawker Hurricane was

accepted, and in 1936, when the renowned Spitfire was launched. These
last two aircraft were the future fighters that were to save Britain – but
would we ever get that far? Guns were next on the important list, and we
would eventually spend many hours on the subjects of the Vickers 'K'
.303 portable machine gun and most importantly the Browning 303,
which was mounted and fixed into the newer fighter and bomber
aircraft.

During this bad weather period we noticed the continued arrival and
departures of various types of mysterious aircraft, which were parked
quite a distance from our activities. Our curiosity was satisfied when a
large aircraft with three engines appeared on the airfield. This was
something the likes of which we had never seen; to us it was gigantic. At
this stage the powers that be announced that this was a French
Dewoitine trimotor airliner, and it was ferrying a number of RAF fighter
pilots to Finland. Naval aircraft carriers were on the way, carrying
Gloster Gladiator biplanes to help the Finnish Air Force to fight against
Russia in the north. This is another grim story of the very beginning of
the Second World War. After this episode, nothing more was heard of
these movements.

The weather worsened. Snow, hail and winds created blizzards such
as we had never seen before. Flying took a back seat, and lectures
intensified. Christmas was celebrated in Perth, and the locals provided
some really good Christmas cheer. One or two lads were allowed home
leave; however, for a few days only, as lectures and study were para-
mount. The civilian authorities laid on a very good Christmas Day meal,
and the big log fires in the club rooms were well tended, which allowed
us to be very comfortable. Arrangements were made to supply transport
into Perth in the late afternoons, and those who did not have their own
transport welcomed this. So Christmas and New Year came and went
and, although our families and homes were always in our thoughts, we
understood what our responsibilities were.

The New Year of 1940 in fact came in with some merriment, as our
friends at the Salutation gathered to make sure we were not homesick.
For the first time I tried Scotch whisky, thinking that, as we were dining
so well, there would be little or no effect. The evening was certainly
boisterous, and the girls had us learning the Scottish dances and reels.
Reels were plentiful as I remember, because, along with a few more of
our course battlers, I was reeling like a ship under full sail. Heaven knows
what we did or did not do on that New Year's Eve! I was awakened at

4.00 a.m. on 1 January by one of my roommates, who was yelling about my snoring capabilities and the fact that I smelt like a distillery. It was only two days later that our efforts to enjoy ourselves were summarised by our now very good friends at the Sally! Two of our lads had disappeared singing their hearts out and had been followed by some older kinder friends. The two had deviated from the street to walk by the River Tay and both had jumped in, as they said, to cool off. The men following had a hell of a job to get them out and persuade them to return to the pub, still singing 'I Belong to Glasgow'. Others had been taken back to the airfield by hotel guests, who excelled themselves as far as friendly gestures were concerned. I was taken back by one of my roommates, who owned a car and was old enough not to drink so much. He explained that they had not been able to get me out of the pub until I had sung all of 'Ilkley Moor Baht Tat' and 'Lay my Head beneath a Rose'. My friends said that it was when I decided to give them 'Oh for the Wings of a Dove' that they had helped me into the car. His first stop was the Tay Bridge, where I apparently deposited my wonderful dinner along with my very first alcoholic drinks into the River Tay. I didn't have to look in a dictionary to find out what my first hangover meant!

Two or three days later I had occasion to return to the Sally again, to apologise for my behaviour. This was accepted in good grace; however, the leg pulling, particularly from the girls, caused my ultimate discomfort, and I actually blushed! When you hear calls from women of 'Never mind laddie, he's only a wee boy', it doesn't do much for one's ego. Never again, said I, and got on with the studies.

With the shocking weather continuing, on 10 January I was told by the adjutant that he had noticed my birth date and I could have a few days leave to go home. By this date I had joined in a card school with some of the senior course who were close to finishing their course and would be posted to Advanced Training Units, where they would be flying more advanced training aircraft such as Miles Master I or Harvards or Oxfords or Ansons, the latter being trainers for bomber pilots. In the course of playing cards, which by now was poker, I had won £25 from one of the senior course chaps. When the news came for his posting, he told me he could not pay me the money he owed. I had lost and won in these games, but, as luck would have it, I was winning more than losing. I told him it did not matter, and he could pay me what he could and forget the rest. He told me he would see me about it in a few days, when his actual posting came through. The day before this lad was to leave, he called me and made the proposition that, if I would accept his old 1936 Morris 8 motor car, he would consider his debt paid. I remonstrated with him and endeavoured to refuse. However, his reply was, 'Look, I've been posted to Wick in the north of Scotland and from there heaven knows what I shall be doing.' One other thing he said was, 'I don't believe it will get me to Wick, so that's the deal.' I accepted. So I became the owner of a Morris 8 that needed some work on it. Some of the lads thought the car was a great 'deal', as cars were scarce and we used the buses, or any transport we could organise.

Before taking my leave, a big party had been arranged at the ice rink, and my friends became very friendly now I had a car. However, I had arranged to take a girl with whom I was slightly friendly, to a village dance in a village about 5 miles from the airfield. This caused lots of misery, but Jock, a roommate, had a bright idea. He would run me to the village of Bellbegie to meet my friend and then he would drive back, pick up the gang and join the party at the ice rink. He would then pick me up at midnight so I could drive the girl home. We had a good evening, now and again walking outside to cool off and watch the snow fall more and more heavily. Finally, we left, in order for the girl to return home and for me to return to Scone Airfield. However, my car was not outside, which was a grim let-down. Now we had to walk along a country lane leading to the main road. However, it was in a 30-degree direction towards the airfield. But, the snow was falling and both on the lane and in the fields it was about two feet thick.

Cursing my damned friends, we plodded off on a slightly scary journey. Thank the Lord I had my greatcoat and cap. We both eventually looked like walking snow statues. As we walked we cracked jokes, and I joined in some Scottish ditties and discussed what I should do to my so-called friends. After a mile, the girl said in her Scottish brogue, 'It's no far noo – the house is a wee bit off the road but there's a light on the door.' After another 30 minutes we reached the gate to her house, which was about 200 yards up the field. The kind lass asked, 'Would you be having a wee drink?' But thinking of shotguns and annoyed parents, I replied, 'No thanks.' However, I did ask, 'Where in heaven's name is the way back to the airfield?' Thank God the snow had stopped and the stars were visible. The girl pointed to a big clump of trees and said, 'Head towards them. There are a few fences to climb, but keep on in that direction and you will find the main road.' Needless to say, I negotiated fields, fences, and animals buried in snow drifts and arrived on base some

$4^1/_2$ hours later, really 'brassed off' and ready for trouble. My only satisfaction was taking off my snow-covered clothes, whipping off my friends' bed sheets, and dumping the lot into a couple of warm beds. The discussion the next morning was really heavy and not printable.

5. A Spirit of Purpose

The senior course moved off in the following weeks, but not before some great excitement. One lad on the course had failed completely and he was so upset that he had threatened to commit suicide. Apparently this lad saw the postings come through and had been placed in the sick bay attended by some medical orderlies. All hell was let loose when one morning we were told that the sick chap who had been failed had jumped into a Tiger Moth that was ready for the day's flight, and had attempted to fly home – somewhere in the English Midlands. He had force-landed in some field, absolutely lost, and was now in the custody of the military police. Heaven help him! We later learned he had been court-martialled and committed to the infamous 'Glass House' at Aldershot, and that was the last we heard of him. This incident really startled us all, as some of our course who had ignored warnings about exam failures now realised what failure could lead to – not necessarily the Glass House, but simply OUT!

Life went on and by 11 January 1940 the weather had cleared, and now all competitive talk was about going solo. We had settled down well and had developed a steady routine of flying, ground subjects, drill and some sporting activities. This included cross-country runs, which made us truly grateful we had done so much marching drill and physical training at our ITW in Bex Hill – and certainly the beginning of September seemed years away! The weather was still pretty grim and there was a break of a few days in the lecture programme.

As mentioned above, I was granted a few days' leave as it was my 21st birthday on 11 January. This gave me the opportunity to try out the wee Morris 8 I had acquired and also to test my driving skills, as I was not used to long-distance driving through strange countryside. So off I went, with a canister of petrol as well as a full tank. I reached Edinburgh without problems, although it was no fun driving. I drove through snow blizzards very carefully, then on to Newcastle and down the coast to Hartlepool.

Between Edinburgh and Newcastle, as I was still travelling over the bleak hilly countryside of the Cheviot Hills with little sign of civilisation, the car engine started to cough and splutter and I quickly checked the fuel gauge and noticed the dreaded sign – the needle was bouncing around the empty mark. It was round about midday, but the snow and sleet made visibility very bad. Never mind, I had the emergency can of petrol, so I ran the car on to the grass verge clear of the road and prayed there were no idiots driving at high speed. Taking the can of petrol and removing the cover to the tank, I endeavoured to pour petrol in but could not get the tip of the can anywhere near the tank because of the spare wheel bolted on the rear of the car. Luckily there was a spanner available. Off came the wheel and I rested it on the rear of the car. Then I could pour the petrol in without loss.

When all the petrol was in the tank, I was now covered in snow and sleet, with fingers blue with cold in the howling wind; it was truly frightening. I got into the car with the can, shut the door, turned the key and, after a few hair-raising coughs and splutters, the engine started. I blew on my hands, brushed the sleet and snow off my face and eyes, then selected the gear and moved off in the car, forgetting the spare wheel. As luck would have it, as I drove through Newcastle the weather lifted and I was nearly home. Entering Hartlepool, I decided to fill up with petrol ready for a few visits to friends. I reached for the petrol pump hose while the mechanic was looking at my filthy car. He asked, 'Where the hell have you come from?' I answered that I had come from Perth in Scotland. 'Hell,' he said, 'you without a spare wheel – you must be mad!' I will leave the story there – but it cost me money and much pride. Needless to say I had a few great days visiting many friends, although not all of them, because my long-time friends were also now in the forces and so were not at home. The return to Perth was much easier, as the weather had improved and I had another spare wheel.

Then we were back to lectures and drill, and also various sports, as the weather was still too bad for flying. We were now into our sixth week at the flying school and I am sure we now knew that we were in a different life altogether. The news we were receiving about the war, the knowledge of what was expected from us, and our progress in flying and lectures had imbued in most of us a spirit of purpose. The rest of January was relegated to full-time ground lectures and studies. We were encouraged to form small groups either in the lecture rooms after hours, or in our own billets or the flying school lounge. Our future was really in our own hands. We had already been told of two or three failures in the senior course, whose members had now completed elementary training and were off to advanced training. It was not too difficult for us to see who our failures were going to be. However, 75 per cent of us had our heads down, making our instructors and lecturers very happy. It would be 12 February before we would be flying again, so atrocious was the weather. However, we knew we needed this time, as our mid-term exams had come and gone, and three of the smart types who had opted for fun and nonsense were on their way to some army unit.

The lectures that were quite new to us all were Rigging (Biplanes), Theory of Flight, Administration, Signals (Morse and Aldis) and Guns. The latter was mainly concerned with the Vickers 'K' and the Browning 303s, which were common to the aircraft. For the guns, we were expected to strip them and then assemble and name the various components. There was also the practical application of firing them, for which we had only the Vickers 'K'. This took place on a range at the far side of the airfield and, as I recall, the weather allowed us only one day for firing. The butts were set up, and the Vickers 'K' mounted on a tripod and made ready for firing. The noise made you really jump, until you became deaf and insensitive to the racket. Some of the lads did very well and some shut their eyes and let go. Nevertheless, the idea was appreciated. Although I had fired 12-bore shotguns and .22 rifles, the Vickers 'K' had a rear sight and a single foresight. When it came to my turn, I sat on the seat, held the gun handles and pressed the trigger. After a short burst to feel the gun's reaction, I fired a long burst at the target, but noticed I was not hitting the thing at all. Then a heavy hand came down on my shoulder and a booming voice yelled 'Stop!' I stopped, looked up and saw the red and very annoyed face of the instructor, who said, 'What the hell are you doing? Have you never fired over sights before?' To which I replied, 'Yes, Sir, but I don't understand.' 'Move off', he said, 'and I'll show you.' He sat down, aimed the gun, and the following burst saw bullets bouncing off the concrete apron about 30 yards from the gun, and ricochet across the open country. The instructor stopped firing and was about to speak to me when the long foresight fell off the barrel. Nobody laughed. The instructor stood up, looked at the gun and said, 'Look at this, the foresight has dropped off.' And so it happened that the foresight was loose and had worked up the holding socket. Consequently the gun was depressed to hold the sight on target. In the end we all laughed, but not before the instructor had made it quite clear how necessary it was to check a gun thoroughly before use.

• *Rigging:* Well, it was 1939/40 and there were still many biplane aircraft in use by the RAF. The Gloucester Gladiator was then a front line fighter, and of course the Tiger Moth and the Avro Tutor aircraft were the main elementary trainers. Therefore we were shown and taught what was meant by rigging.

• *Theory of Flight:* This was truly absorbing, as none of us knew one thing about what maintained an aircraft in flight. I am sure that those remaining of Course 23 were as interested as myself and we gave it all our attention.

• *Navigation and Aero Engines:* These were completely in-depth subjects to which we paid our full attention.

• *Administration:* We had an introduction to this at Bex Hill at the ITW, so we were able to consolidate our learning up to satisfactory speeds with the Aldis lamp and the Morse code.

In a sense we were helped greatly by the continued bad weather and, once we had passed our mid-term exams, we resumed flying with renewed vigour.

6. Feeling Confident

At last the weather improved and by 12 February 1940 we were back to flying. For the next three days my instructors were Flight Lieutenant Lawson and Flying Officer Steele, who took me continually through most of the flying sequences I had learned from Flight Lieutenant Holmes.

On 16 February I was introduced to my fourth and final instructor, Flight Lieutenant Trout (Sammy). This was to be my luckiest day, for Mr Trout was one of the best instructors in the school.

Flight Lieutenant Trout was out of the starting blocks like a racehorse. He greeted me with the words, 'Now, young fella, you'll have me chasing you for some time. I'll teach you what I know and you will pay attention – anything you don't understand, tell me! Now, let's see what you've managed to learn to date. There's a lot of catching up to do because of the weather and the war is hotting up.'

We both strapped into the cockpits and Flight Lieutenant Trout asked me to start up and complete the necessary pre-flight checks, after which I advised him we were ready. Usually in these early days, when we had reached this stage, the instructor would taxi out and take off so as to commence upper-air training. However, not Mr Trout: 'Come on, have the "chocks away" and get cracking, you are flying this aircraft. I shall tell you when I've got her!' 'Hell!' I thought, 'This is something!' So off I started, and I wondered if he had just come back from action. I was to learn that Sammy Trout was too old for action. However, he had been one of the RAF's top pilots and had taken part in many operations in the pre-war Hendon Air Shows – and he really knew his business.

I was instructed after the take-off to go through all the manœuvres I had been taught so far. I managed this for close on an hour, by which time my whole body was aching through concentration. This period had included a number of landings and take-offs, so when we had completed the third landing he requested me to taxi back to the flight line. This first flight with Flight Lieutenant Trout was over and was I praying! When we were both out of the aircraft and I was looking at Flight Lieutenant Trout like a pet poodle, he explained to me the suggestions he was offering – none of them serious, but nevertheless constructive. He then told me to have the aircraft refuelled and take off as soon as possible for 45 minutes solo, and to practise what he had suggested. This day finished with my completing a further 45 minutes solo, and a second 35 minutes with Flight Lieutenant Trout.

Flight Lieutenant Trout arranged for me to meet him in the instructors' office, where he explained what he had assessed to this point. I landed the aircraft very well and the few suggestions he had made on the first flight I had corrected well, and he was pleased.

So, by 17 February, I had completed 34 hours solo and 29 hours dual and was feeling confident with my general progress. The two worrying manoeuvres had been carried out, though they were startling and a little scary. I had experienced (a) stalling and subsequently spinning and (b) stopping the engine in flight and starting again by diving at the speed necessary to rotate the propeller – just a little hair-raising!

Training, both on the ground and in the air, was carried out with our new confidence growing, though we were not overconfident. I had passed the preliminary and mid-term exams. A number of the lads had failed, some the ground subjects and others the flying. We remaining lads offered our sympathy, but this could not assuage the feelings of those who had failed, who were very sad.

We had also survived the continuous and intense cold of the Scottish winter and were none the worse for it. There was always the odd night in the Salutation and at the ice rink, and other shows and entertainment. However, our studies and flying were really in our blood and we relished our training and intended to pass, come hell or high water. During lectures, I received a bit of a scare when the adjutant's secretary entered the classroom and asked the instructor if Sergeant Palliser could see the adjutant as soon as possible. I received some funny looks and raised eyebrows from my friends. I left the class wondering, was this police trouble? I had been pulled up by the police because my car headlights' 'blackout guards' were not fitted correctly. Or could it be the day when I was told there was a nudist camp on the shores of Loch Earn and I had flown rather low over the area? What could it be?

So off to the adjutant I marched, stood to attention in his office and saluted very smartly. I was asked to sit down and was confronted with some papers with a request to explain. They were from the company Richardsons Westgarth, with whom I had been employed. It was explained that a government rule had now been issued that allowed people who had joined the services despite being in a reserved occupation to sign the form, if they so desired, and return to civilian work. The adjutant explained it was my choice. He said, 'Do you wish to sign the form?' To which I replied, 'No Sir. I have passed my mid-term exams and have soloed in my flying. I wish to carry on.' This was a fait accompli.

The third week in February 1940 gave us two days of flying, repeating most of the exercises we had been taught. Then the weather snowed us in again, so there was more consolidation of the ground training, which now included some lessons and explanations of aircraft compass adjusting, together with talks on navigation, which related to our pending cross-country flying test.

By the end of February we could fly again, so on the 29th I undertook more exercises and solo local navigation. Then, on 1 March 1940, I took my first full solo flight from Perth to Montrose on the Scottish east coast. This was truly exciting: steering a compass course, reading a map, watching for ground indicators to determine being on track, and enjoying a good look at the countryside. I arrived at Montrose, which was an advanced flying station, and had the thrill of being shown an advanced training aircraft, Miles Master I, a truly magnificent machine. As I was climbing into my Tiger Moth, one smart alec who had seen me looking at the Miles Master came over to me and said, 'Just starting heh? Would you like my autograph?' I just looked at him and carried on fastening my harness and preparing for my flight back.

Returning to Perth, I had to alter my direction on the compass and ground track because of wind change, and this brought me slightly to the south of my outward flight. Approximately halfway to Perth I saw a huge castle that I had not noticed before and it was quite a sight from the air. This was no historic relic falling to pieces; this was a perfect structure. So I diverted from my flight to a small degree and at 1,500 feet circled round the castle and had a good look.

When I had landed at Scone Airfield and taxied in, I reported to Flight Lieutenant Trout, who discussed the flight with me. I told him about the beautiful castle I had spotted. He looked at me, eyes popping, and said, 'Palliser, were there any flags flying on the castle?' To which I replied, 'Negative.' 'Thank God for that. Do you know what you've done? Flown around Glamis Castle, home of the Queen Mother.' My heart missed a few beats as I stuttered some apologies, including saying that I knew nothing about this problem. Trout said, 'Well hold your breath and so will I and we'll pray that we will have no reports on this matter.' I went back to my billet with my tail between my legs and had to explain my misery to my pals who, of course, went to town on suggestions of what might happen. Maybe a court martial! However, nothing transpired, and Flight Lieutenant Trout dropped the incident. Phew! So my cross-country trial had been passed and now there was much attention to 'blind' flying and night flying.

The month of March saw my return to Flight Lieutenant Trout and more dual flying and tests and many uninterrupted days of flying. It appeared we would be the last course to experience the Cranwell curriculum of lectures and flying. We were given more solo flying, followed by progress tests by different instructors to enable comparisons of results to be submitted to the chief flying instructor. Night flying was commenced during another spell of good weather. This as well as solo and duel flying were pushed hard throughout March, allowing for bad weather, when we would return to ground lectures. The last week in March was awful, with much snow and ice and extremely cold weather. We were grateful for extra heating in the lecture rooms.

For interest I include a numbered list of each flying lesson on which the course was developed and taught:

1. Familiarity with cockpit layout.
2. Preparation for flight.
3. Air experience.
4. Effect of controls.
5. Taxiing.
6. Straight and level flight.
7. Climbing.
8. Descending.
9. Stalling.
10. Medium turns.
11. Gliding and climbing turns.
12. Taking off into wind.
13. The approach and landing.
14. Spinning.
15. First solo.
16. Side slipping.

17. Steep turns.
18. Instrument flying.
19. Low flying.
20. Taking off and landing out of wind.
21. Precautionary landings.
22. Action in event of fire.
23. Restarting engine in flight.
24. Forced landing.
25. Aerobatics.
26. Night flying.
27. Pilot navigation.
28. Formation flying.

In the first week of April 1940 we recommenced flying up to the end of April, as our final ground examinations were completed and our assessments given. On 20 April I received my final test results from Flight Lieutenant Trout and together my results were: Flying Assessment – very good, with total flying, including 14 hours of night flying, 97 hours 20 minutes; ground results – average for all subjects 73.6 per cent. Now, Intermediate and Advanced Training was the next big step.

A get-together had been organised for our farewell on 26 April. The atmosphere was sober and subdued, although there was some leg-pulling by the various instructors. Flight Lieutenant Trout drew me aside and reminded me that I should proceed with aerobatics whenever it was possible, as he insisted it was the best way to know your aircraft. His ultimate advice was, 'YOU must fly the aircraft. The aircraft doesn't fly you.'

7. 'A Big Slap on the Back'

It was expected that we would be posted to different advanced flying centres and, as destiny decided, I was posted to Little Rissington in the Cotswolds in the south of England, together with two other pilots who had become friends, Stan Loveridge and Bill Hughes. The posting was to No. 6 FTS (Intermediate and Advanced Flying), 19th Course, and effective 22 April 1940. However, because of a few days overrun at Perth, we were to commence our journey on 26 April. The three of us loaded up my wee two-door Morris 8 and, with quiet resignation, we left Scone at 5.00 a.m. en route to the overnight stop at Stan Loveridge's home in Gloucester. The run down the west coast of England was very interesting to us lads, who had seldom been outside our own counties. Stan's family welcomed us with open arms and had many questions for us during a long evening.

The next day we completed our journey with some air of trepidation and reported to the guard room at the airfield entrance. Gone was the civilian air of greeting we had received at Perth. This was a full blown unit of the Royal Air Force and was a very different experience. We were taken to a hall where other pupils from many different elementary schools were congregating and we joined in the noisy atmosphere that had developed.

There were thirty-seven lads on this 19th Course and we were destined to be divided into two channels, one training for bomber aircraft and the other for fighters. The last thing I was interested in was being a pilot of a bomber. I had thought of nothing else but being a fighter pilot – as had Loveridge and Hughes. Finally, we were brought to order – and I mean to order! You could hear the clocks ticking. The Chief Ground Instructor (CGI) was accompanied by the Chief Flying Instructor (CFI). They both in turn addressed us on what the future was to be. First, we heard the same promises of what would happen if we did not treat the work seriously and, as in Perth, it was stressed that exams and general progress had to produce excellent averages or else we would be failed. Then the CGI read out the names of each pupil and advised the flying designation that the pupil would be given – namely, fighter or bomber. I am sure many fingers were crossed at this time. However, among the names allocated to fighters were Loveridge, Hughes and Palliser. The atmosphere erupted after the silence, and every expression was to be heard – acceptance or non-acceptance of the designations. There were very few upsets, which was remarkable.

We were then split into two groups, and our group was assembled by the CFI, who addressed general requirements and advised us that we would now be allocated to living quarters and be responsible to various ground sergeants and warrant officers. The CFI advised us that notices would be placed on notice boards, referring to his flight commanders, who would be responsible for our intermediate and advanced training, and also which of us would be allocated to each flight. We were then paraded under the senior non-commissioned officer – Warrant Officer Woods. And what a shock we received as 'Tiger' Woods brought us to attention in a voice that shook the hell out of us. This man, whom I would then have called elderly, was very smartly dressed and sun-burned to walnut appearance. Afterwards, the grapevine advised us that he had served in all countries of the British Empire and had been decorated for service in Afghanistan (Khyber Pass) and had killed enemy fighters with his bare hands. I believed this, as I thought he could have blown them apart with his tongue!

We were eventually dismissed and shown to the various wooden huts, which included ablution facilities, beds and lockers. The first glitch we experienced was when, wearing our new sergeant's stripes, we entered the sergeants' mess, to be met with a most definite 'No Entry' from various regular sergeants of long standing. We youngsters would not be considered as sergeants at any time. We returned to our billets rather shocked. We were obviously a bit on the young side to appreciate the situation. However, the powers that be solved the problem by allocating another building to us invaders. Time and common sense in the end allowed us to understand the problem.

Well, we had experienced our initial welcome. Now we had to pay attention – all the way! Monday 29 April 1940, was a good day to start, and we were advised that the wings exam would take place in eight weeks. We were allocated to 'P' Squad for drill and general assemblies and, together with Loveridge and Hughes, I reported to Flight Lieutenant

Cole, Officer Commanding (OC) 'D' Flight. We were to fly Harvard aircraft. My flying instructor introduced himself as Flight Sergeant Plested, who would begin the teaching on this new aircraft. This session was to familiarise us with the controls and various important features of the Harvard, which was startling when compared to that wonderful little gem, the Tiger Moth, we had left behind at Perth. Wow! The instrument layout, the controls, the size of this huge brute – everything was so different from that delicate lady with two small wings and neat wires holding the aircraft together. This aircraft was of solid metal (stressed skin), with a huge engine and single wing, a giant in comparison. Flight Sergeant Plested laughed at my expression and quietly advised me that converting to the Harvard was not difficult and it should not take me too long to get the hang of it.

I climbed into the front cockpit, which was for the pupil. The rear cockpit was for the instructor. Plested stood on the wing and, leaning over to the side, he explained the various instruments and controls, which had me boggle eyed at the sight and feel. The difference was startling, and I must have behaved like a fish out of water, because Plested tapped me on the shoulder and told me not to be unduly worried, as he understood the change from the Tiger Moth. He then took me along to the parachute section, where I was allocated a parachute (B6) and a locker (125), then back to the aircraft, along with other pupils and instructors. It was recommended that we pupils get together in groups of four or five and discuss what we had been taught. Our group somehow formed very quickly with the addition of two others, Victor Meeson and Tony Page. This resulted in a very happy friendship for the length of the course.

By 2 May I was ready for my first flight, and, with Flight Sergeant Plested in the rear cockpit and myself in the front, we were prepared for the new experience. The Harvard seemed enormous: the height, the length of the wingspan, and a huge radial engine of 580 horse power; it was all a bit overwhelming. Plested's voice came through on another innovation, the wireless-type intercom, between cockpits. A voice said, 'OK, now I have explained the throttle control and engine revolutions and you should know where all the controls are and what they are for, so I shall taxi out of the line of aircraft and then I would like you to take over and taxi to our take-off position.' Out we went, and I was still thinking about the start-up of the engine. It was started electrically, and the burbling noise was like a hundred drains emptying – what a racket!

'Can you hear me?' said a voice. 'Yes Sir', answered another – mine, I realised, with a shock. 'Right,' said Flight Sergeant Plested. 'Now the orders apply as in your elementary training. When I say, "you've got her", you answer "I've got her Sir". OK? And the same when you return control to me. So now use the throttle and taxi to where I shall tell you.' I lowered the throttle about one-thousandth of an inch slowly, when the voice said, 'Anything wrong? We are not moving.' 'Sorry Sir,' says I, and lowered the throttle with more effort and wow – we were moving! The voice said, 'Steady, Palliser, we don't want to be airborne until we reach the runway.' There was a loud gulp from me and then I had the throttle under control and we were off – taxiing, swinging the aircraft with the rudder in a zigzag pattern, so I could see what was in front of us. We reached our point of take-off. The voice said, 'That's the spirit, now I want you to keep your hand on the throttle and place your feet on the rudder bar, hands on the control column (stick) and follow my movements while I take off and explain to you what we are doing.'

We had gone through the primary checks before take-off. Now we made sure our trim control was correct. Then I heard: 'We turn on to the runway, line up straight, receive the "OK" from the control tower [this was new to me] and we open the throttle, keeping the aircraft straight with the rudder. As we reach take-off speed, having raised the tail of the aircraft to the flying position – approximately 75 mph – we commence the climb to our operating height.' Then the first lessons commenced. These lessons paralleled the list shown above, and every detail had to be thoroughly experienced in this conversion to the Harvard aircraft, as it would be thereafter, for any aircraft, until we were fully experienced and qualified as pilots. The first flight lasted 45 minutes, and the experience of how the control differed from the Tiger Moth and applied to the landing of this aircraft was truly exciting. I savoured the power, size and the height speeds available. Certain characteristics applying to this aircraft, such as stalling speeds, the incipient spin effect and general landing, were explained and discussed after our return to the airfield. On the first approach to the airfield for the landing, I followed Plested's instructions, handling the controls with him. However, I did not relate with the reactions needed to land correctly at this time.

We taxied into the flight line-up, where all 'D Flight' aircraft were positioned. Flight Sergeant Plested helped me out of the aircraft and we returned to the flight office, which was in a series of tents on the far side of the airfield. He could see I was as nervous as a proverbial kitten and addressed me with some explanatory lines of, 'This happens to many, changing from the smaller elementary aircraft', and assured me my upper-air handling was good and he was confident of my success. We all returned late that first afternoon to our billets, worried about our abilities to absorb the details that applied to the Harvard. But the value of such a discussion cheered us up somewhat, as we thought about the following day.

The next day we reported for flying, understanding that we had first to parade as a total group for inspections by the senior warrant officer, who was accompanied by the CGI. Remembering our drill experience at ITW in November–December 1939, we presented a 'turn out' to be proud of and we were advised that the senior officers had been complimentary. Before arriving at Little Rissington, many of us had been issued with uniforms that were too big, or too small, or not complete, so we were sent to the main stores, where all our problems were rectified. We all ended up with uniforms and boots that fitted, plus other necessary clothing. Some had not received their sergeant's stripes, and this was remedied. We were now passed out as complete, fully respectable NCO sergeant pilots under training. We were paraded once again before lunch and were informed that ground/technical lectures would commence on 7 May 1940. In the meantime our flying instruction would continue.

Flight Sergeant Plested was there to welcome me, and immediately showed me how to check my parachute and climb into the Harvard. In the late afternoon of the previous day I had had a chat with one of the aircraft mechanics who serviced the Harvards. He took me to the hangar and helped me into the cockpit of a Harvard and then diligently explained all the controls and instruments to me. I sat there for 2 hours and repeated the cockpit drill until I could operate the controls without looking around trying to find them. This was the big secret and it worked. This was worth a couple of beers for the mechanic. So into the Harvard I jumped. Flight Lieutenant Plested followed and he instructed me this time, before we moved, to follow him with the pre-flight check, which I did with some alacrity. This earned me some favourable remarks. I taxied out of the line-up, over to the take-off point, where Plested announced he would take off and I should follow his movements on the controls. When we were airborne and had turned out of the circuit on our way to a clear air position, he commented, 'Heh, that was quite good. I could feel you following me on the controls to a point where I eased my feet and hands somewhat and felt you managing well.' That was something! I felt good.

Now the days were routine: out of bed, ablutions, parade, inspection after breakfast, and off to our flight stations. Our flying times varied from 35 minutes to 1 hour, remembering that there were twenty-eight facets of flying in this instruction programme. In addition to this we now entered the world of the 'Link Trainer'. This was a blue-painted box-like structure with electric controls coupled to the control column rudder and throttle, which passed signals to a machine on a flat table. This mechanical-like robot relayed information on graphs, which showed how you were handling what might be called a model aircraft with a hood. So you were only able to fly as if you were blind to external visibility. I really enjoyed this machine, though many hated it. However, as Plested explained, to qualify on the Link Trainer would enable one to fly at night, in bad weather, and particularly in clouds.

On 6 May 1940 I found myself strapped into the cockpit with a new senior instructor, Flight Lieutenant Foreshaw, in the rear cockpit telling me, 'Now, Palliser, a few take-offs and landings and possibly a solo flight.' My pulse leapt into overdrive and for a few seconds I was struck dumb and then that voice again: 'Have you gone to sleep there?' 'No Sir,' I said, and commenced taxiing for take-off, whereafter we completed all the major exercises, plus two take-offs and landings. Then those words you can never forget: 'OK, let me get out and I will watch you taxi out, go through all the checks, request permission to take off, complete your circuit and landing, and return to the flight line. Good luck!' Needless to say I shouted and sang the whole way round the circuit and made a damn good landing, taxied in and was given a big slap on the back by Plested. Now I was ready for the future and determined to do well in the ground subjects.

With all the flying excitement I must refer to the lectures, as the days were shared between the two to suit the weather conditions. These lectures commenced on 7 May and the programme was as I have mentioned previously. Our advanced programme of lectures was now in the hands of RAF lecturers. The classes were laid out in a most professional manner, and the lecturers were quick to explain the seriousness of the RAF curriculum. Now we had three facets of learning – namely, flying, lectures and link training, with day and night programmes. Included were periods of parades and marching. However, the flying instruction was by far our favourite activity.

Life was not all training and we were able to venture forth to the local villages. Bourton-on-the-Water was our favourite, one of the prettiest villages in the Cotswolds. The local pub was our watering hole. We were intrigued by a model of the whole village, which had been built on a large piece of land at the rear of the pub, and inside each model was another model, right down to a remarkably small size. These visits to the pub were managed with the help of my little Morris car, which had taken a beating from the journey down from Scotland. I later was able to trade it in for a Riley 9 with a Wilson Automatic drive, the deal being effected in a garage in Oxford. This had taken place when, on one occasion with friends, we made a delightful trip to this wonderful city.

During these visits we had a few pints with the locals and, during many conversations, and as the month progressed, we heard some rather alarming news. We missed a lot of news generally, because we had no access to newspapers or wireless. So we were astonished to learn about the war in France and how the German armies were pushing the British and French units west. This was shocking news. We had been so wrapped up in our training that we had never thought of such a calamity. Deep in our heads we reckoned we were doing well and that the war would be over soon. No way! Thousands of civilians and troops were fleeing along the French coast towards the town of Dunkirk, where thousands of troops were already on the beaches praying for rescue.

The Hurricane squadrons, which, as we heard from this news, had done a marvellous job in fighting the Luftwaffe, were returning to England to re-form. Squadrons that had been retained in England were now fighting over the French coast to prevent German bombers and fighters from slaughtering the helpless people on the beaches. It appeared that a call had gone out by wireless and newspapers for volunteers with boats of any size to proceed to the Dunkirk beaches across the Channel to rescue as many people as possible. Later I was to learn that my 16-year-old brother Ted, who was a good yachtsman, had been found a few miles up the Channel from Weymouth, where he lived. A torpedo boat had found him and an officer had asked him, 'What the hell are you doing?' To which he replied, 'Haven't you heard the request for people to go to Dunkirk?' The boat captain explained to Ted that Dunkirk was many miles up the Channel and his boat was just a little too small for such an adventure, so he was towed back to Weymouth, given a pat on the back and sent home. I thought this was marvellous.

Apparently we had lost quite a number of Hurricanes and also Spitfires, which did not help our aircraft numbers and supply in Britain.

The rest is written in history. We spoke to our instructors about this catastrophe, and they filled in some gaps, one of which shook the hell out of us. They drew our attention to the many biplanes that we had talked about in the past: the old Presar front line aircraft. the Gladiators, the Hawker Hart with its three, four or five variants, and also the Tiger Moth and Tutor, and the Miles trainers. We were told that it was very probable, because of the state of the present German successes, that an invasion of England would be the next move by Hitler. The German Luftwaffe, having had a lengthy spell of fighting in Spain before 1939, had learned a lot about fighter tactics, and their experiences made us feel very ignorant, to say the least. With this in our minds we received the additional information that the biplanes were having bomb racks fitted to them to handle small bombs, and these aircraft would be used against an invasion by the Germans when they attacked the coastline of England. You can imagine our thoughts as the pictures of us flying into action in Hurricanes and Spitfires suddenly changed to flying these old aircraft of yesteryear.

So back to training we went. Everything was going very well in lectures, link training and general flying. At times we had a change of instructor. I am sure this was to test our progress and to learn from the changes. However, I remembered Flight Lieutenant Trout's words and prevailed upon Flight Sergeant Plested to allow me to carry out aerobatics, a subject in which he was keen to participate. We completed cross-country flights, and various programmes such as flying over towns and reporting with diagrams the railway facilities and factories, teaching us observation and reporting. Our programme carried on through May and into June 1940, and I felt very confident in my progress. However, some on the course were still feeling a need to be cocky and stupid, which produced poor results.

8. 'Do You Feel Comfortable Sergeant?'

On one day in early June we saw and heard a Lysander aircraft in the circuit. We watched as it completed a landing and taxied on to the main tarmac near the control tower. The time coincided with our lunch break, so we hurried across and talked to the pilot, who let us look around his plane. It looked like an ugly duckling. Some of the ground crew were working on the aircraft and one pointed out to us the .303 machine gun in the fixed wheel cover. This was rather peculiar, but we had a good look. As we started to walk away, we heard a harsh crackle of gunfire. We looked around to see flames and smoke coming from the Lysander's machine gun. Unfortunately, and for some unknown reason, only one chock had been placed against the port wheel and the recoil of the gun was pushing the aircraft back in a clockwise direction and of course the bullets were firing, but luckily across an open airfield. The mechanic who had entered the cockpit had placed his hand on the control column, on which the firing button was located in the grip. Someone (we never knew who, and the pilot refused to be blamed) had set the gun button to 'fire' position. We had to leave at that time and heard no more about the incident.

The first week of June saw everything happen in an alarmingly hectic fashion: the evacuation of Dunkirk and the victories for the Nazi army and air force represented by Dr Goebbels, who was promising terror and destruction for Britain. No wonder, when they had walked over Poland, Austria, France, Holland and Belgium, and had spread havoc through the Scandinavian countries. We were the penultimate easy mark before they turned on Russia. All this created a concern that our course would have to be hurried, as we would all now be required to fight the threatened invasion. Fortunately, this did not happen, and our training continued. However, the full seriousness of the situation made us all pay attention to our training in every way. The talk now was most definitely about WAR!

Together with my four friends, Meeson, Page, Loveridge and Hughes, we had plenty to talk about, as we had just been advised we had passed our halfway exams and were allocated to the advanced flying training, which would or would not see us gain our wings. 'Please Lord let us make it!'

The weather in May and the beginning of June had been marvellous – sunshine and blue skies. What a beautiful area this county of Gloucestershire was to fly over and investigate when off duty. Flying and lectures carried on without interruption, and on 17 June a notice was placed on the official board announcing and detailing the names of those on our course who had been awarded the much-coveted wings. I looked for five names only, and shouted with much joy that we five had made it. There was no further glamour, as was experienced in the flying training schools around the world as the war progressed. From the end of 1940, all flying training would be based in Canada, Australia and South Africa; here there were great parades, awards of wings presented by some senior dignitaries, and bands playing at the end. But not for us. We were ordered to proceed to the equipment stores and pick up two beautifully shaped cloth wings, charged 4d. each, and then we had to sew them on to our tunics. It was the fastest piece of sewing done in my life. And did we celebrate in the local pub in Bourton-on-the-Water!

What a hangover we had the next day. Course 19 had really paid homage to the wings event. Nevertheless, we had to look our parade-smart selves before we reported to both lectures and flying duties. It was a tough day. We were now commencing the advanced flying. We would report to a mixture of instructors, who would be testing us all the time on every detail of the flying syllabus; in short, we really had to prove we could fly the Harvard like veterans. We were flying more country flights, carrying out formation flying generally in 'Vics' of three aircraft in which we had to lead, alternately, at 10-or 15-minute periods. We were to do more flying at Kidlington, an advanced flying airfield on the outskirts of Oxford. We would also practise forced landings in case of engine failure. This particular practice really had you on your toes, as it was carried out without any use of the engine throttle, unless you mucked it up and had to rely on the engine. If so, a 'black mark' was the result.

At the commencement of the advanced training we had been allowed a long weekend leave, which I thoroughly enjoyed with relatives. However, I had included in my weekend case a lovely, comfortable pair of shoes, and into my case also went these damned awful boots, which I

had never worn at home; nor did I like them. Returning to the airfield in
the early morning, I just had time to wash, shave and make sure my tunic
buttons were shining before I joined the morning parade. Standing to
attention, feeling on top of the world, I watched Warrant Officer Woods
walking along our lines, checking everyone's dress and smartness. Then
I felt him standing behind me, with no words, no movement, and my
thoughts were, What can be wrong? Then came a roar like a wounded
lion, followed by the gravel-propelled words, 'Got your slippers on,
Sergeant, heh?' I had forgotten to change my shoes! Well, my ears were
shattered and I was sure my head was singed as Woods spat out for all to
hear, 'Very nice shoes, Sergeant, have you tender feet Sergeant? Do you
feel comfortable Sergeant?' And a blast of more sarcasm. Woods turned
to the accompanying Corporal and said, '6.00 p.m., this elegant lad does
an hour's drill.' Oh dear! Now it was my turn for my friends to have their
amusement at my expense. We had watched quite a few others who had
suffered under Woods. This was my lesson! I would see that walnut face
in my dreams for a long time, and I could only thank my lucky stars that
there was no other punishment – for example, related to flying.

Still in June, we were advised that night flying (advanced) would be
carried out at Kidlington. Six of us were detailed to fly over late in the
afternoon and report to the instructor in charge. We reported after
parking the aircraft ready for flights, and were told we would commence
flying at about 11.00 p.m. In the meantime, we could look around the
area and relax. We were intrigued by the many soldiers who had been
billeted in huts at the edge of the airfield. We spoke to a few and
wondered where they were from. They were scruffy and looked worn
out. They told us they were French Canadian soldiers who had just
arrived after being evacuated from Dunkirk with thousands of others.
Wow! Dunkirk! Tell us about it! Unfortunately, we were summoned to
return to the flight hut for briefing, so we were unable to stay and hear
their stories, although we had the sad experience of seeing a wrecked
Hurricane on a trailer, which had just arrived. This apparently was what
was left of the aircraft of that famous ace, Cobber Cain. There was
much to talk about as we walked on.

Flying commenced at 11.00 p.m. and my flight was detailed for 12.30
a.m. So there was more loafing and resting in the flight hut, which was
equipped with a supply of drinks and sandwiches. Those of us waiting
spoke to the young lass behind the counter. Some asked for beer, at which
she advised that beer was not allowed if we were flying. So we asked what

was in some small kegs on a shelf, to which she replied, 'Oh, that's cider.' Believe it or not, we North Country lads had never been introduced to this beverage, so we asked if we could try this, and the girl agreed. So we enjoyed a couple of small glasses of cider, which was indeed very nice.

Time was moving and by 11.30 p.m. I was feeling very comfortable and raring to go. One of the instructors called me at midnight and suggested I should be ready to take over from the Harvard on the way in. At approximately 12.45 a.m. the Harvard that I would fly came taxiing in out of the pitch black night and the pupil climbed out with a few grunts and groans and said, 'OK, she's all yours.' There was no refuelling at this time, as the flights were no longer than 30 minutes. I firmed the straps of my parachute, climbed in and strapped myself into the cockpit, completed a pre-flight check and taxied to the take-off position. I received the 'OK' signal to take off, turned on to a flare path, which was indicated by reduced light paraffin lamps, and proceeded to take off.

I sat comfortably looking at my instruments and checking on my direction parallel to the flares, when suddenly I felt the aircraft wallow and become airborne at about the fifth flare. Something was wrong! A quick look at the instruments and controls and realised that the previous pupil had taxied in and had not raised the flaps. I looked down, quickly grasping the flap lever, then with a flash my brain thought, 'Hold it, not yet.' I held the controls carefully until I had reached reasonable flying speed and controlled the increase in height slowly until I was at 500 feet, then closed the flaps by degrees until they were 'locked up'. Phew! My fault as well as the twit before me. I had not checked the flaps, which normally in daylight I would have noticed. So this was yet another caution in aircraft inspection. It was an experience that was locked in my mind for ever.

9. 'Don't Mention the Landing in a Field'

Flying instruction and solo flying continued into July 1940, with every aspect of aircraft handling we had been taught. 'Know your aircraft' was the call, and life was never dull. We used to discuss our flying with our friends the bomber pilot pupils, who were flying Avro Ansons, a twin-engine plane that could carry a crew, including navigators and wireless operators if necessary. A great deal of leg-pulling and lighter-vein remarks were made as friendly rivalry prevailed. This helped our spirits when we visited the local pubs. The Ansons were held at the opposite side of the airfield from the Harvards, and of course we had to be very careful in our take-off and landing approaches.

Towards the end of July I had completed one of my routine flight exercises and returned to Little Rissington airfield, making the obligatory approach circuit and confirmed my landing approach to the duty tower. I entered into my final approach for landing, and at approximately 500 feet altitude I heard a heavy rumbling noise which was totally foreign to the Harvard. I looked around and suddenly glanced above me and saw the belly of an Anson hovering over me, with about 100 feet between us. At this time a red flare was fired from the duty tower, a warning to abort the landing. However, I was already holding my aircraft laterally and applied controlled rudder in a flat turn to port. There was no way could I have banked the aircraft in a correct turn, as I would have struck the Anson, as it was closing in fast. This fool, who I thought was one of the pupils, must have made a direct approach to landing instead of the laid-down circuit.

Clearing the Anson, I made a half circuit and landed near our dispersal lines. The flight commander was running towards me and, as I vacated the aircraft, he bellowed, 'Quick, run to the duty tower and have that pilot report to me.' It had not dawned on me that a pupil would normally have taxied to the far side of the field to his own dispersal. This Anson had taxied to the duty tower. As I reached the tower, the pilot was leaving and walking down the steps, shouting something to the duty pilot in the tower. As the pilot reached the ground, I grabbed him and gave him all the language I had learned in my student engineering days, telling him what I thought about the near miss and requesting him to come with me to my Flight Commander. 'He' looked at me and then took off his flying helmet – up to that point I had not noticed that the helmet was not like our issue, nor that the pilot's dress was a black overall suit. I nearly swallowed my tonsils as I looked into the face of 'Amy Johnson' (Mollison). Heavens above! And my language! She simply looked at me and said, 'It was nothing to get excited about and I haven't the time to see your Flight Commander.' She pushed past me and boarded the Anson, in which I could now see two or three more women looking at the pair of us. They taxied towards the Anson dispersal. It appeared that this famous lady was a member of the Air Transport Auxiliary, ferrying all types of aircraft to the many stations in the country, and this flight was to pick up some aircraft from Rissington to fly to other centres. I heard nothing more about this incident. However, I was told by my instructor that I had done well in avoiding a nasty accident. This gave me another yarn to talk about in the pub. However, this was my second worrying incident. It is said they come in threes.

We were now nearing the completion of our course. It was near the end of July and the pace was hotting up. The talk was of pilots being wanted urgently, particularly in 11 Group, the most important group, covering the south-east corner of England. The Operational Training Units (OTUs) were waiting for us. I had completed 104 hours on Harvards, also 8 hours night flying. I had also received an excellent report from the Link Trainer Officer. This related to blind flying using instruments.

Before July ended we were practising more formation flying, still operating with three aircraft in the conventional shape, like an arrowhead. Our turn came on a balmy summer afternoon. There were few clouds in the sky, but a heavy haze had developed. Loveridge and Hughes joined me. The three of us took off independently and joined up away from the circuit. Loveridge, who was leading, maintained a north-westerly direction, and a height of 3,000 feet, with Hughes and myself formatting neatly about 30 feet away on either side, looking carefully at the leader. After 15 minutes we changed the order, and Hughes took the lead. We had maintained a north to north-west course, and the time was now about 3.15 p.m. We practised turns, medium and steep, which was quite a thrill, and also closing up the formation, which was exciting. After 20 minutes Hughes signalled a change, and I slipped into the leader's position. We were now about 80 miles from base and the haze was thickening to a point that lessened visibility to a great extent. I decided to turn on to a south-easterly course, as we were detailed for a 1 hour flight. After 10 minutes of flying I looked around for some ground feature in order to locate our position. I had forgotten to take my map. After all, we were not going too far and we were over territory we had been reasonably used to. I could not identify any feature on the ground, and haze and the sun effect really made things difficult to identify. I attracted Loveridge's attention, as he lived in the Gloucester area, and he looked around and returned a negative sign. He reached in his flying overall for his map, opened the hood of the Harvard – and the draught whipped the map out of his hands. Now it was Hughes's turn, and he simply waved his arms in a negative gesture, indicating he had forgotten his map. This was really serious! We must be overdue by now. The hairs on the back of my neck stood up as I realised that three aircraft would be forced to land somewhere. Damn this haze. However, I noticed a road running north and south and then I saw a field that looked like a possible size for landing. In the corner of an adjoining field were some men building a haystack. With my heart in my mouth and thoughts in my head of what the end result might be, I signalled to the two lads that I would try to land in a field and simply ask these men to point me in the direction of Cheltenham. After my lessons in 'precautionary landings', I was sure of making a good landing and would worry about the take-off afterwards.

I took a sweep around the field. There was very little wind. I commenced an approach at 500 feet from a reasonable distance, easing the nose of the aircraft up a little, lowering the undercarriage and full flap. I held the Harvard with increased engine power into a position just above stall speed. I cleared the hedge and fence by about 6 feet, and then dropped the Harvard, steadied, applied brakes – and prayed. Surely my destiny would not let me down. And it didn't. I managed to stop within 300 or 400 yards. Not wanting to waste time with Loveridge and Hughes circling overhead, I turned the Harvard and taxied back to the corner of the field where the men were working on the haystack. They were already clambering over the fence and waving to me. I reached the corner and turned carefully for take-off. My hood was already open and I shouted to the nearest man and said, 'We are off track with this haze.

Will you indicate, relative to the road, the direction of Cheltenham?' The man quickly pointed at an angle down the road to the south and yelled, 'About 25 miles, you're in the Vale of Evesham.' At the same time another person yelled, 'You had better stay, there's a cop coming, about two fields away.' I said to the first man, 'Mind quickly, I'm taking off.'

Tucking the tail of the Harvard as near to the corner as possible, I lowered the flaps to 'full' after my experience at Kidlington, stood on the brakes, giving the engine full throttle, and let go. Looking back, I saw the men waving, and realised I had blown their hard work apart. I experienced the same lift at 50 to 60 mph and held this wonderful aircraft steady, clearing the fence by at least 15 feet. I maintained an increasing climb away from the field, and reached 1,000 feet, reducing 'flap' position until they were fully retracted. Hughes and Loveridge joined me in formation and in little time we saw the town of Cheltenham, and turned for the run to Rissington. We landed and taxied to our dispersal with the pupils and instructors all out there watching. All the Harvards had finished flying and fortunately we were a rather long distance from the dispersal tent.

I parked the aircraft as quickly as I could and climbed out. Walking over to the other two I said very quickly, 'No time to talk. Say we were lost and had to do some hefty "square search" exercise before we found the aircraft. Don't mention the landing in the field.' We walked together to the dispersal tent, fielding lots of questions from the pupils as to what happened until our Flight Commander, Flight Lieutenant Cole, faced us. 'What the hell happened to you?' I answered, 'Sir, we went further north than we calculated and in returning south we lost our bearings in the very heavy haze. I had taken over the lead and commenced a square search, at the same time maintaining an overlap in a southerly direction. It took some time, before sighting Cheltenham, and then we were home.' I think Flight Lieutenant Cole held his breath for minutes and then said, 'You fools! We were getting ready to send a search party out for you. Do you realise, the three of you, you certainly had us all worried.' He also advised us that the Chief Flying Instructor would probably speak to us the next day. With that, we handed our parachutes and kit in and walked to our billet. I said to my two friends, 'If you breathe a word of this I shall be in serious trouble and might even be thrown off the course. It's up to you. You must realise we three could have been forced to land wherever possible as we were certainly lost.' I shall remember that haze experience as long as I live.

The next day we looked at each other as we left the billet and remarked on what might happen with our interview with the Chief Flying Instructor. However, as we retired from the morning parade, one of the staff sergeants advised the three of us that we should report directly to our Flight Commander. This we did with alacrity. Flight Lieutenant Cole addressed us once more with some penetrating remarks and then requested we three explain thoroughly what had happened. We stressed our lack of experience in being caught in such a situation with the heavy haze and sun effect, and our efforts, not to panic and maintain a routine square search, such as we had been lectured about. I explained how, understanding that we had flown further north than was intended, I turned south and maintained the search to pick up the Cheltenham Reservoir or the town itself, from which we knew our position in relation to the airfield. Flight Lieutenant Cole looked at me and said, 'Are you sure that this is exactly how you were able to return?' I said, 'Yes, Sir.' He pondered for some minutes, then dismissed us saying, 'Well thank the Lord you three returned without incident. I shall speak to the Chief Flying Instructor. You can carry on and report to your separate instructors.' This gave us plenty to worry about in relation to the next possible interview.

For the next few days I was walking on eggshells. Every time someone beckoned me, my heart lost a few beats. I was really scared. My two friends insisted I should not worry; it was all over. However, I was remembering the policeman who had tried to reach us and who would obviously talk to the haystack lads, if for no other reason than to help to rebuild the haystack. I was in a panic. The final day arrived and we were advised of our postings. Victor Meeson and Tony Page were to join me in going to No. 6 OTU Sutton Bridge, near King's Lynn. Loveridge and Hughes were off to another OTU. Our course had arranged a farewell party for our instructors and, as I walked from my billet to discuss the arrangements with others, an orderly approached me and asked my name. I could have fainted. My reaction caused him to ask if I was sick. I reassured him I was OK and asked what he wanted. He replied, 'The Chief Ground Instructor wants to see you.' What could this be? Had the authorities found out at last? Was this the end for me? It was no good thinking about it, so, with Loveridge and Hughes looking sympathetically at me, off I went to report to the CGI.

Once I had seated myself at his request, he explained that a percentage from each course, both fighter and bomber, would be interviewed by him for general course records. He discussed the flying programme, the highs and lows of the syllabus, and then stressed the importance of the ground subjects. The interview ended with a personal reference to my report, which included my weakness in the navigation subject compared to my elementary report. I dared not for the life of me explain that I did not wish to be a bomber pilot, hence my marks. He finally passed my report to me, and allowed me to read it. It was good. However, the last lines really had me gasping. They read: 'Flying above average ability as a pilot, has shown immense improvement and is considered to be the best Group I Pilot on the Course.' I asked if I could receive a copy, but this was not allowed. He did, however, allow me to copy the final words. I had no notebook so I used the back of a photograph I carried of my young brother. I have carried that photo in my papers to this day.

Our farewell party with our instructors and flight commander was a great success. Although the merriment was somewhat tempered by the news of Dunkirk and its aftermath, including the tough times the Fighter Command pilots were having. As I was preparing to leave the party, Flight Lieutenant Cole quietly took me by the arm and said, 'Palliser, you had the experience of being lost. However, your instruction helped you in finding your way back to the airfield. Take care in preparation for such flights and don't get lost in future.' From his approach, the way it was said and the way he looked at me, I thought – he knows!

10. 'Think You Can Handle This?'

No. 6 OTU, Sutton Bridge

Victor had offered to take Tony and myself to Sutton Bridge in his car, as mine had developed problems. It had to be left at the local Rissington garage to be picked up at a later date. We arrived at Sutton Bridge Airfield in the afternoon of Saturday 3 August. We were taken to our quarters and advised to report to the adjutant the next morning.

So, on 4 August 1940 we reported to the officer in charge of flying and were allocated to a training instructor for the initial introduction to the Hurricane. Entering the hangar I had my first glimpse of this renowned fighter aircraft and, true to expectations, it gave me a real thrill. This is what I had read about and seen pictures of in newspapers and magazines. It really looked the part. The instructor wasted no time and asked me to climb into the cockpit, which, for the initial instruction, was resting on trestles with flaps closed and undercarriage retracted. The instructor stood on the wing and commenced explaining the instruments and all the flying controls. He told me to lower and raise the undercarriage by hand, pumping a lever, which was very awkward. We would feel the difference when we could operate this by hydraulics. We then went through the same manœuvre for the flaps, and thereafter the movement of all the other controls, which were similar to the Harvard in the operating sense. The purpose of this type of instruction was to allow us to memorise every instrument and control: we had to operate the controls until we could reach and move them without looking for them. This was the only way to learn for a single-seat fighter. It was vital to be able to look out of the cockpit 100 per cent of the flying time, with no distractions. You cannot spend any time looking for some control when you are engaged with enemy aircraft. I spent some hours going through the movements, until I could handle every control blindfolded. At the conclusion of the day the instructor was satisfied with my efforts, and ordered me to report to a training flight on the east side of the airfield immediately after breakfast the next morning.

The next day I reported to Flight Lieutenant Martin (Dickie, the boy from Luxembourg). He was given this accolade because he had been shot down in France and was sent as a prisoner to Luxembourg, where he was allowed the freedom of the city after promising not to try to escape. Promises, promises! He simply walked back into France and managed to be helped back to England. Quite a lad was Dickie! He talked to me about the practical points of handling the Hurricane from an operational point of view, then walked with me to the flight crew and requested them to have an aircraft ready for my first solo. The flight sergeant advised Martin that the four Hurricanes for training flights were already flying, so I would have to wait. There was one Hurricane parked a few yards away and Martin asked, 'Why not that one?' To which the flight sergeant replied, 'Sir, this is the old 354 with the two-blade propeller, not recommended for first solo.' Martin looked at me, then the flight sergeant, and then said to me, 'Think you can handle this?' Innocently, thinking of how many hours I had now flown, and feeling full of confidence, I replied, 'Sure, I guess so.'

The next thing I knew, I had a parachute on and was strapped into the cockpit of my first fighter aircraft. The flight sergeant jumped on the wing, tapped me on the shoulder and, despite the noise and rumble of the famous Merlin engine, yelled in my ear, 'You OK with a two-bladed prop?' I looked at him and thought, 'Why? I have flown nearly 200 hours in aircraft with two-bladed props. What's wrong with this?' So I yelled, 'Sure.' A tap on the shoulder and my experience commenced. I completed a thorough cockpit check, having made sure before I climbed into the aircraft that the flaps were 'up'. There wasn't going to be a repeat of Kidlington!

I taxied to the end of the field for take-off. There was no runway and, as I taxied, I was alarmed at the virtual slow rotation of the prop. A Harvard prop would be a blur by now, and I could see the damn great hunk of wood revolving so slowly in comparison. But different aircraft have different performances, so I decided not to worry and to carry on. Checking that the airfield was clear and with permission to proceed, I turned the Hurricane into wind and opened the throttle. Nothing seemed to happen for a number of seconds. In my mind I thought, should I jump out and push. Then we were moving, but slowly compared to the Harvard. I looked down, which I should not have done, to see what the revolutions were and what speed we were doing, and when I looked up again, at 50 mph, I was horrified to see the aircraft was hopping along at 45 degrees to port of my original path, and turning more as I looked. I knew what torque was, but this was something else. Another 40 degrees and I would hit the hangars. By now I was doing about 70 mph and I was pushing the right rudder as hard as I could. I lifted the Hurricane off, flying to the right of the end hangar and practically level with the sloping roof. Now that I was hanging in the air, gaining speed, I did not dare to think of raising the undercarriage nor of doing anything else except fly this treacherous monster. Thank the Lord for the 1,100 horse-power Merlin engine.

With great trepidation I completed a wide circuit with undercarriage still down, and prepared for a landing. The circuit had been OK and flaps were lowered at the correct time and the descent was good. However, as I flared out for the landing, and closed the throttle, I thought the engine had stopped. Watching this slow prop, I edged the throttle open, and the damned aircraft proceeded to maintain flying speed and caused me to bounce slightly. But, no worries: the proper correction was made, I throttled back, and achieved a good landing. Taxiing to the dispersal tent, I imagined a thick blue haze was forming. Martin stood, hands on hips, with the ground chaps around him, waiting for my arrival. As I walked from the aircraft, the language around me was explosive. I kept very quiet and held my seething reaction for the moment. I waited for the temperature to die down. Martin had yelled among other things, 'What an awful effort, you may be relegated to the Fairey Battle flight.' That really shook me as the 'Battle' was the very worst aircraft as far as action was concerned and had killed quite a number of the brave pilots in France. My answer in the end was, 'Sir, why did you not explain to me the fact that the two-blade wooden propeller would create massive torque for which I should have been prepared and also that the take-off run would be much slower than the three-bladed De Havilland two-speed prop? A little pre-flight advice would have been welcome and what's more, I returned the aircraft in one piece. No wonder the flight crew were surprised when you suggested using the 354.' Flight Lieutenant Martin suggested I return to living quarters and prepare to fly the next day. But I remonstrated and, as politely as possible, asked to be allowed a second flight in the 354, as I had completed nothing. This was agreed to and the 354 was refuelled and made ready. This time I completed a good take-off, undercarriage up at the right time, and down again, also flaps. I completed the circuit and made a good landing. Flight Lieutenant Martin was satisfied and my day was over, released to return to the billet and then to the sergeants' mess. No more talk of 'Battles'.

As I walked across the tarmac, the flight sergeant who had instructed me in the first ground lesson stopped me and asked who it was that had given them such a fright when taking off. I told him it was me. He grasped my shoulder and said, 'I nearly had a fit when I thought you were trying to run up the hangar roof. The angle of my sight indicated much trouble. I reckon Martin gave you a bollocking!' 'Yes', I replied. 'But he should have explained the torque effect.' I entered the mess for a worthwhile beer and there were Meeson and Tony Page already celebrating their excitement. These two had been sent to another flight and both had experienced good results. However, they had a good laugh and pulled my leg when I explained my predicament. Two days had elapsed since we had been separated, but it seemed like two years. So much for the lessons, time and pressure! That night the three of us, accompanied by another Rissington friend, Joe Morrison, enjoyed an evening in one of the pubs in King's Lynn. The talk was all Hurricanes, and they were surprised to know there was a two-blade propeller aircraft still around.

The weather was such that we were allowed two days' leave – not that we could do much. However, Victor suggested we take one day to drive to his home in Houghton and meet his parents. We had a great day, taking photos and enjoying their hospitality, returning to the airfield late that night. The course was nearing its end, and we were encouraged to fly as much as possible, particularly as we were to experience the three-bladed Hamilton propellers with their two-speed revolution configurations. To please the flight sergeant, I asked Flight Lieutenant Martin if he would allow me to fly the Hurricane 354 once more, as it was really exciting. Martin approved and away I went. Great take-off, smooth climb to 8,000 feet, and then some aerobatics.

Earlier in the course, when the weather was good, I had been asked if I had seen the local skinny dipping in one of the canals leading into the sea. So, when I had finished my exercises, I dived down to beat up the sunbathers and swimmers. On a low level flight I decided to do a slow roll. Big fool me: I was halfway round the roll when I realised I did not have the speed to complete it. I corrected the attempt, giving full power, and, with my heart thumping, limped back to the airfield, hoping that the swimmers would not report me. We had heard so many quite remarkable stories of the wonderful Spitfire, so I guess the four of us had been disappointed when we arrived at the Hurricane OTU. However, the past three weeks had convinced me personally that the Hurricane looked and acted like a real fighter aircraft, and handled like a dream. Never had I felt so confident, but I was to learn more in the months to come.

Indeed, I felt good about my aircraft handling, and on another flight on the 354 I spent 20 minutes on aerobatics, doing slow rolls, both left and right, loops, spins, a flick roll or two, having been given confidence in the Tiger Moth and Harvard. But chatting with Martin after a good day's flying, I must have imparted a degree of cockiness, for he stopped my chatter and said, 'Be careful! Never be over-confident. And remember this all your flying life: there are old pilots and bold pilots, but there are no old bold pilots!' This I have remembered to this day.

On 30 August 1940 the course came to an end, and I was advised that, together with Morrison, I would join No. 17 Squadron Hurricanes at Debden. I had completed a total of 246 hours of training, including 37 hours 10 minutes on Hurricanes, although for reasons unknown we did no night flying on Hurricanes. However, the experience on Harvards had been excellent.

Before we left Sutton Bridge, the four of us, Victor Meeson, Tony Page, Joe Morrison and I, planned to meet at the London Savoy and have a ball on Christmas Eve.

11. 'What a Ruddy Greeting'

No. 17 Squadron, Debden

It was 31 August 1940 and two would-be fighter pilots were walking towards their delegated Hurricanes, which were for squadron replacement. Neither of us was smiling. Morrison must have felt like me: very worried. At last the tales we had been listening to and news from the media had overtaken the excitement of our training. We were off to 'no man's land'.

Off we flew, maintaining a tidy formation, and headed for Debden. We were ordered, as we approached, by the duty tower, to land without making a circuit. This we did and, as we touched down, I nearly jumped out of my skin as I heard an enormous bang. Looking across the far side of the airfield, I saw a huge flash of flame and a section of a hangar rising in the air. Looking forward, I became aware of men running towards us waving their arms and pointing to where we should taxi. In the meantime, chaos was breaking loose on the east side of the airfield, with bombs and machine-gun fire making a racket. We came to a stop with everyone yelling 'Get out and run to the trenches', which were near the operations hut. We both made the fastest run in history. Joe Morrison looked at me as we crouched like scalded rabbits. 'What a ruddy greeting,' he said. 'We could have made a circuit in all that mess, and been knocked out before we started!' I agreed, but I simply could not stop the thoughts belting through my head. I remembered my grandfather, maritime captain Charles Calder, saying to me during a mishap on one of his ships, 'Remember laddie, do your best and your destiny will do the rest.'

The raid was over, and we were taken to the squadron operations (ops) room, where we were greeted by Flight Lieutenant Bayne and Flying Officer Count Czernin ,who remarked, 'How's that for an introduction; you have arrived from Sutton Bridge?' 'Yes Sir,' we said. 'Posted to 17 Squadron.' The time was midday, and we were expecting to be introduced to some of the pilots, and also to be informed of our duties. We waited as Bayne and Czernin conversed quietly, and finally Flight Lieutenant Bayne, who was an 'A' Flight commander, approached us with further shock words. 'Let me explain to you two lads. A signal has just been received to the effect that you both must proceed to Tangmere to join 43 Squadron, which needs replacements. Have a mug of tea and I will give you coordinates for Tangmere on the south coast, near Chichester.'

No. 43 Squadron, Tangmere, 11 Group

Morrison and I arrived without incident, and were separated. I was directed to the squadron ops hut and advised to wait for the officer commanding the squadron for an interview. Incidentally, No. 43 was one of the RAF's famous squadrons going back in history. I waited some 20 minutes, becoming a wee bit agitated, when a flight lieutenant approached me, asking, 'Are you a replacement pilot?' 'Yes,' I said. He gave me rather a penetrating look, requesting me to wait at the end of the passage while he walked to the other end and entered an office. The next thing I heard was, 'Caesar, there's a child waiting to see you. What the hell are we being sent now. He must be of age but he looks about 14 years old!' My guts turned over. I had qualified as a pilot and had achieved good results. What an introduction! He beckoned me to enter the office and introduced me to Squadron Leader, newly promoted, Caesar Hull, a South African. He addressed me in a rather husky voice, which I learned was natural, asking me where I was from and which units I had trained at. The officer who had met me first and who had eloquently described my person was Flight Lieutenant Kilmartin DFC. I would see him later and hear of him many times as the years passed.

Caesar Hull advised me, 'Tomorrow, report to the operations hut, ready to fly.' I would be given a Mae West jacket (this was for floatation assistance should I end up in the Channel). I would also be given a parachute. 'You will be my No. 2 in the first scramble [take-off] and I will talk to you in the morning.' He then organised one of the squadron pilots to introduce me around and also give me some explanation of what to expect. Sergeant Hurry introduced himself to me. He was a long-term airman and an RAF NCO, who had come through much technical training since 1931, and was indeed a most experienced airman. He brought along Sergeant Joe Morrison, who had been interviewed by one of the other flight commanders, and together we met Pilot Officers

Hallowes and Carey, Sergeant Mills, and Flying Officer North. And as we talked to these pilots, we really had our ears bashed listening to so much advice.

That evening I was invited to join a group visiting their favourite drinking place, namely the Nag's Head at Chichester, a few miles from the airfield. This was quite a boozy night, although I drank only two pints of beer, being as scared as hell, thinking of the next day. One pilot, Pilot Officer van den Hove, a Belgian, who had managed to escape from the battles in his country and joined the RAF, had plenty to say. He, along with some of the others, concentrated on Morrison and myself, giving us so much advice we did not know what to think. However, we understood, 'Don't fly straight and level for more than a few seconds, jink and move around all the time you are on your own and, if you are attacked, use the well-accepted formula, "Everything in one corner", meaning you ram the control column (stick) in one corner along with full rudder in a similar direction, and keep moving'. This did not take us any time at all to learn and remember.

Soaked in many months of steady, clear and straightforward flying, I returned that evening to the sleeping quarters, not exactly-panic stricken, but still scared as hell. In half a day I had heard about one pilot who had been shot down in the Channel, another who had been badly burned but escaped by parachute and had been taken to hospital, and two more who had parachuted out and had returned to Tangmere, ready for the next scramble. Dear Lord, what happens now? How I managed to sleep that night, I will never know, but the next morning I was out of bed, showered and dressed, and ready to jump into the cauldron at daybreak.

I joined other pilots in the operations hut. We were now at 'readiness'. Caesar Hull drew me aside and discussed the previous evening at the local pub, and was pleased to hear I had been well looked after by both officers and NCOs. He also asked if the men had explained the attack methods in general combat tactics, to which I replied, 'Yes Sir.' Caesar Hull then told me I was to be his No. 2 (Red 2), a position in the formation, and then explained that, when an attack occurred, the formation would break up, and then it was every man for himself. I could protect his rear only at the commencement of the attack, which would be ordered at the call of a radio comment 'Tally Ho'. He concluded his remarks with the instruction that, should I be separated from the squadron as the action drifted away, I had to return to Tangmere immediately, with no hesitation. I also had to remember to jink from side to side and never to fly straight and level, while keeping a good lookout for the enemy aircraft or any form of attack.

After about 30 minutes of general talk and remarks from the pilots at readiness, the 'scramble' alarm was activated and we ran to our Hurricanes, the engines of which had been started by the ever alert ground crews. Taxiing to the take-off point, I formed up with the CO's starboard side and with No. 3 on the port side. The CO signalled 'take-off' and my first action commenced. Amazingly, the stomach flutter and facial twitches and any other panic signs were gone. Now I was flying! Astern came the rest of the squadron in Vics of threes and we were vectored (steered) towards the Portsmouth and Isle of Wight area. Our orders were to patrol at 18,000 feet, in a designated area, and expected to see at least forty enemy aircraft, bombers and fighters, which were expected to be Ju88 bombers, and also Bf109s and Bf110 fighters, together with the frightening Ju87 dive-bombers. We intercepted this raid as they crossed the English coast and attacked. The squadron naturally broke up, pilots selecting which enemy to tackle. It was incredible. I was with the CO for about 2 minutes and then he had vanished. Now what was I to do? Look for a black cross and fire at any I could see. However, the jumble of aircraft was incredible: Hurricanes chasing Ju87s as they were completing their dives, Ju88s being attacked as they bombed, and Bf109s and 110s attacking us. I fired at two Ju87s and one Bf109 fighter and definitely hit the Ju87s, as we were using ammunition called 'De Wilde', which had a magnesium content, giving a flash if it hit a target. I certainly was not going to stick around to see what happened thereafter. Maintaining the 'whirling dervish' activity, I soon found myself alone in the sky, although I had seen two parachutes going down and one aircraft diving with black smoke trailing. I made sure I was alone and, remembering the CO's instructions of 'Don't hang around, return to Tangmere', I was on my way, jinking all over the sky, determined not to fly straight and level. Tangmere was quite close to where the action had drifted, so I was able to land without a problem, joining the rest of the pilots as they returned.

We had to congregate near the intelligence officer's area and report our experiences. I said I had hit two enemy planes but was in no way sure of the results, and that was that. However, I realised I was not the least bit scared or panic-stricken and had felt cool and fully aware of what was happening. There were a number of scrambles that day, but the CO allocated me to ground duties and talks with some of the standby pilots, consolidating advice on fighter tactics.

That evening, when we had been 'stood down' (which meant there would be no more action), we were off to the Nag's Head once more. There was a slight atmosphere of reserve at the beginning of the evening: it had been really tough, one pilot was reported to have parachuted and was on his way back to Tangmere, and apparently a number of the Hurricanes had received damage from enemy guns. But after a few beers the atmosphere brightened, the usual 'lines' were being emphasised and the antics of the pilots were discussed with some excitement. I was thrilled when I was invited to join in the discussions, and was given plenty of advice and explanations.. So after a couple of days, I felt good in the company of the 43 Squadron pilots. I was never left on my own to hang around and was with these expert fighters all the time.

On 3 September I was once again on standby, and by the end of the day I suggested to my flight commander that hanging around was far worse than flying and I should be allowed to chance my luck.

The next day I was one of those on readiness, walking among those prepared for 'scramble', which came with a rush around 9.00 a.m. As I heard those mighty 1,100-plus horsepower engines start up, the hairs on the back of my head stood up. It was a sound I never forgot. We were vectored to cover the Southampton area at 18,000 feet and were immediately advised of formations of Ju88s and Ju87s, with Bf110s covering them. We attacked them, with every man for himself, and I found myself looking at a 110 coming in my direction on the starboard side. I immediately made a violent steep turn to face him. I saw tracers coming from the 110 and fired my guns at him, which caused him to whip into a tight turn and hurtle over me. I received no hits and am certain I missed him, so quick was the action. I then attacked a Ju87, which was at the time Germany's famous single-engine dive-bomber, and I observed hits on the tail section. However, a Bf109, which seemed to come from nowhere, attacked me and caused me to take violent evasive action. When I recovered my action, I chased a Ju88, which appeared to have been hit. However, in the dive for the Channel, although I fired at him from astern, he avoided me, at the terrific speed of which the Ju88 was known to be capable.

It was incredible. Planes were turning and twisting, with bullets and cannon shells making tracer streaks everywhere. Aircraft were in flames or showing black or white streaks behind them. I made a good attack on a Dornier 17, though I did not see the end result, as I was attacked and the Dornier had dived towards the Channel. We returned with no losses, although some aircraft had been damaged, and with pilots claiming various victories. I claimed nothing. However, my Hurricane had collected some bullet holes in the port wing.

On 5 September I was asked to deliver some documents to Usworth Airfield in the north of England, flying a spare Spitfire that was available for use. By the time I returned, the last squadron of the day had landed at base and was busy with reports. Two pilots had not returned. However, reports were that they were OK. One Hurricane had been lost, though the pilot was safe; another had landed at another airfield. Sergeant Dusty Mills told me later that the total tally for the day was five German aircraft destroyed, and quite a number of 'possibles' were being investigated. The term 'possible' covered a report from a pilot who was certain he had destroyed an enemy aircraft but had not seen it crash. Confirmation must come from another pilot or a report from the area in which it had crashed. It was not easy to have a claim accepted, as it was the job of the squadron's intelligence officers to investigate these claims and to be satisfied with them. Post-war records eventually proved this was very necessary.

The following day brought more of the same for the squadron. I was not included in the actions, and neither was Joe Morrison, so we spent our time in the operations room reading action reports and studying silhouettes of both German planes and our own. In a major dog fight, with many aircraft milling around, it was possible to initiate a burst of firing in a panic.

While we were soaking up more knowledge, one of the ground sergeants regaled us with a serious but funny story. After a bombing raid a few days before we had arrived, the flight sergeant of the ground staff had asked one of his airmen to investigate the badly damaged hangar in which he had parked his clean and tidy Hillman Minx car. The poor lad had returned and told him, 'Sorry, flight sergeant, your car isn't in the hangar'. One of the pilots had said to Spike, the flight sergeant, 'You had better have a look yourself.' So up goes Spike to the hangar, along with a body of troops who were interested. They entered the destroyed hangar and all agreed with Spike that there was no car. As they walked back to the end of the hangar, climbing over wrecked aircraft, they turned to fight their way out, when suddenly an airman looked up and pointed at a metal truss in the roof and said, 'What's that up there?' Spike looked up, and with the loudest bellow in Sussex yelled, 'Those German bastards, that's my car!' He returned to the tarmac screaming blue murder. The car of course was an absolute wreck.

In the late afternoon we heard the Merlins of the squadron returning in ones and twos. We watched and saw Squadron Leader Tom Dalton-Morgan taxiing in and, looking hard at the cockpit hood, I recognised blood on the Perspex. Tom looked our way and his face was one big patch of blood. I yelled to the senior flight sergeant, 'Mr Morgan has been hit, let's get him out.' We ran to the aircraft, which had come to rest. We jumped on the wing and helped Dalton-Morgan out, undoing his aircraft harness and his parachute harness. We both helped him off the wing and waited for the ambulance and the medics. Dalton-Morgan was adamant it was just scratches; he had received no other wounds. However, he said 'Thanks chaps', and was taken to hospital. We heard that a 109 cannon shell had entered from behind his aircraft on the starboard side at an angle of about 15 degrees, had hit the inside of the armoured windscreen, causing a lot of glass particles to whip back into his face, making something of a mess. I didn't see him again, but I understand his injury was not serious and he was soon to fly again.

On 7 September Morrison and I joined the ground staff and pilots, in preparations that were required for our squadron's movement to Usworth in the north of England. As we worked, we waited for that welcome sound of Rolls-Royce Merlins returning from the recent raid. The squadron had been engaged with huge raids along the east Channel coast and the fighting had been very rough. We had been advised of some casualties. Soon we heard the sound of engines and Hurricanes returning in ones and twos and, as they landed, we could see damage on most of them. When the landings were completed, it was obvious that not all had returned. As the reports of the pilots were heard, it was a very sad occasion indeed. It was reported that the commanding officer, Caesar Hull, had been shot down and killed. Dick Reynell had also been shot down and killed. Others had landed at various airfields through fuel shortage. Some had been wounded, and further reports were to be received. It was a terrible shock for the squadron, which was to be rested and re-formed at Usworth the next day.

Usworth, Durham

So, on 8 September, twelve Hurricanes, with those pilots left who were operational, flew to Usworth for a re-formation of No. 43 Squadron.

Immediately a programme was begun to intensify the training of new
pilots for the OTUs. Morrison and I had much to learn and joined in.
The training was first class: air firing at a target, formation flying out to
sea, and patrols out to sea, as reports of enemy aircraft were recorded.
Dogfights were organised, with new pilots and old paired off to gain
further experience.

But 13 September found us preparing for a posting in the south again,
as 11 Group was requesting more replacement pilots. Morrison was
posted to No. 46 Squadron, based at Stapleford adjacent to North Weald.
Mills and I were posted to No. 249 Squadron at North Weald, in Essex,
and in 11 Group.

I was asked a number of times if I was frightened and whether I would
rather have joined the Army or Navy. All I could say was, 'I'm scared
when we are vectored on to the enemy, but in the few fights I have
experienced, I found I was as cool as a cucumber and not afraid of
mixing with the Germans.' My thoughts were that, if I got shot down,
I probably wouldn't know what had hit me. My greatest prayer was that
I would not catch fire.

My new friend Dusty Mills was going to North Weald via his home,
so, with my kitbag packed to the brim, I was off to Newcastle to catch
the train to London and, apparently, a bus to North Weald, as a semi-
experienced fighter pilot. The journey south was a nightmare; the train
compartments were packed, as were the corridors. As we travelled south,
I was sitting on my kitbag with my RAF greatcoat on my knees and was
wearing my complete sergeant's uniform, collar and tie. Going to the
bathroom and then coming back to find one's gear was a major
undertaking: I was lucky, as mine had been looked after by a soldier who
was enjoying the seat.

12. 'Yes I'm Old Enough'

No. 249 (Gold Coast) Squadron North Weald, 11 Group

As we approached London it became hotter and hotter, and the overcrowded compartments and overflowing toilets made life very uncomfortable. When the train pulled into King's Cross, there was a mad stampede to get out. The station concourse was also teeming with hundreds of naval, army and air force men and women all yelling and pointing, trying to reach the platforms or exits for trains or buses. After I had used all my strength pushing and shoving and jumping up and down to see where I was heading, I managed to yell out, 'Where's the platform to North Weald?' A station porter shouted to me to join him, so, after some more shoving and cursing, I managed to get beside this chap. He asked me if I was the one yelling for North Weald and, once I had confirmed this, he grabbed my kitbag and said, 'The train's no good for you, you'll be better catching the bus.' I wondered if this was a joke, as I had heard of tricks being played on servicemen. However, as I reached the bus door, just as the driver was ready to leave, the porter gave me a shove and yelled, 'This bugger is for North Weald.' It was standing room only on the bus, a Green Line vehicle. With the standing room being full, I was breathing down the driver's neck, but at least I had managed to cling on to my greatcoat and kitbag. But I felt as though I had just been pulled out of the Thames, for I was soaked with perspiration.

I remembered now that the No. 43 Squadron pilots had continually remarked about the fine warm weather that never seemed to change and how easy it was to find the German aircraft – though this of course meant that the 109s and 110s could also see our planes.

The bus was going to a place that I think was called Ongar and, in so doing, passed the North Weald Airfield. It was now about 2.00 p.m. and I was hot, hungry and fed up with the journey, which had been the worst nightmare ever. Finally the bus driver yelled to me, 'Here you are son, God bless you', and dropped me at the airfield gates. I gathered my items, straightened my tie and my hot uniform, and reported to the guard house: 'Sergeant Palliser for No. 249 Squadron.' The corporal on duty gave me a queer look, so, before he could give the old Cockney crack, I said, 'Yes, I'm old enough.' When I had satisfied this well-uniformed corporal and was cleared for entry to my future, I asked him where the squadron adjutant was. Smiling nicely, he pointed to a spot where I could just see some huts and tents over the horizon, the other side of the airfield. I asked if there was a van or some vehicle that could give me a lift. There was another smile as he said, 'Sorry Sarge, there's nothing.' So I asked if I could borrow one of the bicycles I could see outside the guard house. There was another smile and a very polite refusal; they were all in use.

I stood outside the guard house and calculated that the No. 249 dispersal was between 1½ and 2 miles around the perimeter track and carrying my load that far would be the end of an awful day. But the easiest way to carry an overcoat is to wear it and shoulders can take a nice heavy kitbag. And what's a nice stroll anyway on such a lovely summer's day! I added a few more tasty curses to my vocabulary, which I increased during the train journey, and walked. I did not time the journey but it seemed to take for ever and I was sure my boots were waterlogged. Eventually I arrived at the place of my questionable future. As I dropped my kitbag and tore off my greatcoat, a sergeant/pilot came up to me from the tent area and asked my name. He introduced himself as Sergeant Beard and explained he had just landed from a patrol and action. Sergeant Beard suggested that I should leave my greatcoat and my kitbag with him, smarten up and mop the facial perspiration, and introduce myself to the adjutant and the pilots in the ops hut. This advice caused me to make the biggest faux pas of my life. No doubt I was stressed from my entry into the war and the awful journey to North Weald and of course I had not been born into RAF protocol. But I stepped into the operations hut to see about a dozen pilots with flying suits and 'Mae Wests' at the ready. Larking around, one giant of at least 6 foot looked at me and shouted, 'Hey, look, a little sergeant has arrived to win the war.' I answered, with all the wrath I had accumulated, 'Hell! The petrified forest!' Everyone I could see at the time was 6 foot or over. I stood, terrified, at the dead silence that followed my remark. Then a future friend, Pilot Officer Tom Neil, yelled, 'Hey, Tichy, you can't talk to officers like that. What do you want?' I apologised and, I suppose in a funny Yorkshire voice, said, 'The adjutant please, I have been posted here from 43 Squadron to join No. 249 Squadron.' The next remark was from another pilot, who said, 'But they are at Usworth now.' I answered, 'Yes, they flew there on 8 September, after a terrible time.' The next question was, 'Did you join them there from OTU?' 'No,' I said, 'I joined them at Tangmere at the end of August.'

At that point the adjutant, Flight Lieutenant Lohmeyer DFC, a First World War aircrew whose uniform bore a navigator's 'wing', arrived and asked me to join him in a small office in the hut. As he led me in, there was a loud raucous blast of sound from a motor horn and then I heard yells and curses as the pilots 'scrambled' – this being the operation word shouted when they had to run to their Hurricanes and be airborne as quickly as possible. At least I was used to this action now. Flight Lieutenant Lohmeyer talked about the squadron, explaining that the Africans (Gold Coast) had donated towards No. 249 in some way, hence the name '249 Gold Coast Squadron'. He then asked about No. 43 Squadron and finally advised that I would join 'B' Flight, led by Flight Lieutenant Parnall. It was suggested that, with my relatively short time in No. 43 Squadron and having been involved in the actions on the Channel coast, I should be fully prepared to join the actions as soon as I was ready. Final advice was that I should join the NCO pilots in their bell tents and they would advise me of the accommodation, meals and general conditions relating to the sergeant pilots. I had to introduce myself to Flight Lieutenant Parnall when he was available in the afternoon.

Certainly, the interest on my arrival was not up to the standard of No. 43 Squadron, and this, added to my error, made for an uncomfortable start. Sergeant Beard was still near the tent with my kit and, as I approached, he asked me what the disturbance was about. I explained how I had introduced myself to the officers. I had not seen a bell tent since my scout days. However, I kept my thoughts to myself and listened to Beard, who had introduced himself as 'John', so 'John' it was. He started describing the dos and donts of No. 249 Squadron activities. First he explained that No. 249 was a new squadron, formed mainly at Church Fenton, and also in Leconfield and Boscombe Down in the Midlands. It had been passed as a squadron ready for operations, arriving at North Weald on 1 September. They had experienced a great deal of action at this time and had suffered their fair share of casualties. The bell tents were our sergeants' quarters. There were metal beds with palliasses, blankets and pillows. For our ablutions we had water facilities and a field toilet. Our food would arrive in thermos boxes and we would help ourselves. We would be advised by our flight commanders of the action status – 'readiness' meant we would be ready with Mae Wests and flying helmets on, able to run like hell to our allocated Hurricane, which would have the engine running ready for take-off.

Flight Lieutenant Parnall advised me to discuss the flight roster with John Beard, who appeared to be the senior sergeant, and he would explain the situation. 'You will soon learn to find North Weald after an action,' he said. He turned away and entered the operations hut. I made my way back to the bell tent, to find most of the sergeants had returned and had obviously been told by Beard of my altercation in the ops hut. Did I have a torrid time as an introduction. However, it was all in fun and we all had a good laugh. Dusty Mills of 43 Squadron had finally arrived. As he had been with 43 Squadron for some weeks and had already shot down three enemy planes, Mills also remarked on the lack of interest in his arrival. Dusty also welcomed my presence and talked about the awful last operation with 43 Squadron, and the loss of Caesar Hull and Dick Reynell, just as the squadron was to re-form at Usworth the next day.

The hectic September day closed with strong indication of what the next day would offer. The evening and night brought heavy and continuous bombing, as the Luftwaffe tried to knock out the airfields. Not only were there bombs, but the anti-aircraft defences were throwing up a barrage that was loud enough to break one's eardrums. We NCOs in the bell tents felt the full effect of shrapnel, which on occasion cut through the tents.

13. 'Fuel You Idiot'

On 15 September we were ready at dawn, and had our first grumbles about the tents. The reply from the adjutant was, 'Let's finish today and we'll see what can be done.' It was OK for the officers; they were billeted off the airfield. The morning scramble, with which I was not involved, was airborne. Reports were that three fleets of 100-plus German bombers, with large escorts of fighters, were heading for the south-east area, and all airfields and factories would be attacked. The morning reports contained actions by all pilots, a number claiming victories confirmed, while others had succeeded to inflict heavy damages on Heinkels, Dorniers and Messerschmitt 109s and 110s. The morning had been helped to a great extent by the terrific weather we were experiencing – blue sky with small fleecy white clouds, 'cotton wool', at about 12,000–14,000 feet.

In the afternoon, Blue 3, the formation I was with, was scrambled. We climbed and vectored to our patrol position, covering the area between Maidstone and Canterbury, holding 15,000-feet altitude. We were advised from Fighter Control that we should increase our height to 18,000 feet and vector south, south-west to intercept a raid of 400 plus with heavy fighter escort. At approximately 3.30 p.m., after attacking and damaging a Heinkel bomber and then a Dornier, I broke away as a 109 attacked me. I found myself in cloud for a few seconds and, upon breaking through, I saw a Dornier 217 being attacked from astern and I saw strikes on the port wing and the engine, causing black smoke to stream from the plane. However, the Spitfire must have exhausted his ammunition and he dived away. I attacked the Dornier 17, which was below me, and dived behind and below, firing into the starboard fuselage and wing. I noticed good strikes around the rear gunner's position and pilot area. On breaking away, I witnessed three open parachutes. I claimed a half confirmed.

The thrill of my first confirmed, shared victory was deflated when I realised I had exhausted my ammunition. Checking further, I saw my fuel gauge was screaming, 'Fuel, you idiot! You're down to emergency!' I was lucky the fight had reduced my height to about 7,000 feet and below the cloud formation. I knew I was north of the Thames. However, where were North Weald and Flight Lieutenant Parnall? There was no time to think: I had to find a field to land in. I commenced a circular search, checking every field for a possible landing. I could not write off a priceless Hurricane! With about one-sixteenth of an inch on my fuel gauge, I spotted a semi-triangular field that had reasonable length, except that on the side of the landing path there was what looked like a bomb crater. A quick calculation was necessary. However, I remembered the incident of my experience with the Harvard at Rissington and the haystack. I made one slow run over the field and calculated there was a chance. I flew to a position north-west of the field, giving myself a good long run at a very low level, and commenced a precautionary approach for landing. The fuel gauge was registering zero as I applied as much power on the engine as possible to enable me to hold the nose up with full flap, practically on the stall angle.

The ground seemed to be flashing past but this was do or die, and I must save this wonderful aircraft. Suddenly the hedge of low bushes was there; nose high, full throttle burst, and I was past the hedge and about 6 feet off the ground. So throttle closed, holding steady, I dropped to the ground. I did not think of speed, putting on maximum brakes and hold-ing steady as I passed the crater, which turned out to be a natural large depression in the ground. Speed was now much slower and, praying that the field was clear of items that might damage the aircraft, I stopped about 400 yards from the far hedge. As the propeller was still turning, I turned and taxied as near to the hedge that I had just missed as possible and positioned my aircraft for a take-off. The fuel gauge was still on zero, but it was over-recording. When I recovered from this stress, I noticed a boy running across the field towards me and quite a number of people following him. I had retracted the flaps and switched off the engine. I had left the hood open on the approach. I now unlocked the harness and parachute and checked the gun button was closed, even though I knew my ammunition had been exhausted.

This had been the most hectic day in No. 249. With No. 43 we had not experienced the numbers of German bombers and fighters we had encountered today. Now I had time to think of what would happen to me. This was my first day with No. 249 and Flight Lieutenant Parnall. I still had to return to North Weald and it was already late afternoon.

The boy advised me there was an anti-aircraft battery on the far edge of the field and no doubt they would help me to contact the nearest airfield. Young John was joined by a man who was a farmhand. They offered to keep an eye on the plane, as there was quite a crowd gathering. I reached the anti-aircraft battery and an officer offered to phone Hornchurch, which was the nearest airfield. I waited until I was advised that a truck was on the way with fuel, then I walked back to the aircraft. There were many people around, but John and his friend had been able to advise them to stay clear of this Hurricane. I spent some time with the people asking many questions. The truck arrived, and the sergeant introduced himself to me and he said that they were ready to fill my fuel tanks. I explained that I needed only one 25-gallon tank, as full tanks would possibly be too heavy for the take-off ahead of me.

When the aircraft was ready, I thanked John and his friend, and climbed into the cockpit, and gave the 'ready' signal. I would take off in the direction I had landed, and I had placed the Hurricane in that position before I had finished my arrival. The ground crew from Hornchurch started the engine, let it warm up for some minutes, and finished the full cockpit check. But before I moved the throttle, I put the flaps 'fully down'. This was against all the tenets of flying for 'take-off'. However, I remembered Rissington, where I had saved three Harvards, lost in the industrial haze, from forced landings. So 'full flap' it was. Having been given the course for North Weald, I opened the throttle against 'full brakes', let go the brakes and prayed as hard as I could. It seemed to take for ever for the speed needed for take-off to develop, and the bushes were ahead when I felt the release from the ground at about 55–60 mph. Instead of being tempted to pull the nose up, I held a semi-flat position, and this wonderful Hurricane rose like a lift and cleared the hedge with a few feet to spare. That marvellous Merlin and the Rotol propeller at nearly 3,000 rpm had proved themselves. I flew straight on until I reached about 500 feet, then I closed the flaps slowly and turned to the field at about 1,000 feet and beat up the crowd that were still on the field cheering.

It was dusk when I arrived back at North Weald. As I taxied into the dispersal, thinking of what Parnall would say, I was greeted by my sergeant friends and I reported to one of the officers, who recorded my return. Thank God I had saved a Hurricane. Flight Lieutenant Parnall was nowhere to be seen, and the next day he made no remarks at all. Three days later a letter arrived for me from John Farndon, full of excited thanks for using his father's field, and stressing that I would be welcome anytime.

That night saw most of us sergeants ready for bed. Stroud, Mills, Davidson and I sat in our luxury beds in the modern dwelling with some light from torches – we had to be careful in the tents because of lights showing. We discussed the tremendous effort of Hitler's Luftwaffe, which was the beginning of an effort to commence invasion once the airfields had been knocked out and the civilians in the southern counties shocked beyond belief. We listened to the BBC radio reporting the terrible bombing of the City of London and the outer areas. Battersea, the railway bridges between Victoria and Clapham, and also the West London area had suffered extreme damage, especially the secondary industries. Lambeth, Islington, Motcham, East Croydon, Shepherd's Bush, The Strand, Hammersmith, Westminster and three of London's important hospitals had all suffered from huge high-explosive bombs. The loss of life was appalling. The people in London particularly seemed to be blessed with the Cockney humour as they stood up to this onslaught night after night.

Mills brought our attention back to our day when it was reported that squadrons of Hurricanes with higher-altitude patrolling Spitfires had destroyed 185 German bombers and fighters. This news the newspapers were happy to report. However, they took no notice of our 11 Group leaders, who were carefully checking the claims that many German aircraft had been attacked, as they fell out of the formations, by a number of fighters, who would claim the final victory as the German plane blew up or was vacated by the bloody murderers in their para-chutes. The final tally was 60, which in any language is very good.

I asked my three friends if they had seen the one Heinkel diving in flames as a crew member had jumped out. However, his parachute had streamed in one long figuration and I could see the single line from the body of the man that had stopped the parachute from opening. I could only feel sadness as he dropped to his death. We all spoke at the same time. 'What did you think when our air ground controller announced over the radio, "These are yours Ganer Squadron, 400 plus with heavy fighter escort of 109s and 110s, both Messerschmitt planes"?' Then we talked about what we had individually achieved in the attacks. All four of us had successfully damaged or shared in the destruction or damage of Heinkels, Dorniers and fighters. The squadron had received no casualties. The day, as announced by RAF 11 Group commander, was extremely good. There would be many more days like this one to come.

The following day, 16 September 1940, the weather had deteriorated, which changed the pattern of squadron requirements. A section of six aircraft patrolled and attacked smaller numbers of German planes and the flight to which I belonged was stood down.

The states of readiness in the squadron were:

(a) Stood down   (Released)
(b) Available   (20 minutes)
(c) Readiness   (5 minutes)
(d) Standby   (2 minutes)
(e) Scramble   (Run like hell; ground staff had engines running in this case)

When flying on patrol with the squadron, one pilot would initiate a wireless-type instrument, which would, when actuated, send a signal representing the squadron name. No. 249's name was 'Ganer'. This signal would relay the squadron's position on a grid map in the Group Fighter Control – Fighter Command – 11 Group. If you were selected to be responsible for the signal, you would switch on the instrument and the squadron position would be monitored as long as the patrol lasted. If this was not operating, the question would be asked, 'Is your cockerel crowing?' The worry for the pilot with this responsibility was that, when the dial signalled, his headphones were silenced while the locating beam was related to HQ's beam. Then the pilot could be in the middle of an action, milling about, shooting and dodging enemy dogfighters, and never hearing what was going on around him. Naturally, in a fight, pilots would be yelling and screaming at other pilots, 'Look out!' 'Watch your tail!' 'Look behind you!' When the quadrant completed the 30 seconds, the pilot then heard the full force of the action and wondered 'What the hell was that?' as he heard 'Look, it's on your tail!' and all sorts of expletives. This could be an awful shock to the system.

All this was related to the wonderful Hurricane Mark 1 single-seat fighter aircraft, which I had the very good fortune to have the privilege of flying. The Hurricane was the first single-seat wing aircraft, launched in 1935 as Britain's first front-line fighter. However, it was efficient only up to an altitude of 20,000 feet. It was armed with eight Browning .303 machine guns grouped close together, four in each wing and able to fire approximately 1,100 rounds a minute, and designed to have a solid trajectory at 250 yards. This was thought to be a short distance for an aircraft with a top speed of some 320 mph, although, in a dogfight or heavy manœuvres, speeds were much lower. We soon wondered why the powers that be did not think of the alternate American 0.50 guns, with a much heavier bullet and an effective range of 400 yards.

The Spitfire, launched in 1936, was truly a remarkable aircraft, smaller than the Hurricane and about 40 mph faster. In a dive it was much quicker than the Hurricane, which allowed it easily to follow a Messerschmitt after it had dived to get away. It had eight .303 Brownings, which, because of its thin high-speed wing, had to be fitted far apart on each wing. It was a great aircraft to fly and had no problems at all – 'a real lady'. However, it carried all of the 95 gallons of high octane petrol in a tank located behind the instrument panel and virtually on the pilot's lap. This could be catastrophic if the plane was hit by enemy fire, as the pilot had 3 seconds to leave the cockpit. Many of the burn cases were inflicted on Spitfire pilots.

As a contrast, the Hurricane fuel tanks were in each wing, with the root section of the wing blanked off, while the tanks were self-sealing. The Hurricane also had a small 25-gallon tank behind the instrument panel, which we generally emptied as we climbed to the operational area.

The German fighters were the Messerschmitts. First there was the Messerschmitt Bf109, a single-seat fighter that had been proved in the fighting in Spain during the 1937–8 campaign. Armament was two 20mm cannons and two heavy-calibre machine guns. It was about the size of a Spitfire and probably a little faster. However, the handling characteristics were much trickier than the Spitfire. It had a high-speed wing design and was much faster in a dive than the Hurricane. But in a dogfight it was outclassed by both the Hurricane and the Spitfire. The Messerschmitt 110 was a twin-engine fighter with a pilot and rear gunner armed with two 20mm cannons and a 7.9mm single-barrel gun for rear protection. This aircraft was outclassed against both fighters.

Following a lull in the attacks, we were scrambled on 18 September and vectored on to a very large raid of Heinkels with the usual escort of Messerschmitt 109s and 110s like a swarm of wasps. A question from HQ was, 'Have you sighted your raid?' At this a shout came from one pilot, 'Sight them? We could get out and walk on the bastards.' We attacked head-on, which scattered the Heinkel bombers and broke us up into individual combat. The sky was one mass of aircraft gyrating, diving, climbing and attacking when they were able. As usual, once these fights started, you were on your own. I attacked a Heinkel from port side, climbing into him to fire into the wing root. I managed a 2-second burst and skidded quickly underneath him as the rear gunner gave me a burst, which flipped across my port wing. I turned and fired at the tail section, and also aimed at the rear gunner, which I must have silenced. However, my shots took bits off the aileron section of the bomber, and I had to turn quickly away to avoid fire from a 110 with four cannons in its nose.

After this, the main fight was drifting eastward. All I attained was various damages on the bombers and a 110 that attacked me from my starboard side – a quick turn under him and a sharp burst of fire saw pieces fly from his port elevator when I dived away. I was down to 10,000 feet by now and the carnage was as usual frightening – parachutes here and there, different aircraft on fire, diving earthward. I saw one Hurricane in trouble, trailing thick smoke, and I wondered if one of the parachutes was its pilot. As usual, in about 30 minutes I had used up most of my ammunition and fuel, and so I turned to return to North Weald. I had damaged a number of enemy aircraft, but I could not claim any sort of victories. With the nerves in my legs trying to shake my knee caps off, I landed and reported on my experiences, and waited for the next scramble. A number of the officers were engaged in some worrying conversation, and I heard them explaining the loss of Flight Lieutenant Parnall, who had apparently returned to North Weald with aircraft problems and had immediately taken another Hurricane and flown off alone to join the squadron. However, it was thought he had been attacked by a roving 109 and shot down. Witnesses had seen him crash in a local field. A fourth scramble had us tearing to meet a raid on the south-east coast, but the raid had turned back and we returned to base.

On 19 September we were sent off in pairs, as the weather had deteriorated with dense cloud forming. We did not encounter any hostile enemy and finished the patrol. The weather caused a general lull in the flying from both sides. Also on the 19th an Australian pilot, Flying Officer Millington, a friendly officer with a record of eight victories, joined the squadron.

After a number of lulls in the operation because of weather conditions, I joined Flight Lieutenant Beazley as Red 3 in his section on patrol near Gravesend. We attacked a Dornier 17. Beazley opened fire and I opened fire at the rear of the Dornier. Red 2 joined in this attack. The German dived away into a cloud and came out of the cloud to be

met by further fire from the three of us in different attacks, after which
white smoke and glycol were seen streaming from the starboard engine.
We experienced no return fire. The Dornier dived into the cloud again,
badly damaged. The three of us had poured bullets into this aircraft.
Flight Lieutenant Beazley claimed a 'badly damaged' Dornier 17 for the
section.

The weather really had changed the assaults. More attacks and patrols
were being carried out with sections of two aircraft dodging through
clouds and rain. And the enemy in small numbers were undertaking
raids on factories and airfields. We had some excitement during this
weather when one night a single bomber flew over the airfield and
dropped a huge landmine. We woke up to hear panicky voices telling us
to get dressed and get to the south side of the airfield, while the bomb
squad discussed what they could do to disarm the thing. We could see it
about 500 yards away from our bell tent. The team reckoned that, if it
had exploded, it would have wiped out all of us sergeants in our tents
and quite a number of aircraft, along with the operations hut. We went
out to the airfield and over to the local village for a few hours while these
army heroes worked on the mine and disabled it. It was a huge cylinder
about 3 feet in diameter and 8–9 feet long, sitting in a clump of trees with
the parachute still attached. Some weeks later we heard that a similar
mine had fallen elsewhere, and two of these brave lads had been killed,
trying to disable it.

A week or so later, on 27 September, we were scrambled, the whole
squadron of twelve taking off, with Wing Commander Victor Beamish
following. He joined us on many occasions. We patrolled the Wickford
area and were then ordered to patrol the Maidstone area, where a large
number of Messerschmitt 110 twin-engined fighters, escorted by many
109s, had crossed the coast between Dover and Brighton. They were
operating in a manner to entice our squadrons to maintain attacks and
use ammunition and fuel, so that we would be retiring to rearm and
refuel when another huge raid came in behind. As we approached the
area in a clear blue sky with a few light clouds high in the sky, we saw at
about 12,000–15,000 feet over Redhill an amazing sight of approximately twenty Bf110s in a huge defensive circle, with dozens of 109s high
above, showing no effort to come down and protect them. Maybe they
were thinking they would run out of fuel, and had to face their return
over the Channel. Whatever the reason, Flight Lieutenant Barton, who
was leading the squadron, led us in a diving attack, with 46 Squadron

following. Attacking with Red Section and diving from 19,000 feet, I split up the circle and set upon a 110, firing two 3-second bursts as he was turning. I saw the return fire cease as he was in a steep turn, and then saw smoke and oil, as the machine dived into the sea, about 4 miles off the coast, south of the Redhill area.

I then attacked a second 110, aiming on a quarter attack, which developed into a beam as the 110 turned. The port engine ceased to turn and a smoke stream commenced; no return fire was noticed as the 110 went into a shallow dive towards the Channel. I did not follow and see it crash, as another 110 appeared close, and I attacked, again firing into the wing root on the starboard side until my ammunition ran out. I was fired at by the rear gunner and felt a shock on my feet as a shell hit my rudder area. When I landed and taxied in, one of my ground crew told me my rudder was badly damaged. My second claim was later confirmed to have crashed.

After we had returned to North Weald, there were many exciting reports given to the squadron intelligence officer. Apparently the squadron had shot down eight 110s, and 46 Squadron had claimed four. I claimed three, but only two were confirmed. Our excitement was dampened when it was reported that Percy Burton was missing. I had seen Percy Burton's Hurricane as I left the fight with the third 110 and had noticed his aircraft's contortions as he chased the 110, and he was very close. I was in the section behind him on take-off and recognised his squadron letters, as other pilots must have. This saddened me, as Percy was one of the officers whom I talked with on occasion when we were at readiness. He was a South African and a rather quiet and gentle lad. He had talked a lot about South Africa and was happy to answer the many questions I had asked him, as I was interested in South African history. His death had quite an effect on me, when I realised that one's life is always minutes away from ending.

In late September we were finally allowed to leave our bell tents and make ourselves comfortable in the half-built hut with a strengthened roof and an open fresh-air view to the west. The east end of the hut was closed, with an ordinary door touching a large mound of earth, the toil of the government builders who had worked on the perimeter track. So at the beginning of October we had a roof over our heads and felt a degree of safety. Electric lights were fitted with low-power globes and the switch was mounted on the side of the hut, at the open end. We washed and shaved with the aid of bowls of water, generally cold, and to shower we had to walk around the perimeter track on the east side of the airfield to the sergeants' mess building.

By now new sergeant pilots had been posted to No. 249. It was suggested we should draw lots to decide who slept where from the closed end to the open end. The beds were placed from east to west, each side of the hut, leaving a walking path between the bottom of the beds. The last man to arrive at night switched the light off. A tarpaulin was fastened to the open end. At times some of the WAAF girls would visit us and offer to do some shopping for soap, razor blades and other bits and pieces. We had not left the airfield for many days. However, some nights we would borrow an available car and visit the Sun & Whalebone Pub on the Bishop's Stortford Road, about 5 miles from the airfield. We had to be satisfied. However, we thought deeply about our treatment.

After three nights of this we were awakened at about 3.00 a.m. by the sound of awful screeching and scraping, and then a bump shook the hut. We all shot out of our beds and raced around to the perimeter end of the hut to see a No. 25 Squadron short-nose Blenheim night fighter with its nose buried in the mound against the hut. How we blessed the mound, which we had asked to be moved! We all gasped when we realised that, if the big heap of soil had not been there, we would have been wiped out. We helped to get the pilot and air gunner out, noticing that one of the propellers was missing. No. 25 Squadron Blenheims were being used for night fighter action, and these old aircraft were famous for shedding propellers. By that time, the ambulance and a fire engine had arrived. However, luckily there was no fire. When the excitement was over, dawn had broken, and the whole mess was there to behold.

14. 'Scramble, Scramble!'

We entered October with a change of weather conditions, so we changed to patrols of two Hurricanes chasing single bombers roaming around in the clouds. We were reasonably comfortable in our new half hut. I wondered what my mother would say if she saw me now! However, we laughed it off and accepted the continuous staccato blasts as our mechanics started our Hurricane engines. It was a thrill to hear the 1,100 Merlins making their never-forgotten rumble as they were readied for the first scramble.

One week after this we were summoned to a meeting to be told that accommodation off the airfield had been arranged, and we would move shortly. During this last week in the half hut, a new pilot had arrived – one Macejowski. He was immediately christened 'Mickey Mouse'. He was one of a number of Polish and Czechoslovakian pilots who had escaped from Europe and found their way with difficulty to England. All of them were pilots and had flown antiquated aircraft against the Luftwaffe, with dreadful results. However, they were thrilled with the Hurricanes and Spitfires that they could now fly, and they proved to be very good fighter pilots. Mickey was a funny lad, full of good humour and full of stories of his journey and subsequent arrival at No. 249. He could never wait to go to the local village or even into London when he was off duty, proving to be a real terror with the ladies. One night he returned to the hut in our last week, very late. He jumped into bed and refused to switch the light off. A big argument commenced, to be finished when John Beard, who was the senior in the hut, produced a revolver and shot the light off. I think we all had a good laugh.

October continued with persistent inclement weather, rain, showers, low cloud and high cloud, which produced a number of active German raiders, with individual bomber raids on the airfield. We were ordered to patrol in pairs to try to locate these bombers. No. 249 Squadron had been praised by the commanders of 11 Group, and three of our officers

received the Distinguished Flying Cross (DFC). Our friend Sergeant
John Beard received the Distinguished Flying Medal (DFM). Flight
Lieutenant Butch Barton had certainly earned his, as he never missed a
flight. He was a Canadian, a quiet and reserved person. Pilot Officer
Gerald Lewis received a bar to his DFC. He was a South African and
had just joined our squadron, coming from No. 85 Squadron. Pilot
Officer Bill Millington had also joined No. 249, coming from No. 79
Squadron. Bill was an Australian. They were three good pilots from
three different countries of the British Empire.

The weather was certainly changing from what had been a mostly
good September, with rain and clouds forming and more cumulus stratus
to fly through. The half hut was certainly protecting us from shrapnel.
However, it was far from a joke to live like this, and the officers knew it,
with little sympathy. Sergeant Smithson, one of the original 249 pilots,
returned from hospital after recovering from some injuries from enemy
action. Known as 'Smudge', he was a very pleasant lad, full of fun, and
came back none the worse for his ordeal.

As October progressed, there were many individual scrambles or
patrols with single or two aircraft. The Dornier 17s seemed to be very
active, delivering individual raids on the airfield and factory targets. The
Dornier 17s were less cumbersome than the Heinkel. Our patrols took it
in turns to fly dawn patrols, taking off at 4.00 a.m. and patrolling the
11 Group area and sometimes flying halfway across the Channel to check
the cloud coverage. These patrols gave me time to understand the
Hurricane, with its 1,100-horsepower Merlin engine, smooth controls
and the reaction when used savagely as if it was being attacked. It was a
wonderful feeling to think, 'Look at me, 21 years old and a full-blooded
RAF fighter pilot!' The duty of a dawn patrol was to estimate the cloud
structure in tenths, ten-tenths being total cloud cover, then cloud density
and different types of cloud at different levels of cloud formations. This
was reported to ground operations to assist in their calculations of what
might be expected from the Luftwaffe. Twice on these patrols I had
broken through a cloud layer to see a Dornier sneaking across the top of
a cloud layer in a position between Dover and the Thames estuary. The
first time I had opened the throttle and unfortunately passed over a
section of broken cloud and was spotted by a Dornier, which turned into
a thick mass of cloud. I followed into the position it had turned into, and
maintained a huge circle just on top of the cloud layer in case the
Dornier exposed itself. However, after 5 to 10 minutes the Dornier was

nowhere to be seen, and I went on with the patrol, returning to base. The second patrol of this nature took place with Flying Officer Beazley, the gentleman of the squadron. Flying just on top of the cloud layer, we spotted a Dornier 17 at right angles to us on a west-to-east course. I buried myself into the top of the cloud layer, edging a little to the west, and John Beazley stayed between the cloud layer on the same course. So far we had not been seen. But as I closed on him to about 400 yards, his rear gunner must have spotted me. It dropped into the cloud as I fired a 3-second burst hoping for some luck, as from that distance it was fairly possible to hit the Dornier. I dived down under the cloud layer, maintaining a south-easterly course, then climbed up above the cloud once more to see the Dornier again flying south in clear air. Beazley saw it at the same time. We closed again with full throttle, fine pitch, and 3,000 revs on the Merlin engine and, closing on it again at 300 yards, we fired together from port and starboard sides, closing fast. And now we could see the strikes, as again it dived back into a cloud, with both of us following. We noticed that the rear gunner had not returned fire, which probably meant he had been injured or killed. And we now noticed a black streak of smoke and flame. We returned to North Weald and reported the action; we knew we had damaged the Dornier. A report was received from a ship in the Channel that a twin-engine German aircraft had crashed in the sea about a mile from the ship. That was the last I heard. However, Beazley had claimed a victory, it being shared with me. This was confirmed.

Towards the end of October, more pilots joined the squadron. Among them was Pilot Officer Tommy Thompson from No. 85 Squadron. I was happy to see him, as we had met at Hastings in 1939 when we were introduced to the RAF. Despite his commission, we had much to talk about. We welcomed two Czech pilots, two French, three Polish and three South African. Now we were truly cosmopolitan.

Squadron Leader Grandy was injured and was posted to the Air Ministry for a senior position. The squadron was to be led by Acting Squadron Leader Barton. Butch Barton, as we all knew him, was a Canadian, and to my own delight he was of short stature, as I was, among the giants. Butch was a quiet reserved man, a deep thinker, strong willed and afraid of nothing. The whole squadron accepted him as our leader with much pleasure. His rank would be confirmed later in the year.

There was a noticeable change taking place in the squadron. Discussions between officers and NCOs were increasing, particularly after an action, where tactics and results were welcomed. Flight Lieutenant Gerald Lewis and Pilot Officer Terry Crossey, both South Africans, had already talked with me on a number of occasions after I had shown interest in South Africa – always a subject of adventure. Pilot Officer Bill Millington, the Australian, was a really nice lad who, like Crossey and Lewis, had time for officers and NCOs. So No. 249 had become a family in many ways – but only in the operations area when at readiness.

Another welcome change came when we were advised by Flight Lieutenant Lohmeyer (adjutant) that at last our concerns relating to our awful living conditions had been noted. Arrangements had been made for all NCOs to be billeted about 5 miles from the airfield in a beautiful home on a large country estate belonging to Sir Godfrey Thomas. We would enjoy home living, and our meals would be delivered from the airfield. This change included NCO pilots from No. 46 and No. 257 Squadrons. Transport would be organised by the RAF at North Weald. It was now near the end of October, so the move was a godsend, as winter was beginning to show its arrival. It was goodbye to bell tents and half huts!

On 29 October, after a busy day with two heavy scrambles, at about 1630 hours the squadron was ordered to scramble a section in the company of some of No. 257 Squadron, which had been ordered to fly in from Stapleford Airfield to join up with No. 249. The section in which I belonged was at readiness for instant action and we were milling around joking and comparing actions with the No. 257 NCO pilots. I was laughing at a joke 'Tubby' Girdwood was telling me, when all hell broke loose. The operations corporal was screaming, 'We're under attack, we're under attack. Scramble, scramble!' As he shouted, we were running to our aircraft, and I shouted to Tubby, 'Finish the joke when we return.' Our airmen mechanics had already started the engines, I jumped into my aircraft and out of the corner of my eye I saw Tubby on my starboard side, about 100 feet away, climbing into his aircraft.

Now bullets and cannon shells were tearing up the field around us, and I was just airborne when I heard a sickening crack on my starboard side, like a 6-inch gun being fired. With a quick glance I saw Tubby's aircraft, hit by a bomb from a Messerschmitt 109. At the same time I felt an awful vibration in my engine and I realised I had been hit by something. I had to level out at zero feet and do a quick flat turn to port to enable me to land before my engine blew up. I landed in minutes beside the perimeter track, climbed out and ran back across the airfield, where a large number of people were looking at what was Tubby's Hurricane, which was now a ball of fire. The Hurricane had been hit by a bomb, which had burst underneath and had blown the plane up in a sort of loop, which ended in the furnace. Tubby could be seen, shoulders and head visible. I yelled 'That's Tubby Girdwood', and I started towards the aircraft. However, some of the No. 249 Squadron pilots who had not been able to get airborne held me, shouting, 'Don't be a fool the aircraft will blow up any second!' The fuel tank was full of high octane. We had to retire further away, as bullets from Tubby's guns were now exploding in the fire. We stood and watched helplessly and witnessed the terrible sight of a friend being cremated before our eyes. This was the worst experience and most shocking episode of my whole career.

As for my own Hurricane, it was found that shrapnel from the bomb that had killed Tubby had sliced off a few feet of one of my aircraft propeller blades. This type of attack was replacing the huge fleets of daytime bombers. A number of Messerschmitt 109 fighters fitted with one 500-lb bomb and using their cannons and machine guns, roaring at a target at top speed, could cause much trouble. The damage to the airfield and building, and the loss of life and injuries to personnel, were serious indeed. However, our pilots who were airborne in the first section were in a good position to chase and attack the fleeing 109s. At least four were shot down and a number damaged. The pilots of No. 257 Squadron were able to share in this action, with good results. A sad, sad day with the loss of a young volunteer and friend.

The truck that now took us sergeants to and from our luxury residence and the airfield had arrived. As I joined the number of sergeants, I was stopped by the airman mechanic who had checked my Hurricane and had the engine running when I had jumped in and became airborne. He said, 'Sarge, did you realise that you did not put your parachute on and the aircraft straps were folded on the back of your seat, untouched?' I had thought of nothing else but getting airborne and avoiding the bullets and bombs that were everywhere. I was lucky my flight commander was not aware of my error. Then we were off to Sir Godfrey Thomas's lovely home. After a wash and with a tidy uniform, the regular 249 sergeants were off to the Sun & Whalebone public house on the Bishop's Stortford Road, which was also close to the airfield. Charlie Brewer, the jolly, big, plump Jewish owner, welcomed us with open arms and offered free beers all round. He was as alarmed as we were, as he had been on the edge of the attack and had had full view of the action, ground to air. He was in tears when we described the action when Tubby had been killed and repeated his old remark, 'Why must you kids be part of this war?' We joined the local civilians, drinking, discussing our flying and playing darts, which we enjoyed. Among the civilians was a middle-aged lady with her daughter Jean. They explained their home was in Bishops' Stortford, a few miles north of London. the constant bombing of London and suburbs had caused the husband, a lieutenant colonel and a director of the Bryant & May Company, to rent a section of one of the local farmer's houses, for a long period. A lot of families had done the same. Most nights the atmosphere in the pub was very jolly, particularly for us, as we all came from different areas of Britain, with our funny accents. With our new evening residence and this evening activity, life was indeed a great deal happier. However, the war was still on, and in the early mornings our breakfast arrived with the vehicle, waiting to carry us back to the airfield.

During the first week of November, Dusty Mills and I were ordered to patrol a convoy of ships leaving the mouth of the Thames and heading north. These convoys were being attacked fairly regularly by Dornier 17s. We approached the convoy carefully, commencing a run around the last of the ships and up the starboard side of the convoy. There must have been sixteen or eighteen vessels in two lines. We signalled the colours of the day and reduced speed to 180 mph. We split the patrol, Mills flying down the portside as I patrolled up the starboard side. We were level with each other, approximately half the way up and down the line, when I heard a bang; then another and another. The convoy was firing at us, so we thought. However, they had spotted a Dornier approaching.

The weather was terrible. Low cloud, rain and heavy winds made visibility very tricky. The German passed across the front of the convoy, when I realised he had seen Mills and myself and had dropped his bombs on the leading ships. I saw Mills had reacted and was turning to chase the Dornier, and I was already heading towards it with full throttle. The Dornier turned for cover in the rain. However, we were closing in from either side. I fired a 2-second burst. I could see I was just out of range but closing. Mills was in a similar position when we lost sight of the German. We maintained our direction, practically side by side, when we spotted him turning. Now we were in 300-yard range and we both fired, I suppose about two 3-second bursts, and the Dornier caught fire, streaming heavy smoke, and crashed about half a mile on the coast side of the convoy. We patrolled for about 30 minutes in case there was a second bomber. There were no further reports of enemy aircraft. We could see little bursts of steam from the ship's funnels as they sounded their sirens for thanks to us.

Returning to base from this convoy, pleased with our success, we were close to the mouth of the River Thames when we received an order to patrol westerly along the river to endeavour to see signs of an aircraft that had been recorded as crashing into the river. We both had been flying under 1,000 feet as the weather was so bad, and we had experienced icing conditions in the clouds. We came down to about 500 feet and in one area we witnessed a number of small craft circling a spot in the river. We reported this back to North Weald. Later we learned that the aircraft was an Airspeed Oxford twin-engine trainer that was piloted by Amy Mollison. She had apparently been warned of the icing conditions, but had ignored the warnings. This had probably caused the crash. 'Sorry Amy.' We returned to North Weald and claimed a success, later confirmed, another shared victory.

On 4 November I had returned from a negative patrol in awful weather, which had closed in, with darkness and pouring rain. Squadron Leader Barton asked me to make my Hurricane ready for another flight, as reports indicated a number of German Dorniers were above the cloud and bombing blindly over the London area. I was ordered to scramble and reach the top of the cloud layer and report any enemy activity. If it was a single Dornier, I was to endeavour to attack it. I looked at Butch Barton and said, 'I have just landed an hour ago, experiencing heavy cloud at a pretty high altitude.' He told me we must stop these raiders with their indiscriminate bombing, particularly over the City of London. Thank God for my advanced training in instrument flying.

I was airborne just after 6.30 p.m., and entered the cloud at approximately 500 feet, cursing and yelling blue murder at this awful patrol. I was immediately in the hands of one of the senior controllers, who were very very reliable in these conditions. I was scared – was this my day for trouble, not from Dorniers but from the shocking conditions? It was like being locked in a huge dark room, pitch black. All I could see was my instruments. I was climbing on a south-west course at 160 mph towards the London area. But the Hurricane was truly a reliable and wonderful fighter aircraft, and I trusted it to the hilt. And, apart from some nasty bumps in the atmosphere, it was flying quite smoothly. I broke through the cloud mass at 12,000 feet into very black sky, with no moon; however, there were stars.

Control had altered my course a number of times, and now the instructions were placing me in a circular pattern over the London area. The information was clear and concise, which made me feel quite confident. But after I had spent about 20 minutes trying to see a Dornier in this blackness, my controller advised me that the positions of the German aircraft had vanished from the control centre plot of 11 Group. I should return to base. Back to the black box with the controller talking me down once more. The magic of this sort of flying can hardly be explained, as the calm voice ordering my speed of descent and course came through my helmet, with me repeating the orders, which allowed the control to be maintained, and so I kept my position in this blackness. Now I was in the North Weald area, absolutely blind, my eyes sore from the intense concentration on my instruments. The control vectored me to a position approximately 10 miles north of the airfield, bringing me around the area of the 300-feet-high radio masts on the North Weald border. The information was that there was still a heavy raid and visibility was down to 200 feet. I gasped. How do we do this? I must have bellowed this reaction, as the controller's voice came through: 'Ganer Blue One [my call sign], you are 10 miles north of the airfield, now flying south at 132 degrees, altitude 2,000 feet. Reduce your speed to 140 mph, course 170 degrees, descent angle 500 feet per minute.' I couldn't see a thing, and my hands were squeezing the control stick very, very hard. 'You are on a straight run in, now lower your flaps, reduce speed to 80 mph. Lower undercart, throttle in fine pitch, height 500 feet, hold your speed at 80 mph and you should see the dark mass of the runway any second.' And damn me, there it was. Talk about prayers. I brought the stick back into my belly slowly and then I was down, and it was pouring with rain.

I brought this wonderful Hurricane to a stop, turned and entered the perimeter track, and taxied back to our dispersal. The duty pilot greeted me, helped me with my report, and one of the squadron cars drove me to our new billet. The time was now 7.50 p.m. This flight felt as though it had lasted for ever. The secret of this navigation was tied in with the controller's orders to me, which had to be repeated by me. This allowed the electronic waves from two signals crossing, showing exactly where I was positioned. I changed quickly and joined the lads, who were leaving for the jolly Sun & Whalebone, where I managed to partake of a nice ham sandwich and a pint of beer. Jean, my friend, was being told what an idiot her boyfriend was, with jokes being made about my wet and blind flight. The darts match had begun, and Jean partnered me, playing for a round of drinks. Jean was an excellent player and I was not too bad. The competition was jolly and the atmosphere fine and warm, and the night was very pleasant.

Around this time I managed to have my Riley Saloon car returned in good nick. One of my pals had borrowed it when we were at OTU Sutton Bridge being introduced to the wonderful Hurricane. A problem had arisen when he was showing off the Wilson Automatic gearbox to his girlfriend. He drove the car forward and said to his friend, 'Look, you just move the gear lever down and the car reverses.' The result was a £20 repair bill for me and no car from August until now, November. He paid half. I was now taking Jean out for short runs to the villages around the district and we had enjoyed a number of picnics. This made for a very happy release from the awful tension of flying and fighting, with the constant thought, 'Will I make tomorrow?'

Now we had entered November, Acting Squadron Leader Butch Barton called us all to a meeting in the readiness hut. He informed us that the Air Ministry had announced a change in the Luftwaffe tactics. They had ceased operating massive bomber fleets, owing to the serious loss of their bombers and fighters during daylight. Their tactics were now to bomb cities and selected industrial targets throughout Britain, by night. Sporadic attacks would be maintained by day, with small groups of bombers and fighter bombers, like the raid on North Weald on 27 September. He also mentioned that the War Office had calculated that Goering and Hitler had accepted that their losses overall had forced the cancellation of attempts to take over Britain. British air power had not exactly won the war as such. However, the Royal Air Force had stopped any attempt at invasion! In addition to this, the RAF Bomber Command had been sending up large forces to cover the whole coastline of France, Belgium, Holland and the Nordic Territories, searching out barges, boats and every possible troop vessel. The result was that, by the end of September, the German invasion fleets were matchwood in every harbour, river mouth and river along the European coast.

The 'Battle of Britain' had saved Britain. However, major battles were ahead. Other than the United Kingdom airmen from the following countries were now involved as well: Australia, New Zealand, Canada, Belgium, Poland, Czechoslovakia, Rhodesia, South Africa, France, Ireland, Jamaica, Newfoundland, Pallestine, America.

The Americans made their way to Britain via Canada. The American Ambassador, Joe Kennedy, had given his very angry reports to his home country that Britain was finished. It was a waste of time helping Britain, he said. His calculation was that Hitler would win easily, and the UK had no chance. This tirade went on for two years. He also advised that American airmen should not be allowed to join the Royal Air Force and they were to be stopped from entering Canada, which was accepting them. This effort is in many of the history books.

There was no rest for anyone. November was no different, the fight went on. However, there were new suggestions that the RAF would now plan attacks on and into France and Belgium; the tide was turning. The RAF had forced the thin end of a mighty wedge for the rest of the free world to use.

In the meantime, Winston Churchill was angry, because our night fighters were not delivering satisfactory attacks on the German bomber night raids. Now the night assaults were increasing, cities such as Liverpool, Birmingham, Coventry, Southampton and Plymouth were suffering as poor London had done. Fighter Command was ordered to commence 'back-up' fighting using single-seat fighters. The Spitfire could not fly at night, because of the long straight nose with the exhaust flames blinding the pilot. The Hurricane with a shorter nose curving down slightly could accept Inconel plates fitted between the exhausts and the pilot's sight. Inconel was a high-temperature steel plate. So here we went again!

On 7 November 1940, after a number of early morning 'scrambles', which proved to be false alarms, at midday the whole squadron was scrambled to patrol the Thames estuary. It was reported that a fairly heavy raid was plotted approaching the estuary at 18,000 feet. When we arrived in position, we could see nothing. However, as I was weaving over the squadron, I completed a tight turn and, looking down, I could see the ships in the estuary and bombs exploding.

I advised Barton, who immediately led the squadron, diving fast to about 2,000 feet. We were given a 'Tally Ho' call and waded into the mess of Junkers 87 dive-bombers, which were covered by 109s. I saw a 109 diving below me. I dived to attack him, carried out a stern assaults and closed fast. At very short range I fired a long burst and could see strikes from nose to tail, and the 109 crashed into the water. Sergeant Smithson reported he could confirm the incident. At this time we were using 'De Wilde' .303 ammunition. The bullet point had a design that held an explosive tip. When the bullet hit any part of an aircraft, there was a flash and a minute explosion. The ammunition was recalled at the end of 1940. I attacked two Stukas (dive-bombers) and managed to see strikes and pieces falling. However, I had to be satisfied. The action cleared as other squadrons appeared. The Germans suffered heavy losses.

A week later, on 14 November, after a midday discussion on tactics, Squadron Leader Barton drew me aside and advised me that he wanted me to make the first 249 night fighter operation related to Churchill's request to the squadrons. At 5.00 p.m. I was ready to fly to Debden and report to Squadron Leader Peter Townsend, who was now in charge of the night fighter squadron. I had previously checked a change in armament for the eight guns and had requested to increase De Wilde ammunitions, and also tracer, at the expense of ball ammunition. At 6.00 p.m. I landed at Debden and reported to Peter Townsend, who welcomed me as joining the first attempt to use Hurricanes. I entered the operations hut in which there were three other pilots from different squadrons. Peter Townsend pushed his lovely Alsatian dog off a basket chair and offered it to me, handing me a pair of very dark lens glasses. The other pilots were already wearing theirs, as these glasses helped us with night vision. My orders were to be airborne at twelve o'clock, midnight, and once airborne I would receive radio orders from the group controllers. It was the same discipline. Orders would come from control, I would repeat the order for radio waves to plot my position, and eventually vector my return to North Weald. Sandwiches and soft drinks were available, and I could snooze in the basket chair or walk around the hut. Unfortunately we could not read. However, chatting to the other guinea pigs was quite interesting and passed the time quickly.

At twelve midnight I placed the glasses on the table and took my leave from Peter Townsend, who wished me luck. I had asked one question when we were waiting. 'What do we do if we find our own airfield fogged in?' Peter answered, 'Control will vector you to another airfield.' And 'What if they are fogged in?' 'Well, we suggest you calculate your position, maintain altitude at 15,000 feet, and fly on an easterly course and bail out.' OK. I climbed into my great Hurricane and felt much safer. I was airborne at twelve o'clock midnight and climbed up to the patrol line, heading north to cover eventually an area between Liverpool, Birmingham, Coventry and the Debden area. Instructions from control were to fly at 12,000–14,000 feet, 200 mph, patrol in a zigzag pattern, enter the slipstream disturbance of the bomber stream, and hope to see the enemy bomber. Unfortunately the twin-engine Havoc aircraft was not able to fly with us, otherwise we would have been helped by this aircraft, which was fitted with a very powerful 'Lay Light' (searchlight), which would have lit up the sky ahead of us and in we would go. So I settled down to maintain a long boxlike zigzag course with my eyes wide open, looking for dark shadows that could be a Heinkel bomber, which I would endeavour to destroy. I had fuel enough to allow me to fly for 2 hours before aborting the flight, so I could cover quite an area of the country.

As I approached the Midlands of England, I could see the red glare of fires and, as I got closer, my heart was in my mouth, watching fires the likes of which I had never seen before. As I first saw Coventry and Birmingham, I tried to see the Heinkel aircraft silhouetted between me and the inferno. However, no matter how hard I tried, I saw no aircraft. I screamed all the curses I could and I was experiencing a lot of turbulence of the air. However, the fires must have developed most of the turbulence, as the heat could reach my aircraft. Back and forth I flew, sometimes slowly, other times faster, as I thought I could see the enemy. I cried, I screamed, I flung the Hurricane up and down, as there was the light from these fires. I flew towards Liverpool, but my fuel was telling me it was time to proceed south to be able to return to North Weald. Never have I felt so useless in my life. My thoughts and prayers were pouring out of my system for those people – now I realised what London had and still was suffering. As I approached the Debden/North Weald area, I was brought back to my own problems, as the controller advised me to increase speed, as the Thames fog was developing towards North Weald. I entered the North Weald circuit just after 2.00 a.m. and, as I landed and was taxiing into the dispersal, the fog rolled in. I slept the rest of the night until 7.00 a.m. in the ops hut, as the fog was so dense it was impossible for a truck to take me to my new billet. I felt as though I had been pulled inside out.

Yet another week later, on 21 November, Thompson and I were ordered to scramble and fly to a position at 5,000 feet, and to patrol the tip of south-east England, where a convoy of cargo ships was turning from the Channel to proceed to the Thames. We intercepted a Dornier flying in from the Dunkirk direction. However, we positioned ourselves between the convoy, on the east side, and the Dornier. The pilot obviously saw us and immediately dropped his load of bombs in the sea about a mile from the convoy, and turned and fled like a scared rabbit.

We maintained position for about 50 minutes, and then another section of Hurricanes from No. 257 Squadron carried on the patrol. We returned to North Weald, with the convoy safe and, as far as we were concerned, no action.

At this time of the year, as we were entering December, the weather was worsening and patrols were being reduced until more serious reports were received. When December arrived, we were on standby. I decided to have a walk around the perimeter track to visit the sergeants' mess and use the external phone. I had not forgotten the arrangement I had made at Sutton Bridge with my three friends. I had found out which squadrons they had joined and I phoned. I was shocked at the answers I received. Victor Meeson in No. 56 Squadron had been killed on 20 September 1940. Joe Morrison of No. 46 Squadron had been killed on 22 October 1940. Tony Page of No. 257 Squadron had been killed on 8 November 1940. I was shocked beyond belief. All I could do was enter the mess lounge, find an armchair and cry my eyes dry.

I walked back to the No. 249 dispersal in a complete daze, thinking, 'Will I last the year out?' None of us had reached 21 years old yet. As I was walking back, head down and feeling so awful, I heard a voice say, 'Sergeant Palliser, straighten up there, you're not walking tall like you normally do.' I could not stop the tears in my eyes as I braced myself, and saluted the famous wing commander of North Weald, a wonderful person who had led the North Weald wing, Victor Beamish, a flying legend. We stood looking at each other. I apologised for my head being down and my miserable appearance, and quietly I explained to him the news I had just received. The silence seemed for ever as I waited to be criticised. But he put his hand on my shoulder and sympathised like a father. I was amazed with his reaction. He dismissed me kindly. However, he stopped me and said, 'Palliser, you have been a good sergeant pilot and are a strength to No. 249 Squadron. Have you ever thought of accepting a commission?' I held my breath for some seconds and said, 'Sir, I come from a good family and I was a student engineer before I joined the RAFVR. I believe I have, along with other sergeants, been treated like a second-rate citizen. Yes I would accept a commission.' He replied, 'Wait until the new year', and walked a couple of paces. Then he called me again. 'I will speak to the Air Ministry.' Looking into my eyes with his steely gaze, he asked me, 'Are you frightened at all?' I replied, 'Sir, I am bloody frightened, until the fighting commences.' I was commissioned in April 1941, Pilot Officer.

15. A Patrol Too Long

No. 249 Squadron was scrambled around mid-morning on 5 December. We were ordered to our allocated patrol line, which was between Maidstone and Canterbury in Kent. Our altitude was approximately 15,000 feet. We were eventually ordered to increase height and proceed towards the Dover area. A number of German 109s had crossed the Channel, flying very high, and were approaching the south coast. As we increased height to approximately 20,000 feet, Sergeant George Stroud and myself commenced a weaving manœuvre, with Stroud weaving behind and below the squadron, myself behind and above, and the remaining ten flying in Vic formation – two Vics of three and one of four aircraft. This action enabled us two weavers to see clearly as we flew back and forth across the squadron, and so the patrol continued.

We saw the 109s some 2,000 feet above us and the squadron circled to gain height. The 109s appeared to turn south over the Channel and the squadron manœuvred inland towards the River Thames area. The 109s then turned to cover us once again as we climbed and veered south to try and engage. The 109s turned back once again, this manœuvre being repeated a number of times. As the main body of the squadron changed direction, the weavers had to be very careful to stay close. In keeping our eyes on the enemy, it was all too easy to let the point of contact with the squadron widen, and so to find ourselves too far away for comfort.

During all the manœuvrings we had been airborne for approximately $1^3/_4$ hours, which was nearly double our normal patrol time. Squadron Leader Barton eventually queried this with ground control, who responded with the order to return to base. Stroud's fuel gauge must have been like mine, nearly zero. As we reduced height, now heading north, the 109s attacked. Stroud was hit, although I did not see the end result. However, he had to bail out, and suffered burns. We were more or less over the Thames at this time, and I was now on my own, as the squadron had split up, with every man for himself, as we were all short of fuel. At this point I saw tracer trails over my port wing and at that moment my engine coughed and spluttered momentarily. At the same time I throttled right back and applied hard right rudder and aileron, and saw a 109, which came under me and climbed as he over-shot. I gave him a quick burst but had no time to see the effect, as I was now in a spin. Now I was north of the Thames at an altitude of approximately 5,000 feet with the engine spluttering away as I recovered from the spin.

I realised I would have to crash-land and saw a field with a secondary road running alongside. I prepared for a gliding landing, undercarriage up, and managed to judge the landing well. The field was of soft wet soil, with no crops. Unfortunately I had not fastened my body harness and I had still held on to the throttle lever, with the result that when the aircraft hit, the radiator bit into the soft soil, the tail came up and then dropped down. My head hit the reflector gunsight and my thumb nearly disappeared into my wrist, still holding on to the throttle. Luckily, I had, at this moment, put my forearm across my head to minimise damage to my face. However, my head snapped back and I felt as though my neck was broken.

At this time I saw two men running across the field towards me, having left a parked military vehicle at the side of the road. I was having difficulty opening the hood and they helped me open it, and also assisted me out. I was dazed through the smack on the head and my hand was very painful. However, no visible injuries appeared. The two men were customs people in khaki uniforms, and they told me they had heard the spluttering and bangs from my aircraft and could see I was in trouble and heading for the field – hence their much appreciated help. It appeared I had crashed near the small village of Stanford-le-Hope, through which these men were travelling on the way to Southend. They took me over a railway crossing and dropped me at the fairly big wooden structure of a roadside café. I was helped up a number of long wooden steps into the building, where they explained my problem to the café manager. Over the road from the café was a house which was also the police station. The policeman came over and I explained what had happened. I asked him if he would contact the nearest airfield (Hornchurch) and advise them of my crash, together with my name and squadron number and the fact that I was stationed at North Weald. While I was waiting, the café manager or owner asked if I needed medical attention. I advised him that I would be OK and that I would wait for a pick-up from Hornchurch. I had pulled my misplaced thumb into position and, apart from pain, it seemed all right. My head and back were sore but did not feel serious.

The policeman returned with the news that a vehicle would be coming from Hornchurch soon. In the meantime I was offered a cup of tea and a comfortable seat. I was chatting to the policeman when one of the locals called across to me saying, 'Heh, lad, what happened to your mate?' I looked at her, absorbed the question and answered, 'I have no mate. I'm on my own. I fly a single-seat fighter, namely a Hawker Hurricane.' She came back at me with a squawk of shock. 'You're on your own? A kid like you in that there aeroplane – you on your own.' 'Yes,' I replied. She then yelled to her audience, 'On his own, look at 'im – a child and they don't give him a mate. I'm going to write to my MP about this. Here you are, lad, have a piece of my cake.' Amid the laughter of the other people, it felt as though the war was at a standstill.

A vehicle arrived and I was taken to a Red Cross building close to Hornchurch, where I was checked over by a medical orderly and stayed the night. When I undressed for bed, two deep cuts were revealed in my right leg. They were treated and bandaged. The next morning a car arrived for me to return to North Weald. What a day. It was a real blunder, being airborne for nearly 2 hours, forgotten by ground controllers. Sergeant George Stroud had been shot down, I had force-landed, and four other pilots, Flying Officer Lofts, Pilot Officer Crossey, Flying Officer Cassidy and Pilot Officer Solak, had been forced to land at other airfields. This was a lesson for HQs.

Two or three days after the crash episode, Squadron Leader Barton was confirmed in his rank, which pleased everyone. Grandy was now a very senior officer in Fighter Command. Barton had been requested by headquarters to supply a pilot to be ready to test the new Hurricane and Spitfire Mark IIs, which would now be fitted with the new Merlin 20 engine, with increased superchargers and 1,350 horsepower. What a thrill it was to hear of this being offered to us at this time; we certainly needed them! I was briefed to fly these fighters individually, and the expectation was that our fighters could reach at least 35,000 feet as fast as and as high as the new Messerschmitt 109s and the Focke-Wulf 190. Our fighters, with armament that was to be either four 20mm cannons or twelve .303 machine guns, would be the future. In the tests we were equipped with barographs and various recording instruments to be analysed by the aircraft designers. There were only a few tests, of which I can remember only three. For the last test I had been down with a lousy cold and was feeling grim. But I was approached and ordered to complete the final tests, as we had proved we could reach the 36,000 feet height comfortably – with bags of oxygen. The weather was cold but clear and I was airborne at approximately 10.00 a.m. with the order, 'As fast as you can and as high as possible.' This was always when enemy action was possible, although the weather was very uncertain. So I steadied the aircraft engine revolutions at 2,800 rpm and, at approximately 160 mph, pointed the aircraft to heaven.

I reached 36,000 feet, although I am simply unable to remember the time it took. I realised there was power left to increase the height, maintaining circles at this altitude, round and round over south-east England and the English Channel.

The view well above light alto cirrus clouds was marvellous and I tried to yell with satisfaction at the terrific feeling I felt. I found I could not utter any sound whatsoever. I had now reached just over 40,000 feet and at the same time the controller's voice clearly reached me, saying 'Ganer Red 1, where the hell are you? We have your plot but you are not responding.' I made a valiant effort to talk, trying to force my voice, but to no avail. Then I developed an uncontrollable cough. I had had the odd cough as I climbed. However, that was par for what I was already suffering. But this was something different. I could not talk, I could not stop coughing, and suddenly I felt sick and vomited into my oxygen mask. I felt a salty taste and raised my left hand off the throttle and eased off my mask. It was then I saw plenty of blood, which shook the hell out of me. Had I been shot without feeling the attack? No! Now control was talking hard and fast, as they could receive no voice from me. And the plot they had on my flight was still steady. In the end I thought, to hell with the plot, I was going down to 'Mother Earth'. My coughing had stopped but there was copious blood on my gloves and flying suit and this was not my imagination. The worst part of the descent was that it was too slow at times, as my ears were playing up with the increase in pressure.

Well, I managed to land sometime around midday and I was driven around to the sick bay to be cleaned up and examined to find the cause of the bleeding. I was examined as best as a corporal medic could do, and, as the blood had stopped dribbling, his judgement was that I had burst a blood vessel in my nasal area. He also suggested that, after I had given my report to the CO, I should return and stay in the sick bay until the next day. I trundled off to the operations hut looking like a butcher's shop, because he could not clean my flying Sidcot; that had to be replaced. I arrived at the ops hut and was surprised to see the CO and some of our pilots talking to what looked like army officers with wings. The whole group fell silent, and then everyone, including our visitors, was asking every question in the book relating to being 'shot down'. Butch Barton took me aside and I told him what had happened. He said, 'Give me your report and get back to the sick bay and I'll see you when we can get rid of these American pilots.' They had arrived to talk to our pilots in action. When they heard me tell Butch I had managed to get to an altitude of a fraction over 40,000 feet, the senior American blurted, 'Say guys, that statement is impossible. We are told a body would explode at that height without a pressure cockpit.' I tried to laugh as I thought, that is probably close to the truth.

After I had left the sick bay the next day, Butch had a long talk to me, and the records from my plane were sent to the 'Boffin'. However, the barograph reading proved the altitude of 40,000 feet. Butch stood me down for a few days so I could have a proper doctor's opinion. I enjoyed the break. The doctor gave me quite a comprehensive examination and was satisfied there was no more bleeding and any mucus was clear. He accepted the fact that in winter it is always likely for some chest complaints, and coughing relates to this. I was ready for more action.

December had been a mixed month. New pilots had arrived to replace our losses, one of whom was a real friend, Bill Millington, shot down while flying well into the Channel, chasing a damaged 109. He was reported as crashing just short of Dover; it was very sad and he was a great loss. Sergeant Stroud, one of my boozing pals, was still in hospital with severe facial burns. A new task had surfaced, as Churchill with the Air Ministry chiefs calculated one big change for 11 Group to make plans to go on the offensive. The Battle of Britain was now. The Battle 'for' Britain was won. The major battles were ahead. This made no difference to the night raids or the daylight raids, with small groups of bombers and 109 fighter bombers. The fighting would never cease.

Squadron Leader Barton, together with another pilot, performed what was called a 'Rhubarb'. Two aircraft would fly together, particularly in this bad weather, and attack airfields, railways, troops, tanks and any such target. This was tricky. However, we were about to receive the new Hurricanes and Spitfire Mark IIs – Hurricanes with 1,300-plus horsepower and fitted with four Hispano 20mm cannons or twelve .303 machine guns; Spitfires fitted with similar engines, two Hispano cannons and four .303 machine guns. At last! The Mark II Hurricanes arrived in the squadron and I was allocated one with four cannons – was I thrilled! It was the first time I would be flying my own aircraft. I immediately asked permission to have a check flight, and enjoyed flinging this Hurricane over the airfield, completing an aerobatic routine before landing. The next morning I was advised that one of the new Mark II, GN-H, would be my Hurricane for a few days and maybe longer. What a thrill! A young airman armourer, who was good at painting some funny motifs on the side of the cockpits, asked if he could paint something on GN-H. I had always laughed at a cartoon in one of the London papers, featuring a cheeky character called 'O'Reilly Foul'. So he painted this funny head on the cockpit side of GN-H.

I completed a couple of patrols over the next few days, feeling proud of my painting. Then, at readiness of the first scramble of the day, I saw one of our new Polish pilots walking to my aircraft and climbing in with the aircrew, ready to start the engine. I ran across and asked what was going on. He replied that the CO had asked him to fly some documents to Martlesham, home of Bader's No. 242 Squadron, and he had told him to fly GN-H. I called to my flight commander, Neil, and asked what was going on, to be told that Butch had ordered the flight, it was to be only there and back, and the aircraft would be returned in time for me to fly it. As I watching the Pole, Skolski, taxiing out and taking off, it was as well that my silent curses could not be heard. However, it was a thrill to listen to the rasp of the new engine. The weather had clamped down, and flying was relegated to time spans of between 30 minutes and 1 hour, so the day was quiet. About midday, the phone in the ops hut rang, and I heard Neil's voice yell, 'Where, when?' I walked into the hut and asked what had happened. These December days, with Butch now confirmed as CO, had brought about quite a friendly atmosphere in the squadron. Neil said Skolski had crashed near Martlesham, having been flying low in bad weather. He had flown into electric wires that were built around the countryside. Skolski was only slightly injured. However, GN-H was a 'write-off'. So bang went 'O'Reilly Foul' and my aircraft. Once again pilots flew whichever aircraft were free each day, and only Butch and the two flight commanders were to have a specific one, if available. After all, there was a war on – didn't we know?

16. Steady and Strong

The December weather was awful, and the patrols were scratchy. Even the Luftwaffe was taking things easy. We were still enjoying the hospitality of the Sun & Whalebone. The lady of the beautiful house had been interested in our comings and goings and she was very satisfied with our manners and the tidiness in her home. So we were now offered a small drawing room, and she supplied cards for us to enjoy bridge or whist or the demon poker. One particular day we had been stood down and the arrangement was made for a good poker game. There were quite a few of us either playing or watching. Suddenly the cry came: 'There's no beer left.' I was a watcher at the time, so volunteered to go to the Sun & Whalebone, borrowing Sergeant Dennis Steadman's Ford 8. I knew a short cut through the lanes between the farmer's fields. I zigged and zagged through the field. It was much harder than I anticipated – pitch black and the headlights on the car were the usual metal shield with slots to provide some light.

I managed to pick up the beer, taking longer than I had calculated, and I realised that the return was going to be a problem. I set off praying I would remember the twists and turns, which, on the return, seemed to emanate in the darkness at funny angles. I managed three-quarters of the way when up went the searchlights and ack-ack guns commenced firing. Obviously there must be a venturesome German bomber trying to be a hero. Suddenly about half a mile away there was a vivid flash and a tremendous bang, as the first bomb dropped. Must be close to our airfield. I was back into the car after checking my position, when two more bombs exploded in a line heading in my direction.

I decided I had located the route of the last few turns and I pushed the speed (don't laugh) to about 10 mph, and saw what I calculated to be the last bend before the straight run to the house. I made a right-hand turn and, before I could correct the error, there was a loud bang and the car tilted up in the air, making an awful sound, and stopped, with the

First solo flight. (All pictures in this section: Charles Palliser)

Sergeant Parker ready for take-off.

Sergeant Palliser waiting for friend Sergeant Meeson – leaving Rissington for Sutton Bridge.

Left to right – Sergeant's George Stroud, Tich Palliser, Dusty Mills, Harry Davidson.

Talking it over after a fight – young pilots exchange experiences.

Ready for scramble.

A Magister to Oxford – the squadron's runabout.

Commanding Officer Butch
Barton practicing.

Sergeant Davies – 1940.

No. 249 Squadron – Flying Officer Pat Wells on top watching ammunition loading. Sergeant
Palliser third from left, in charge.

Sergeant Davidson.

Squadron Leader Butch Barton and Wilfred.

Sergeant Palliser with Pipsqueak, Pilot Officer Cassidy with Wilfred, Pilot Officer Wynn, Pilot Officer Fayolle, Sergeant Mills.

Sergeant Tubby Girdwood. Attacked in the middle of taking off and he was burned to death. We watched and saluted.

Palliser shot down, December 5, 1940.

One blade spared – shot down December 1940.

                                        Willow Farm,

                                             Ingrave,

                                                  nr. Brentwood,

                                                       Essex.

                                             16th September,1940

Dear Mr. Palliser,

        Just a line to enquire if you got home safely last night, as
it was almost dark.   I didn't get near enough to you to say goodbye.

        When my eldest brother went up to the field to get the cows
this morning, on the ground was the shape of a Hurricane, this patch
was where it had stood yesterday.

        Please let us all know as soon as possible whether you did get
home all right, as we all should like to know.

        Well dont forget that if you are in trouble again over us,
you are always welcome.into our field, and if you are passing in
a car any time dont forget to call in.

                        Please reply as soon as possible.

                             Yours Sincerely,

                             John Farndon

                                (John Farndon.)

p.s. I am the one that had the brown jacket on .

R.S.V.P.

Letter from a young boy after I crashed landed in his fathers' field.

Winter 1940/1941.

Winter. We were offered half a hut instead of bell tents.

Gas practice – North Weald.

My tail rudder damage after flying from Dunkirk, February 1941.

YEAR			PRACTICE		YEAR		PRACTICE	
MONTH	DATE				MONTH	DATE		
1940								
SEPT.	15.	½. D.O. 17.	DESTROYED.					
"	21.	⅓. D.O. 17.	DAMAGED.					
"	27.	1. M.E. 110.	DESTROYED		TOP HALF OF RUDDER BLOWN AWAY BY CANNON SHELL			
"	27.	1. M.E. 110.	PROBABLE		(LATER CONFIRMED)			
OCT.	21	½. D.O. 215.	DAMAGED.					
NOV.	11	½. M.E. 110. JAGUAR DESTROYED.			DEC. 5th ORDERED TO PATROL BEYOND ENDURANCE OF			
"	15	1. M.E. 109.	DESTROYED.		FUEL. JUMPED BY 109³ AND CRASHED AT STANFORD-LE-HOPE.			
1941 FEB.	10	1. M.E. 109.	PROBABLE.		2ND SWEEP INTO ENEMY TERRITORY. BLENHEIMS BOMBED DUNKIRK.			
JUNE	12	⅓. C.A.N.T. Z.506.	DESTROYED.					
"	18	½. MACCHI. 200	DESTROYED.					
OCT.	19	½. SAVOIA 81.	DESTROYED.		LONG RANGE PATROL OFF LAMPEDUSA AND TRIPOLI.			
DEC.	20	1. JU. 88.	DESTROYED.					
"	20	1. M.E. 109.	DAMAGED.					
"	24.	1. J.U. 88.	DESTROYED (SECTION)		SECTION MASSACRE.			
"	24.	½ J.U. 88.	DESTROYED.					

Extract from my logbook.

Sergeant Parker at the shower.

What was left of three Hurricanes three days after arrival on Malta from the *Ark Royal*.

A long range Hurricane after a four hour flight from carrier.

Flight Lieutenant Neil rests in new quarters.

Sergeant's Mess at Ta'Qali.

L-R – Pilot Officer Crossey, Pilot Officer Moon, Pilot Officer Hulbert, Pilot Officer Palliser, Sergeant Rex, Pilot Officer Cavan.

From top left to right – Neil, Crossey, Mills, Matthews. Party attended by the girls of good Maltese families.

Palliser returns to Ta'Qali from action – June 1941.

Flight Lieutenant Jack Hamlyn DFC, who flew me from Malta to South Africa.

Arrival in South Africa to instruct in flight tactics.

Tich and Ruth Palliser, married 23 January 1943. Terry Crossey was the Best Man.

Arrival at training school.

Very last flight as we head for Bulawayo for air display, August 1947.

Airborne and approaching Bulawayo airfield No. 2 – Palliser ready for the final display of aerobatics. After this, Palliser resigned from the RAF to return to engineering in South Africa.

Hospital ship *Oranje*, returning me to the UK, July 1944.

Instructors school.

rear wheels spinning and going nowhere.

I opened the car door and I slid down the side of a heap of something and landed, bottom down, into a big pool of mud and melting snow – and I had on my only decent civvy clothes. In the dim lights from searchlights shining in the cloud, I saw the Ford 8 balanced on the top of a heap of some farm produce. The rear wheels were about 2 feet off the ground, the car bonnet about 6 feet in the air. The headlights had suffered and were no longer shining. Now what was I to do? Luckily the bottles of beer were intact, so I removed my jacket, flung it into the open car door and groped my way to the rear of the car.

I pulled and hacked at what turned out to be turnips piled in a winter heap, covered in straw. Standing back, I now saw I should have turned left not right; the bombing had made me panic for a few seconds. I had to get the back wheels of the car on to the ground. The front seemed to be OK, as the front bumper had taken the brunt of the impact. So, on hands and knees, I dug into the turnips, flinging them between my legs, over my shoulders, left, right. I was a horrible slimy mess. I had no idea what the lads back at the house would be thinking, or whether Sir Godfrey Thomas's wife would be panicking. What a mess! I must have worked on those damned turnips for half an hour or more before I finally had the rear wheels firmly on the ground. The car was also at a reasonable angle, so I climbed into the car and, with my next lot of prayers, the engine started, and I was able to back the car through the opening of the lane and drive, with difficulty, slowly down the last of the lane to the house. The next day I phoned the farmer and apologised for the trouble. I explained my pilot friends and I would try to repair the damage when we could leave the airfield. The farmer told me not to bother. He said, 'I thought one of last night's bombs had done the damage.' He said he would rebuild the heap and wished us good health and flying.

The poker game had finished, and some of the lads had driven to the open road to the pub and had not returned. The howl that penetrated the courtyard could have been heard miles away, but the remarks and laughter when they saw me in the house were memorable. My clothes were thick with mud and anything else that was around, and the leg-pulling lasted for ever, as the poker lads were from Nos 257, 46 and 249 Squadrons. I could have asked for a transfer; instead, we all had a beer. Lady Thomas was told about the incident days later. She sent for me and gave me a big hug for my troubles – a wonderful lady.

Early in December, Butch Barton was officially promoted to lead the squadron, which he had done since Grandy's injury. Pilot Officer Neil was promoted to acting flight lieutenant. This quiet period was livened up by the first offensive patrol led by Squadron Leader Barton and a long-time member of No. 249, Pilot Officer (Dickie) Wynn, a pilot who was always ready for action. We had been advised to take advantage of this quiet period to fly in the new Mark II Hurricane and to practise low flying in the local area. Obviously there was something in the wind.

The day arrived when Douglas Bader, CO of No. 242 Squadron, and Stanford Tuck, leader of No. 257 Squadron, flew into North Weald for a special meeting of the North Weald Wing (three squadrons including ourselves), with Squadron Leader Barton of No. 249 Squadron, under Wing Commander Victor Beamish. The next day we were organised to form a 'wing', and fly a high-altitude formation patrolling over the French coast – this to invite the Luftwaffe to come up and fight. With Wing Commander Victor Beamish joining us, we formed a three-squadron patrol in a huge Vic formation, with Bader leading the wing, Butch Barton leading 249 in No. 2 position, and Tuck in No. 3 position. I was in Blue position to Tom Neil and was prepared as usual to break away and patrol over the wing as 'look out' responsibility, with Sergeant Mills flying under the wing, replacing poor Sergeant George Stroud, still in hospital after being shot down previously.

We climbed steadily in a beautiful formation, which, from the ground, must have thrilled people watching from the towns and villages as we ascended. We passed over Portsmouth, the Isle of Wight, Bournemouth and Weymouth – towns and cities that had suffered the German bombing raids for the previous eight months. Over Plymouth, we turned south towards the French coast, west of Boulogne, reaching an altitude of 30,000 feet. Some distance west, we turned east, well inside the French coast, and held the thirty-six Hurricanes at 36,000 feet. What a thrill for all of us, as the Mark II aircraft were absolutely steady in formation. No Luftwaffe could be seen. However, we were leaving behind huge white condensation trails, which lingered for miles behind us. I made a signal with my hands, as we were on total radio silence, that we might be followed by the enemy fighters hiding behind us under the cover of thick white trails. Flight Lieutenant Neil waved me to patrol above and Mills to fly below the wing. What a sight it was to see the formation from above, steady and strong.

As I patrolled above, I saw a Hurricane suddenly break away from its

position and, as it turned away, it rolled on to its back and dived vertically
down, away from the wing. I whipped around in a tight circle, thinking
of an attack, but there was no sign of enemy fighters. Oxygen! My
thoughts flew to the possibility that the pilot had suffered a problem in
his oxygen line, or had forgotten to adjust for the height at which we were
flying. Mills and I rejoined the formation, as we were now over an area
between Calais and Dunkirk. The leader signalled a return and we
turned for the south-east coast, above Dover. Over England, the
squadrons returned to their own airfields, and the patrol was at an end.
The next day the senior officers gathered at North Weald, where Wing
Commander Beamish, accompanied by officers from the Group,
discussed the patrol and particularly the performance of the Mark II
fighters. The Royal Air Force had prepared for the offensive operations
into Europe, and we were advised of a real offensive effort being
organised for 10 January 1941. The feedback from the squadrons was
really exciting. The control of the aircraft at such a fantastic height, the
power of the Merlin 20 engine and the introduction of the Hispano
20mm guns were most welcome. The general feel of the Mark II engine
had earned nothing but real praise – roll on the offensive!

17. 'What Guns!'

On 10 January there was much activity at the airfield. Our twelve Hurricanes were lined up on the airfield in front of the ops huts and the briefing of the twelve pilots, including Wing Commander Victor Beamish, commenced mid-morning. The squadron would be airborne at noon, and would be airborne in sections of three aircraft – Red, Blue, Yellow and Green, four Vics led by Squadron Leader Barton. No. 242 Squadron, led by Squadron Leader Bader, would take off from its base, Martlesham, and Squadron Leader Stanford Tuck, with No. 257 Squadron, would scramble from Stapleford Tawney. Six Blenheims, twin-engine bombers, would leave their base. All squadrons would form the total formation in a huge Vic formation, with the Blenheim bombers behind and in the centre of the Vic. Most of the territory between North Weald and Dover would be used for the total formation to form and head for France. Bader would lead, Barton would be No. 2 position, and Tuck would be in No. 3 position, with the bombers behind and close. This formation would cross the Channel aiming for Calais at a tricky height of 500 feet to fly under the German radar. Two squadrons of Hurricanes from other bases would fly way above us to maintain 'top cover' and Spitfires would be scrambled to make very high cover when the action commenced. Orders were that the three escort squadrons would split when we reached the coast, and that the bombers would remain at minimum height and fly straight to their target, which was a forest, named Forêt-de-Guines, where German tanks were stationed.

The action commenced. Bader led us straight down to Calais Marc Airfield. For some reason he flew us across the airfield at 1,000 feet, which frightened the hell out of us when the German defence commenced firing with their Bofors guns, which were lethal in their hands. No. 249 dived to zero feet and fired at the parked fighters on the airfield, some of which were already taxiing to take off. I made my attack across the centre of Calais Marc, hitting two of the Messerschmitts that were nearly airborne. Then I made a screaming turn to starboard to come down the western edge of the airfield to strafe the guns, which I was sure had already hit some of the leading Hurricanes. Stanford Tuck had led No. 257 Squadron to minimum height, and was knocking hell out of the parked aircraft on the east side of the airfield. Barton yelled, 'Watch the Blenheims', and I joined the other No. 249 pilots towards the Forêt-de-Guines, which was only about 5 miles away. The top cover Hurricanes were attacking 109s as they were airborne. Hell's Angels was a baby to the actions now – thirty-six fighters screaming around the area at zero feet. For once I thanked God for having 109s with yellow painted noses, otherwise we would have been shooting at our own aircraft. We saw the six Blenheims leaving the forest and we made for the Channel. We circled around them, maintaining a very low flight and were now over the water.

I had hit two 109s as they attempted to take off. I saw two parachutes that looked like Germans and had seen two Hurricanes of Bader's squadron get hit. The upper squadron had now entered the fight, and our three squadrons were now making sure that the bombers were OK. All six appeared to be unharmed. As we crossed the Channel, we encountered heavy fire from four German patrol boats anchored about 3 miles off the Calais coast. Two of our Hurricanes were hit, one flown by one of our old team, Flying Officer Cassidy, who returned with a damaged tail. Pilot Officer Tommy Thompson had a piece shot off a propeller blade, but made home base. Meanwhile, Victor Beamish dived down and attacked one patrol boat and, as he pulled away, he saw a 109 on the tail of Pilot Officer McConnell's Hurricane. McConnell was wounded and his aircraft was hit. He baled out in a big hurry, his Hurricane crashing in the Dover cliffs. McConnell was picked up by a rescue boat and taken to hospital with a broken leg. Discussions on the action were carried out by Wing Commander Beamish and the leaders of Nos 249, 257 and 242 Squadrons, and we were stood down and were driven to our quarters away from the airfield. I believe Squadron Leader Bader was asked why he had led his squadron across Calais Marc Airfield at 1,000 feet. The answer was, 'I had to see what targets had to be attacked.' He lost three pilots, hit by Bofors guns, and one of those was an old First World War senior officer who had pleaded to join the exercise. Sad! We heard no more.

We were soon into February, and on the 4th three Hurricanes were scrambled, Squadron Leader Barton, Tommy Thompson and myself. When we were off Clacton at 10,000 feet, we sighted a convoy, and we were notified that an unidentified aircraft was 25 miles from the convoy. Just then we identified a Bf110 over the convoy. Squadron Leader Barton immediately dived to 2,000 feet, just above the cloud. As we approached, the fighter bomber (twin engine) sighted us and released his bombs, wide of the convoy. Barton, leading the dive, made a head-on attack, then turned on his tail and delivered a further burst as the 110 fled into the cloud layer. I followed and also fired several bursts. By then both engines of the Bf110 were emitting black smoke, and Barton followed it into the clouds, where I waited for it to reappear. But as soon as it did, he spotted Butch and myself and dived once again into the cloud. Soon Tommy Thompson, who was also below the cloud, spotted a large splash into the sea.

The patrol continued, and ack-ack firing signalled the appearance of a second Bf110, which was sighted 2,000 feet above. Squadron Leader Barton, with full throttle, climbed and pursued this 110 and opened fire. The 110's port engine stopped dead as it entered a cloud, with Barton close on his tail and firing short bursts. Barton forced the Messerschmitt down to sea level, where it ditched in a shower of spray.

I was then given four days' leave and told to report back on 10 February. I visited my family for three days and enjoyed a decent rest and the excitement of getting together. The idea of engagement was introduced. Although this was a possibility, the thought of marriage was 'NO'. We were too young.

I returned to the squadron on 9 February and was satisfied with the few days away, as I was not worried about flying. I reported to Flight Lieutenant Neil, who grabbed me by the shoulders and yelled, 'Yes! Tich Palliser is back!' When he removed his hands, looking around at the other pilots, I said, 'What's all the excitement about?' Dusty Mills poked me in the ribs and said, 'Tomorrow is another go, this time Belgium and Dunkirk, and you are in it.' Therefore a large briefing discussion was held on this raid. 'Circus 4' was to have six Blenheim bombers to bomb Dunkirk docks and some hinterland targets. There would be four squadrons escorting, including No. 249. We all flew Mark II Hurricanes, for which we were grateful. And our aircraft had a mixture of Hurricane IIs A, B and C. 'A' was fitted with eight .303 Browning guns, 'B' had four Hispano 20mm cannons and 'C' had twelve Browning guns. My aircraft was a 'B' with four cannons, two in each wing. This was the first time I had flown with cannons. As I studied the barrels protruding from the wings, I thought of what they could do with a much larger bullet than the .303 and a muzzle velocity of 3,000 feet per minute. This meant we could increase the distance to engage to 400 yards or more, compared to the .303 at 250 yards. What guns!

The operation would be similar to that at Calais – three squadrons to attack and cover the Blenheims, with a top cover squadron to take care of the battle area. As the bombers attacked with their bombing runs, a number of Bf109Es dived on No. 249. A Hurricane was shot down, flown by newly commissioned Pilot Officer Davis. He baled out wounded and was taken a prisoner of war. The rest of us were flailing around the air shooting at every 109 sighted. As I broke away from the squadron, we were now over Gravelines, west of Dunkirk, and over the beaches of the Channel. I circled at 3,000 feet with Red 3 and saw three 109s. I picked out one and fired at about 400 yards, and saw huge pieces of his port wing fly off. I turned and saw one of our Hurricanes being attacked by a 109. I dived, giving a quarter attack to his starboard side. After two 2-second bursts half the 109 blew up as he tried to turn away. The recoil effect of the cannons was a shock. While I was following him down, I gave one more burst, and that was the finish. I was now only 20 or 30 feet above the water.

I followed the badly crippled 109 close to the beach, when a tracer came over my wing. I turned violently, and a 109 flashed past. I pulled the aircraft round slightly and fired at the fleeing 109, when my two starboard guns jammed. The recoil of the port cannons meant that the firing had stopped on the starboard side. My aircraft performed like a motor car skidding. I had opened my cockpit hood, as we were flying low. My head bumped into the frame of the open hood and my goggles, which I had pushed to my forehead, fell down over my face. I had to do some smart correcting. My controls must have been damaged. Probably the 109 behind me did get some shots into my Hurricane. I nearly put the tip of my wing into the Channel. When I straightened up, I saw Flight Lieutenant Lewis, a South African who was flying as Yellow 2, and had been fired at by the 109 that was on my tail. He later substantiated my claim that the pilot had been killed and had been seen to crash on the beach.

That had been close! What a flight! Our losses were small, with few injuries. As we were straggling towards Dover, my aircraft felt somewhat sluggish in the controls. However, the engine was smooth, and we landed at North Weald in the late afternoon. I taxied towards my parking position, guided by the ground lads. I switched the engine off, and relaxed, having a few deep breaths. My rigger jumped on to the wing and said, 'Are you OK, Sarg?' I answered in the affirmative, but my mind was racing twenty to the dozen regarding the results of the action. When I climbed out of the cockpit and jumped off the wing, the rigger suggested I should look at my Hurricane aft of the cockpit. I was looking at a hole in the fuselage about 18 inches in ragged diameter and going round to the starboard side, a hole about 3 inches in diameter – a cannon shell hit, obviously. The wooden longitudinal stringers on which the canvas structure was attached from cockpit to tail were broken and some parts were missing. That was the strength of the Hurricane. Next he pointed to the tail, or what was left of it. The rudder had lost at least 12 inches off the top and the elevator was 50 per cent in ribbons. No wonder I had felt the aircraft wobbling and vibrating as I nursed it to the airfield, but, believe it or not, I had had no difficulty landing. Butch called us into the ops hut, and we discussed the action, which was accepted as a great success. We had lost one pilot, who became a prisoner of war. A number of Hurricanes had sustained various damages. However, the six Blenheims had returned safely. The other squadrons, Nos 257 and 242, would be analysing their own results.

From March into April 1941 the winter weather played havoc with operations. Any actions were limited to pairs of aircraft risking the storms, carrying out raids on the French and Belgian coasts and strafing anything that moved. More pilots were arriving at the squadron, which eased our continual scrambles and allowed us more breaks to wind down. Thank the Lord for small mercies. The squadron carried out another escort mission on the last day of March 1941, with the Blenheims bombing two merchant ships a few miles off Cap Gris Nez. We had no interference from enemy aircraft and we all returned safely. During this period the weather and cloud conditions were really hazardous. Returning to North Weald from a convoy patrol, I was flying No. 3 to Flight Lieutenant Neil and No. 2 on the starboard side of Neil was one of the original members of the squadron, Pilot Officer Wynn, a thorough gentleman. As we approached the airfield, Wynn's Hurricane did a violent turn to starboard and, as were at a height of only 1,000 feet, nosedived vertically into the ground. Flight Lieutenant Neil wrote to his family, 'What a tragedy that the smiling, level headed "Dicky", who had been with the squadron from the start and who had fought bravely for the last seven months, being shot down and wounded with a nasty neck wound, and crashing more than once through engine failure, should die in such a way.'

Amazing changes were taking place at this time. New pilots continued to be posted to the squadron – Sergeant McVean, Sergeant Ron Rist, and an Australian, Sergeant R. L. Davies. Within 48 hours, three of our five Poles had gone, including our merry favourite, Macejowski, whom we had nicknamed 'Micky Mouse'. It was so much easier to say! Polish squadrons were being formed, as their numbers increased – they were all brave and very good pilots. Old faces reappeared after injuries, and many new faces were arriving. In November 1940, No. 249 had been adopted by the people of the African Gold Coast. The people had collected a substantial sum of money from the West African colony and had offered this gift to the squadron. Our pilots decided we should have a squadron crest, such as the older squadrons were honoured with. And so we designed a squadron crest, and the design was submitted to the Air Ministry for consideration. This included a central design that depicted an elephant, as portrayed on the official coat of arms of the Gold Coast. It also included a motto, 'Pugnis et Calcibus', which translated as 'With Fists and Heels'.

A newly promoted officer, Wing Commander Ron Kellett, was appointed as Wing Commander Flying, North Weald, on 10 April 1941. Wing Commander Victor Beamish had received further promotions. Wing Commander Kellett immediately accompanied six No. 249 Squadron Hurricane IIs on a high-altitude sweep over the Le Touquet, Boulogne, and the Calais area. As in my tests the previous December, flying at 33,000 feet in the unheated, unpressurised aircraft soon began to affect the pilots. Flight Lieutenant Neil described the conditions: 'It was unbelievably cold. Through the frost caked metal frame of my hood, some 30 yards away, I could see only the top of the helmet of my nearest companion, who was no doubt equally cold.' Such was the cold that Wing Commander Kellett was posted sick on return, and was obliged to relinquish his new command.

The comings and goings continued. Flight Lieutenant Lewis, with whom I had had long chats about South Africa, was posted on 14 April. Then, on 17 April, we received the news that No. 249 was shortly to proceed overseas to the Middle East as a 'well tried and skilled fighter squadron'. This accounted for the intensity of movement of pilots. Poles, Czechs, French and Belgians were not allowed to serve overseas. More pilots arrived. We wondered when the flow would cease. It was announced that the skilled squadron leaders would discuss the possible interest with their pilots, with the idea of leaving for the Middle East as a complete unit. Naturally, some pilots who were married might wish to remain in the European theatre and, as was already in motion, it would be arranged for them to join UK Squadrons. The majority of No. 249 were eager for the change. Malta was not mentioned at this time. More new pilots came. Flying Officer A. G. F. Harrington, with no experience whatsoever but very polished, was the first to arrive. Thereafter, the new No. 249 was rapidly taking shape, with lots of excitement!

Dusty Mills and I had finally been awarded our commissions, and by 27 April 1941 we were pilot officers. We were thrilled, and did not forget that we had been together in No. 43 Squadron back in August 1940. Sergeant F. Etchells arrived along with Rex, Lawson, Parker, Rist and McVean. All were new and inexperienced. The old squadron pilots, the men who had established the squadron, were the experienced survivors: these included Squadron Leader Barton, Flight Lieutenant Neil, Flying Officers Beazley, Wells and Cassidy, and Pilot Officers Crossey, Thompson, Palliser and Mills.

18. 'There's a War on Mate!'

Leave had been granted, and all pilots had to report to Euston Railway Station on the morning of 8 May 1941 for the journey to Liverpool, where we would board the aircraft carrier *Furious*. I handed over my flying logbook (Air Ministry instructions) to adjutant Flight Lieutenant Lohmeyer, along with my metal luggage box with my civilian clothes and other belongings. These would be transported by ship with the ground crews and recovered when they arrived in the Middle East. I made arrangements to stay in our quarters near North Weald, as I would spend the last few days with Jean, my fiancée. I had packed changes of underclothing, socks, and so on, in an issue parachute bag, which would accompany me on my flight off the carrier. We had a rather sad few days, and Jean presented me with a lucky rag doll of Lupino Lane, a comedian from the London theatre. On 7 May a friend drove me to London, where I booked into the RAF Officers' Club, which enabled me to appear at Euston Station in good time on 8 May. Now that I had my breath back, would this be 'out of the frying pan into the fire'? I muttered a small prayer and joined the others, all excited: forward to the Middle East and the Sahara Desert!

So, on 8 May, we boarded the train at Euston Station and played the fool, joked with each other and arrived in Liverpool around lunchtime. Cars and small vans were ready to take us to HMS *Furious*. What carnage we witnessed from the constant German bombing raids. Every building was a shambles, and fires were still raging, as bad as in London. We arrived at Gladstone Dock, Liverpool, laden with our luggage. We were quietly directed to the gangway to board HMS *Furious*, and quietly advised to salute the quarter-deck, which was when we stepped on to the actual ship. Our joking remarks and playful attitude had ceased. There was a weird and tense atmosphere, and everything seemed to be happening at the double. Our sergeant pilots had been taken to their quarters somewhere in the bowels of this giant well-worn ship. Now our officers were hastened to their quarters, where they would be billeted for the journey to the first base, Gibraltar. Our Hurricane Is were already in the giant hangar in the body of the vessel. They would be assembled as the carrier sailed and would be placed eventually on the flight deck. Squadron Leader Barton and the two flight commanders would be shown to cabins, and the rest of us would enjoy the comfort of hammocks spread longitudinally under the lines of pipes. Our bags would be stored safely and packed in our allocated Hurricanes when we finally flew off.

Talk about mystery! We were now chatting to each other about how we would fit into this manœuvre. We were finally able to talk to some of the ship's officers, who more or less apologised for the hustle and bustle we had experienced. The reason for the pressure was because there had been a terrible night of bombing by the Luftwaffe. The chances were that there would be another raid as the Germans attempted to sink the *Furious*.

The morning was bright with a slight haze. We gathered together and were conducted around the ship. We walked along, in twos or threes, poking everything. And why not, seeing as we had to be incarcerated inside this steel monster. She looked a picture of a fighting battleship. Everything around us was geared to work and speed, as they prepared for a hasty departure. And sure enough, just after midday, the escort destroyers moved out into the river and the fussy old tugs came alongside. We were captivated by the speed and crew movements and the show of efficiency. What memories this brought back to me. I could remember being with my grandfather, Captain Charles Calder, on the bridge of his ship as I commenced my first sea voyage when I was a child. I hoped this would not be my last. But at present it was so quiet that it was hard to realise this was truly a war, and one that looked as if it would be long and bloody.

We were out of the river and heading north. We knew our first leg was to Greenock to join a massive naval manœuvre. At this moment, when we had left the Mersey river mouth, I calculated we had passed over the position where the T Class submarine, the HMS *Thetis*, sank with all hands except the captain. The officer we had worked under at Greenock in 1938 was in charge of the work on the *Triumph, Trident* and *Tribune* submarines. Lieutenant Commander Pennington, who had left us to join *Thetis* for the maiden tests, had been killed, and our work was finished. Our contract had been fitting the huge pressure chargers designed by

Brown Boveri under licence to the company in which I was a student engineer, Richardsons Westgarth in Hartlepool, Cleveland, in north-east Yorkshire. There was always something, somewhere, to jog one's memory!

We were approaching the entrance to the River Clyde, and above us we saw a Spitfire patrolling as we moved to our berthing position among many different naval ships. After such a worrying day, as at any time we could have been attacked by the Luftwaffe, the strain was eased as we were told to prepare for our first night in hammocks. What an experience! I had a lower hammock and had a hell of a job balancing in order to be comfortable. Just as I breathed a sigh of relief, I heard a clang and Tommy Thompson, who was about 3 feet above me, tried to sit up and hit an 8-inch-diameter pipe above him. Practically every morning until we reached Gibraltar, he hit this pipe as he tried to get his 6 foot 2 inch frame out of the hammock. The batmen who helped us with these damned hammocks were delighted to roll us out of them each morning. I just cannot remember those nights and mornings, how we undressed and dressed, handled the ablutions and anything else. All we heard from our naval mates was, 'Serves you right for choosing an aircraft carrier to get to your destination.' 'There's a war on mate!' Every morning we heard this as the batmen brought us mugs of tea – how do you drink tea in a hammock?

The next day, 9 May, while final preparations were completed, we were given permission to spend the afternoon ashore. The weather was changing and quite cold. There was little to be interested in, so we returned to the *Furious* and went to the wardroom, where we were allowed. This was most interesting and very comfortable. We sailed at 8.00 p.m. and I was fascinated at the quick and quiet way the various work was carried out. The weather had turned really nasty – dark and windy with rain. However, we found a sheltered spot, and watched all the manœuvring and listened to the orders; we were very impressed. Our escort destroyers led the way out of the river, and the heavy escort larger warships came up astern. We noticed one large ship, probably a battleship, but we were not told the name – a mystery ship.

Now we were heading north-westerly to enter the Atlantic Ocean and out of sight of Northern Ireland. Darkness fell, and it was so cold we were happy to enter the wardroom and sample their pink gin, which was not bad! The wardroom was warm and laid out with very comfortable furniture – rather like a good city club. Those naval officers who were not on duty were all eager to talk to us about past operations and ask us

if we knew where we would end up in the Middle East. We knew
nothing. However, it was suggested that, as the talk was about the three
squadrons, there might be a major action in Egypt with a new fully
operational 'wing' (three squadrons) blowing along in the sandy desert.
There was no doubt about the friendship of these naval lads, and there
were promises of more interesting talks and walks around this mighty
aircraft carrier. We were set to do more battles with the hammocks, and
a possible mug of tea from our energetic batmen. All night this mighty
ship's engines pushed us further into the Atlantic Ocean, the weather
deteriorating somewhat, as we felt the reaction and movement as we
tried to sleep.

On 10 May we were awakened with a smacking on the underneath of
the hammock, far from gentle, and a new day of mystery commenced.
Breakfast was good; there were no complaints. About 9.00 a.m. we were
gathered in the wardroom, and a senior officer advised us that we were
not to meander around the ship, although we would have decent time to
be accompanied by various officers. He explained the many duties carried
out and the places where sailors and officers were ordered to go when
battle warnings were received. We were then given assisting duties in any
enemy action – helping in gun positions, with many guns of all sizes in
all parts of the carrier. I was delegated to the hospital area, helping with
injured personnel, seeking the wounded and generally running up and
down gangways to offer help. This was exciting for me, as I would meet
a cross section of many medical people, and I was not affected by blood
and injuries; I had already had my fill.

HMS *Furious* was an ugly brute, and certainly not as glamorous as
battleships, cruisers or destroyers. She was like a bloody great steel works
factory. The flight deck was a tremendous flat deck of steel from bow to
stern, the measurements of which I do not know. However, it was like
half an airfield runway with the same length and width. Underneath the
edges of the deck those who did all that was necessary for the ship's
operation were accommodated. The good fortune for us, as we moved to
the Middle East, was that between them, two aircraft carriers, the *Furious*
and the *Ark Royal*, which we would meet in Gibraltar, were able to carry
some fifty-eight Hurricanes. The *Furious*, old as she was, had a full-width
lift with which to rise and lower aircraft from the tremendous hangar and
workshops. The size of the hangar is hard to explain: it was a mountain-
ous cavern with masses of steel girders and was as big as the largest
hangar on the airfield. The *Ark Royal*, a more modern carrier, had a 'lift'

that accommodated only half the width of the flight deck, so she could assemble and carry only one squadron. While we sailed, the naval teams would put together our Hurricanes, wings to fuselage, long-range tanks to wings, and every other component, including fuel tanks in the aircraft, which would hold approximately 170 gallons of fuel, allowing us a cruising speed of 180 mph, and a distance of approximately 500 miles, more than enough if there were no problems.

When the Hurricanes of No. 249 Squadron had been assembled, they were raised to the flight deck and parked neatly at the rear end of the deck, where the controls, tanks and engines would be tested and retested as we sailed our way to Gibraltar. After this was done, the Hurricanes of No. 229 Squadron would receive the same treatment. However, they would be retained in the now spacious hangar until we were transferred to the *Ark Royal*. All this time we were kept busy learning as much as possible about the work we had been assigned should we be attacked by German battleships or Luftwaffe aircraft.

There was always time to perambulate around areas of the carrier, to see something of interest. For instance, we found a walkway down the side of the deck with a narrow netted protection, which allowed one to stand on the side of the flight deck and watch the Navy aircraft take off and land as they patrolled the square miles around the flotilla of naval vessels. From this position, we could look straight down to the ocean and see a cross section of marine life following the ship. A particular interest was watching hammerhead sharks of frightening size cavorting with smaller sharks. They were truly ugly monsters! We still could not understand why the battleship on our starboard flank was not named. It certainly looked like the *King George V*, the Navy's latest battleship, with 15-inch guns among others. It seemed that the speed we were maintaining of 12 knots was to suit this vessel.

The days passed rather slowly, which related to the constant tension and thoughts of possible action. During this time we queried, with our naval friends, how great it was to have the *King George V* battleship in our escort from the UK. There was much laughter as they told us that the *King George V* was actually in the North Sea. An old battleship, the HMS *Centurion*, was disguised as the *King George V* in the hope that it would scare off a possible German attack. The great guns we could see were all wooden pieces, and there was little more armament on the ship. The naval lads laughed. We were less amused. We were informed of what was happening in the UK and Europe generally, and much was filtering through about the German battleships that were sheltering in western harbours and were expected to make a dash up the Channel to the safety of the Nordic fjords. There were also reports on the movements of the famous *Bismark* warship – there was plenty for us to discuss.

We passed through the Bay of Biscay, out of sight of land and the possibility of being seen by German agents, and the first leg of our voyage was closing. The day before we arrived in Gibraltar, our captain received a signal from Admiral Sir James Somerville of Force 'H', who was in command of the operation, saying that, on arrival in the harbour, we were to berth stern to stern with HMS *Ark Royal*, so that our Hurricanes could be transferred to her. During the night of 18–19 May, No. 249's Hurricanes were moved to the *Ark Royal*, as described by our CO, Squadron Leader Barton: 'The transfer of Hurricanes was achieved by simply lowering a huge wood and steel platform between the balanced decks of the two carriers. This was completed without damage and the aircraft were arranged for final check and take-off.' At this time we were advised that the rest of our NCO pilots and ground personnel were on their way around the Cape of Good Hope via the Suez Canal, bound for Egypt. Sergeant George Stroud, who had recovered from his burns, was with them. They had our logbooks and personal clothing. We would never see these again, as our personnel were absorbed in the Western Desert forces.

From Gibraltar, the two carriers sailed in company. This movement was given the code name, 'Operation Splice'. On 20 May, in the evening, the operation moved slowly from Gibraltar and sailed into the night darkness, back through the Straits of Gibraltar, and a westerly course into the Atlantic, much to our amazing surprise. We were now a major naval force with Force 'H' and Force 'K', with destroyers, cruisers and other warships in a huge screen around us. As far as we could tell, we were cruising at flank speed, as if we were going to the Azores, then, on the morning of 21 May, we turned and hurtled back towards Gibraltar. We had been on a reciprocal course in daylight for a long time when an alarm was sounded. As we turned on to this reciprocal course, a Portuguese shipping trawler was seen on the horizon. A destroyer belted across to this small ship, took off the crew, so it was explained, and sank the trawler. This crew could have alerted the Spanish and German authorities, who were based in La Lynya in Spain, next door to Gibraltar. We continued our direction and passed through the Straits of Gibraltar about midnight, and with full speed; the whole operation was heading in the direction of Malta, our next stop.

We had been advised that we would leave the *Ark Royal* at dawn on 21 May. We expected to be flown off the carrier to enable us to have a flight of between 2 and 2^1/$_2$ hours. However, at dawn the alarm was raised, and the news was given to us that the German *Bismark* had sailed and the *Ark Royal* was given immediate orders to sail to the North Sea for major action. We would have to fly off earlier than anticipated. We were issued with small paper maps showing Malta in relation to the North African coast and the island of Sicily, near Italy. Naval pilots flying Fulmars, single-engine two-seater aircraft, would lead each of the three squadrons. The twenty-one 249 pilots would fly off one at a time, as we had been allocated and positioned on the flight deck in order of take-off. Squadron Leader Barton was first. I was number 7. In yet another demonstration of the efficiency of the naval personnel, we were given no time to think about the take-off. Two sailors with short wands in their hands stood either side of the Hurricane to guide us into position and directed us to 'Go, go, go!' To complete the take-off we would hold the aircraft at full throttle, feet on the brakes, flaps set at 14 degrees down, feet off the brakes, and off we flew. I was watching the CO, who left the carrier but sank beneath the bows of the ship, before eventually coming into sight. I nearly swallowed my tonsils as I thought he had not made it! I accelerated and was actually airborne before I reached the end of the flight deck.

All twenty-one of us took off without mishap. We flew around the carrier in formation until the Fulmar was airborne and set to lead us. We were circling and wondering what had happened to the Fulmar, when we saw it returning to the *Ark Royal*. Its undercarriage would not retract. Another Fulmar became airborne, which joined us after we had used a lot of our fuel through circling the now retreating carriers. RT (radio transmission) had to be used to finalise instructions as we recommenced our journey eastward. Now we understood that the rest of the Hurricane squadrons had flown off the *Furious* and their formation had lost another Fulmar through a burst oil line. What would happen next?

19. 'What a Small Island This Was!'

No. 249's formation formed up behind the second Fulmar, a two-seater aircraft similar to the old Fairey Battle aircraft, and we now stretched out more or less in a line abreast, with the Fulmar leading. We all must have been damned worried at the mileage we had lost and the fuel consumption. Way out on our port side, Nos 213 and 229 Squadrons were spread out like ourselves, behind their second Fulmar. We now proceeded at about 100 feet above the Mediterranean so that our engine noise would not alarm the Vichy French on the African coast. That was not particularly comfortable, as we had to keep a keen watch on each other's Hurricane and remember to operate the fuel supply from the wing tanks to the engine. Now we were about 550 miles from Malta, when we should have been 450 miles. The group I was in, led by Squadron Leader Barton, settled down to reaching Malta around midday, and we were very happy to see the cliffs of the island ahead. We were ordered to land on Ta'Qali Airfield on the north end of the island, and the other aircraft landed at a larger airfield, Luqa, in the centre of the island. Some aircraft that were very low in fuel landed on the third airfield, Hal Far, on the south-west of the island. What a small island this was! And there was a smaller island called 'Gozo' to the north. Incidentally, a number of aircraft in Flight Lieutenant Neil's section actually ran out of fuel as they taxied to the dispersals after landing.

Before we had our breath back, we were given the bad news that No. 249 Squadron was to remain on Malta. The other two squadrons would depart the next day for Cairo, Middle East. What had we landed in now?

We were told that one of the No. 213 Squadron Hurricanes had been lost. It had apparently been flying very low when the pilot, who was trying to read the small map we had been issued with, hit the water, damaged the aircraft propeller and crashed. He was captured by the Vichy French and interned, unhurt.

Those of us who had landed at Ta'Qali were informed that this airfield was to be our base. We also heard that the island had been subjected to a lightning attack just before we had arrived. Someone remarked, 'What a pity, we could have had our first fight.' To which the quiet voice of Squadron Leader Barton remarked, 'Thank heavens the attack was over. None of our Hurricanes was armed.' The silence was penetrating.

By early afternoon the pilots from Luqa and Hal Far had arrived at Ta'Qali, and one could have cut the atmosphere with a knife! Flight Lieutenant Tom Neil (Ginger), as usual, was in full voice, complaining as to how he had a shaky flight with quite a number of problems. However, the important difficulty, apart from the shock of our remaining on Malta, was that we realised our ground crews, luggage and logbooks would not reach us. All we had was what we stood up in and small items that were in the parachute bags, which were tucked away in our aircraft. We were also advised we would be taking over the clapped-out Hurricanes of No. 261 Squadron, who were to leave after defending the island since August 1940. So they would accompany Nos. 213 and 229 Squadrons to Egypt. A few of the new Hurricanes, which we had flown to the island, would be left. Big deal! Pilot Officer Pain, a former member of No. 249, advised us that some of the old Hurricanes were held together with dope painted linen and metal repair, with pieces cannibalised from some of the aircraft unable to fly. The situation was impossible.

Officers and NCO pilots milled around like lost souls until somebody arrived and explained about our accommodation. Officers were taken to a large house, more like a medieval castle, called Torri Combo, about a mile north-east of the airfield. The NCOs were taken to a similar building about half a mile south-west of the airfield. I arrived with Terry Crossey and Dusty Mills, with Tom Neil following, and we entered the courtyard of this large house. We were advised to choose a room and make that a billet. I shot up the stairs of the house and found a nice room with two beds and a window opening to the east. I dumped my bag on one of the beds, then left to find out where Crossey and Mills were locating. They had chosen a room in what had been the servants' quarters across the patio from the house. I explained to them how I had found the room in the house and Crossey said, 'That must be the room that Tom Neil has taken.' I said, 'So what? We only sleep there.' Terry Crossey then advised me that I would not be comfortable in the same room as Neil. I would be better off joining them in their large room. I said, 'No way! Tom Neil would not mind.' Eventually everyone found a room, and we then collected in a large living room to discuss our fate.

At the end of the day and after much discussion and a fair amount of wine and whisky, bed was welcome. I crept to my bed before Tom Neil appeared and, with a last gasp of a very exciting day, I fell asleep in this lovely airy stone fortress. At 2.00 a.m. I was awakened as a terrific scream was echoing in the room. I looked through my mosquito net across the room, where Tom was sitting up facing me, looking very white and disturbed. I said, 'What's the matter?' He opened his mouth and, with a full moon lighting up the room through the wide window, he looked my way and he let out a scream a mile long – I am sure it could be heard all around the island. Scream followed scream as he looked at me without any movement. I leapt out of bed, hurting my toes on the stone floor, and hopped across to Tom's bed, pulling up the mosquito net. It was hopeless. He sat up rigid, looking straight ahead, screaming and yelling enough to frighten the hell out of me. Pretty soon others ran into the room. Terry Crossey apparently knew all about Tom's nightmares and took over and quietened him. In the meantime every hair on my head was pointing skywards. By 3.00 a.m. things were quiet and Tom was asleep again. And where was I? Over in the other quarters with Terry and Dusty, who were both laughing their damned heads off. Lesson number one – don't be too clever!

20. The Battle of Malta, 249 Style

It was 22 May 1941. With twenty-one pilots at our disposal, we were well off and had plenty of choices to build a flying squadron of twelve Hurricanes, if we had that number of Hurricanes among what was left after the departure of the other three squadrons. Squadron Leader Barton split the flying programme into two flights. He would command 'B' Flight and Tom Neil would lead 'A' Flight. This allowed 50 per cent of the pilots to be off duty at any one time. Each flight would operate for half a day. A day-on and day-off roster was organised in conjunction with another newly formed squadron, No. 183, which would share the defence of the island with No. 249.

On 25 May, the first flight of half the squadron had been taken to the airfield in an old small bus with torn and dirty seats, much to the pilots' disgust, and they were dumped at the south-east corner of the field, where a dirty and ragged dispersal bell tent greeted them as the Field Operations Unit, Ta'Qali. A number of Hurricanes had been lined up near the tent area when, at about 2.00 p.m., the warning sirens were heard. The squadron was not ordered to scramble, so some of the pilots went to their Hurricanes and got into the cockpits. Suddenly, Bf109s arrived and attacked the static Hurricanes. I was off duty this time and only heard the roar and snarl of the 109s and the subsequent noise and crackle of the machine guns as they blasted the line of aircraft. Flying Officer Harrington's plane was hit by a cannon shell in the fuel tanks, and a bullet went through his parachute. However, Harry (Harrington) was not hurt. Sergeant M. McVean, a new pilot, jumped from his cockpit in such a hurry that he broke both his legs. Also, Flying Officer Pat Wells, who had just returned to the squadron after injuries sustained at North Weald, suffered a bullet through his right ankle. Three of our ground crew were also injured. What a start to our new arrival. Six Hurricanes had been hit and two were totally destroyed. This debacle did nothing for the confidence of our new pilots.

Squadron Leader Barton visited the headquarters of the RAF in the city of Valletta and met the Air Vice Marshal Hugh Pugh Lloyd and the Group Captain Senior Air Staff Officer (SASSO) and had down-to-earth discussions on warnings of enemy aircraft and immediate scramble information, which had not been given to us in the first raid. Barton expressed his views by quoting the way the controllers in 11 Group operated. Squadron Leader Barton came back to Ta'Qali assured of big changes from headquarters. News was given that the German fighter and bomber squadrons had been withdrawn from Sicily to be moved to the Russian front. The Italian air force was now moving in to attack Malta.

On the morning of 7 June No. 249 was patrolling an early first in our new responsibility. Raiders approached the island, and we attacked, with Squadron Leader Barton intercepting a BR20 bomber, shooting it down in flames. Flying Officer John Beazley and I attacked a second of the enemy bombers, and it was recorded that it had crashed into the sea.

The next day Squadron Leader Butch Barton organised the first raid on Sicily in return for their effort just after our arrival. We had six Hurricanes loaded with eight 40-lb bombs, four under each wing, and the armourers had been requested to include patterns of incendiary ammunition in the gun belts. We were airborne at dusk to dive-bomb Comiso Airfield in Sicily, which was the major field from where the assaults on Malta had come.

It was dark as we commenced our attack in an open Vic formation, Butch first and with me following. We were really side by side covering the airfield. We dropped our bombs as near as we could to the groups of Macchi fighters and bombers. Dave Davies did not see his bombs burst. Beazley's Hurricane went U/S with a glycol leak. The flak was heavy, and the streams of shells reached up to us like pretty tennis balls. Light, not so pretty, flashed past the cockpit – red, green and white streaks of death. The moon was bright, and so we were able to see some of the results of the raid and some of our damage.

We followed with another raid, setting off at 4.30 a.m. The moon was slightly obscured, but it was fairly bright. Butch Barton took off first. However, his tail nav. light failed, which made it difficult to fly in formation. Dave formed up on myself, and we flew straight off. After half a circuit, Beazley joined us, acting as escort along with Cassidy, who was now in the Malta Night Fighting Unit (MNFU) and had missed me as I had switched off my nav. lights. Dave and I overshot Comiso Airfield and finally bombed Victoria Airfield, and then a town west of Comiso. Our bombs hit planes and vehicles on the eastern side. I lost Dave in the dive and carried on home to Malta, as we had been ordered. I saw the CO being fired at by light flak as I crossed the coast, going out. The CO had found the target OK. When we had returned, Dave told me he had dropped his bombs on the same areas as me. Quite a success!

On 12 June Valletta Harbour was attacked by Macchi 200 fighters. One Macchi was shot down by myself, shared with our Australian, Sergeant Sheppard.

The next week, on 18 June, nine Macchi 200s approached Malta during the early afternoon. No. 249 scrambled and intercepted them. I was leading a section of three, including Sergeant Sheppard. I was flying a lousy Hurricane, which caused me to drop back somewhat, but I was still climbing. One Macchi saw me lagging behind and dived to give me a head-on attack. Sergeant Sheppard immediately turned and followed the Macchi. When the Macchi was close enough and had not fired, I gave it a 3-second burst and hit his starboard wing, and debris burst from his aircraft. Sheppard closed behind and gave him a long burst, which made a hell of a mess of the cockpit. The Macchi crashed into the sea. Sheppard and I claimed a victory, which was confirmed.

June ended after a number of skirmishes when raids were reported on radar but never materialised. There were a number of attacks on Sicily by the other two squadrons that had now been formed, which gave No. 249 some time to reorganise the two half squadrons and the new pilots. This allowed fighter tactics practice and ordinary patrols around a 20-mile radius of the island. This lull also allowed us to improve tremendously the liaison with the Valletta operations and the radar communication. It was well accepted that the Luftwaffe would return soon and life would be hell.

On 26 June I was admitted to hospital with food poisoning. The food we ate was awful fish. Our chef did what he could from the supplies available. The fish were collected generally after enemy bombs had been dropped in the harbour or surrounding sea – they were killed by explosions. A month and a day later I returned for duty to the squadron. Good medication did the trick!

The lack of Italian action was disconcerting. The weather was reasonable to good, and on our patrols in a radius around the island we were experiencing small raids of Italian aircraft. Numbers of them appeared on radar reports, but they turned away on most occasions as they sighted our patrols. We were now rostered in a way that would allow us to have days off to visit Valletta, the capital, and we took full advantage sampling the cafés and clubs. That was well worth the visit! Talking to the Maltese people and particularly the anti-aircraft gun soldiers, we received explanation of this peculiar lull in the offensive raids. Since the Luftwaffe had left the scene, the Italians were terrified of the Malta barrage.

The only important targets for bomber attacks were Valletta itself and a famous British giant aircraft carrier, HMS *Illustrious*. This ship, on a par with the *Ark Royal*, had been badly damaged in one of the great naval battles in January 1941 and had been attacked along with the Force 'H' fleet of battleships, cruisers and destroyers in a fierce operation 100 miles from Malta. The Germans concentrated on the *Illustrious*, approaching with a large formation of between forty and fifty Ju87 vertical dive-bombers and Ju88s, the most fearsome aircraft in the Luftwaffe. The *Illustrious* was badly damaged. However, she was escorted from the fighting and managed to return to Malta, where she was berthed in 'French Creek' in Valletta's 'Grand Harbour'. When the Germans found out what had happened to the *Illustrious*, they concentrated their efforts on destroying her as she lay in the huge dry dock. We experienced their last raid on the week of our arrival, after which the whole German air force was withdrawn to go to the Russian front.

Because of the terrible concentrated attacks, the Maltese anti-aircraft regiments had built a barrier of every type of gun around Valletta and the whole of the huge harbour adjoining this great walled city. The barrage was considered to be heavier by far than those of London. In fact, the Maltese claimed one could walk on the field of bursting shells. This was obviously why the Italian raiders preferred to bomb the small towns around the island and the airfields. We had not experienced this barrage. However, it would not be long before we would, as we received the news from headquarters that the Luftwaffe in improved strength was returning to the Mediterranean theatre.

On 31 July 1941 we were scrambled to intercept a raid approaching the island. We met six Italian SM84 bombers escorted by about six Macchi 200s. We attacked over the small island of Gozo, a few miles north of Malta. Immediately we bounced them, the bombers dropped their bombs on Gozo and turned to retreat. I managed to damage one bomber as a Macchi attacked me. I turned and dived away, and the Macchi fled. I climbed back into the melee and attacked another

Macchi, which was now streaking for Sicily. Aiming high, I fired a 4-second burst and saw strikes on his tail section. By this time the fight was over, with three Macchi fighters shot down and two bombers on fire and heading for the sea.

Another raid on Comiso was organised for 8 August, this time with six Hurricanes. We first flew on a course west of Sicily and attacked railways and oil tankers, plus an engine pulling a line of loaded trucks. Staying low at a speed of 250 mph, we headed overland to Comiso, attacking every aircraft and vehicle in sight. We had surprised the defence, coming from west to east overland, and afterwards, with a slight turn to the south, we were streaking for Malta – no casualties.

It was a fine day on 14 August. There were no reports of activity over Sicily from Valletta headquarters. I was delegated to take charge of any activities. At this time the Malta local authorities had kindly removed our operation tent and built a sandstone building of huge interlocked blocks, which were bulletproof. We also had chairs and tables to eat meals – comfort for all! I was sitting in a chair when one of the pilots advised me that two naval officers were approaching our operations dwelling. I walked to meet them, asking what I could do for them. One, Lieutenant Commander Wanklyn, who, I now noticed, had the ribbon of the Victoria Cross on his chest, asked if it was possible for him and his fellow officer to have a flight around the island as, being submariners, they would like to see what Malta looked like from the air. They had heard that we had a small training aircraft, a Miles Magister two-seater, and they had also approached headquarters for permission, as there were no enemy plots on the action table, and the morning forecast appeared to be clear. Overpowered by such a hero, I rang headquarters and was given the 'all clear'.

As I was responsible should a readiness appear on the screen, I had one of the pilots get the Magister made ready and fly each officer around the island and point out the various places of interest through the Gosport tubes for communications. This was accomplished, and after we had offered them coffee or tea (we had no biscuits), they thanked me profusely and invited me to ask the squadron leader, who was now Tom Neil, if he had pilots who would like to attend a party two days hence, to be on the huge fuel-carrying submarine, HMS *Thunderbolt*.

Needless to say, the eight of us, including Flight Lieutenant John Beazley, Tommy Thompson, Cassidy, Mills and Leggett, ended up in the bowels of the submarine, greeted by Lieutenant Commander Wanklyn

VC and officers of other submarines in Marsamuscetto Harbour. The party was absolutely terrific, and after I damaged two or three whiskies I asked if I could look around this giant submarine, as it was of interest to me. Wanklyn came to me and asked why I should be so interested. I replied that before the war commenced I was a student engineer in a large maritime engine works in Yorkshire, in a town called Hartlepool. I was a junior in a test department designing and manufacturing large pressure chargers for the diesel engines of T Class submarines. This work was related to the designs of the Swiss Company, Brown Boveri. The period for me was the end of 1937. In 1938 our senior engineers were working on the commissioning of the *Triumph*, and *Trident*, in Greenock, while another submarine, the *Thetis*, was nearing readiness for testing in Liverpool. Our small special progress office consisted of a manager and two qualified engineers and myself as a gofer. My work was to take part in certain results of test work and visit the site on a few occasions carrying reports. This allowed me to see around this, to me, wonderful submarine battleship, which I never forgot. Our office was accountable to Commander Pennington, who appeared to be in charge of this project. This ended when HMS *Thetis* sank during the test in 1938. Commander Pennington was killed with all the crew and civilians except the captain. Our work was completed and I applied to the naval authorities for service in submarines.

I was asked many questions about my pre-war experience as the party increased. Tommy Thompson, Cassidy, Mills and a new member of the Squadron, Leggett, and myself were the last to leave and we were pretty groggy! Beazley, Neil and the others had left earlier. The time was nearly 11.00 p.m., and we staggered out of the submarine on to a completely empty wharf. There was not one vehicle to return us to the airfield and Torri Combo. The submarine berth was in a much smaller harbour on the north side of the city, and on the other side there were some stone steps leading from the city side down to the water's edge. As we argued the situation, Cassidy pointed to a number of small wooden boats that ferried people from this wharf to the city steps during daytime. They were tied to a bollard on the wharf edge, and the oars were in the boat. We untied the ropes of one, jumped in and pedalled, taking turns, as it was difficult. We were within 100 yards of the steps when, with loud shouts and waving big poles, the Maltese boatmen were alongside us and literally pushed us out of the boat. They grabbed the rope that hung partially over the end and turned away, back to their jetty.

We managed to laugh like hell and swam for the steps, which were easy to see in the moonlight. By this time it was nearly 11.00 p.m. and amid our swimming, slowly in our waterlogged uniforms, Tommy said, 'It's nearly 11.00 p.m. Don't you remember the Navy let off the underwater explosions every hour.' This was to deter Italian frogmen from placing explosives on the ships in the harbour. I think we all yelled and struck out for the last 20 yards from the steps. I have never swum so fast in my life and, along with the others, we hit the steps like a tidal wave, sitting down to catch our breath. Still laughing, pulling and pushing, we stood up, turned to climb the steps, and 'Crunch!' The explosion nearly knocked us off our feet. We all looked at each other, blessing our absolute luck. The underwater explosion against enemy frogmen was on time. Sobered up, we climbed the steps and reported to the military police who patrolled all night, told them some of our story, and with big grins and remarks like, 'Just like you RAF types', we were driven back to our quarters near the airfield. Next morning we handed our soggy garments to our senior batman, who would see them dried and pressed. Squadron Leader Butch Barton lectured us 'idiots', as he told us to get to the aircraft dispersal next to the ops building.

On 17 August I led a section of six Hurricanes in loose formation to patrol a circular distance around the island in a 20-mile radius, which covered protection of the local fishing men in their small boats. There was no activity to report on our return to Ta'Qali. In the previous two weeks, more Hurricanes had arrived on the island, and some Mark IIs were included as well as a new Mark I.

August finished with no activity. However, rumours were once more warning us that the Luftwaffe would be back soon.

21. 'The Pilots Were Not Amused'

Enemy activity was infrequent into October, but we maintained fighter tactics. New pilots were arriving, so we spent time with them practising cannon firing and dive-bombing with the Mark II aircraft.

On 6 October 1941 a night bombing exercise was being briefed, with six Hurricanes. Ginger Neil and Squadron Leader Barton managed to take Mark IIs for comfort. However, the remaining four of us had Hurricane Is, which had arrived recently. The destination was Comiso again, and the target stood out well in the moonlight. Earlier raids had taught us the layout of the dispersals and the hangars, which we bombed once again with 40-lb bombs. It was a pity that we did not have the equipment for one 500-lb bomb! The time was 11.00 p.m., and the defence was poor. There were no casualties, as we returned to Ta'Qali.

Three days later, on 9 October, there was yet another attack on Sicily – this time at 4.30 a.m. It was very dark, and targets were hard to identify. We strafed the town of Vitorio near Comiso. The targets were industrial, still with no heavy defence, only light ground machine-gun fire. Another raid and we would be invited to dinner!

By 14 October the Malta Night Fighter Unit (MNFU) had been formed, taking five pilots from our squadron and 185 Squadron and, as luck would have it, the four Hurricane Mark II Bs. Four common aircraft were allocated to them. An old friend of 11 Group, Squadron Leader Innes Westmacott, as squadron commander, had selected Tommy Thompson, Cassidy and Mills – now 249 would be a new squadron. One new quite young pilot, Barnwell, had arrived and was also allocated to the MNFU. He looked to be 16 years of age. However, he was the youngest member of a well-known English family who had other sons who were fighter pilots in the RAF. In the first week he had shot down three Italian bombers and was awarded the DFC; he was a glamour youngster.

One particular night, Barnwell was on patrol again when the radio picked up a signal from him that he had engaged another bomber. He yelled that he had hit the enemy. Then he shouted, 'I am hit and am baling out.' It was estimated he was about 15 miles north-west of Malta. At dawn I led a section of three and conducted a low-level search for about an hour. However, we could see no debris or dinghy in the water. The other search team had no success either. We had to accept that a nice brave lad was lost.

It is about time to recount some pleasure among the agony of fighting and the loss of quite a number of our companions and friends. During the previous four months we had enjoyed the welcome of many of the Maltese families, to the extent that one of my old friends, Terry Crossey, a South African, was courting one of the daughters of a government official and by the grace of God it could prove to be a serious relationship. Meanwhile, the family of Sir Phillip Pullicino, a representative of the British government, resident with his wife and eleven children in a lovely large home in Rabat, made it quite clear they would make us feel at home. Another prominent family on the island who invited us to their home was the family of Count Scicluna, who owned the Maltese Brewery. His place was like a castle on the Mediterranean coast and included a small zoo, tennis courts, swimming pool and a pathway to the coast for boating and swimming. He had a beautiful ocean-going luxury cruiser, which was housed in a palatial large sandstone building. His wife, while she was entertaining a number of us, explained that the cruiser was looked after by a resident family. The boat was now, of course, laid up for the duration. The Countess had explained to us that the Count had many hobbies and was seldom seen when visitors were around.

On one visit, I had joined in the swimming and squash, and afterwards was enjoying a walk around the open area of the home. I saw this fine sandstone building with the door open, so I ventured in and let out a quiet gasp at the large cruiser. It was a beauty. I noticed a man in a boiler suit working on a bench obviously on something from the boat. He turned to me and rubbed his hands on a rag and said, 'You are a visitor I suppose?' I answered and said, 'What a beautiful boat. Do you enjoy working on it?' He told me he could show me around the boat if I was interested. I told this man, who was obviously a maintenance engineer, that I came from a maritime family and would enjoy looking around. We enjoyed about an hour of inspecting the engines and the framework, propellers and controls, after which he advised me he must go as he had some more work to do. I said to him, 'You're lucky and must be proud to be looking after the Count's grand vessel.' He smiled and said, 'Yes, I am Count Scicluna.' He laughed at my expression and took me by the arm as we walked out into the open vista of his home ground. He explained how he loved to work on his boat and cars, which were the best that one could imagine. Walking me into a section of his house, which, I suppose, was one of his studies, he entertained me for a couple of hours, questioning me on my flying and previous young life. This was one of the most interesting days I had.

Another family, the de Giorgis, of whom the father was in the oil industry, as well as entertaining us to various meals with their family, also had a lovely house in St Paul's Bay in the north of the island. This was used only on summer vacations, and the squadron was offered a number of days at a time to rest and enjoy a beautiful fully furnished villa, with a small sailing boat for pleasure. There was also the Malta Club and various nightclubs. So when we were off duty we were never bored. This was a great help, considering the strain we were under with operations. During the beginning of October I had joined the ever-increasing receivers of 'that' letter telling me that Jean, my fiancée, had met a major in the Army and she hoped I would understand and accept the situation. I was surprised but definitely not shocked, as our correspondence had not been all that good. I answered her letter with a simple: 'I understand, and as we accepted the idea of marriage before I left England, anything could happen when we were separated.' I wished her well. The heavy fighting and conditions dampened any feeling I might have generated as I closed the door on that episode. Anyway the loss of quite a few of my squadron friends and the strain caused me to think I would never leave Malta.

On 17 October 1941 a different role was planned. We were to escort six newly arrived Blenheim bombers to attack Syracuse seaplane base and huge oil and other tanks on the west of the city. The Blenheims bombed from 12,500 feet. Three Macchi 202s attacked the bombers as we entered the action. They would have arrived from Comiso. It was a wild melee as we warded off the Macchis. However, it was claimed a Blenheim was shot down, and the guns of the Blenheim caused one Macchi to crash into the sea, where the pilot was apparently rescued. We could claim only to have damaged the other two, which disappeared quickly. These two Macchi 202s were the new Italian fighters and were very good. Our Hurricanes had slight damage but no pilot was hurt.

The following day Air Vice Marshall Sir Hugh Pugh Lloyd called a meeting with Squadron Leader Butch Barton on the subject of the

Luftwaffe now returning to Sicily and Rommel's new push in the desert. Troops and materials of war were being ferried by cargo planes or conventional bombers, through Sardinia and to the African coast, to supply Rommel. He wanted us to patrol an area from Sardinia over the island of Lampedusa, which was in their hands, using Hurricane Mark IIs with cannons and long-range tanks. Butch discussed this with the squadron and appointed me to be his No. 2. But first we had a few arguments about how long-range tanks reduced the speed and fighting ability of the aircraft. The Mark IIs had improved enormously with the new engines, so it was agreed a patrol would be arranged for 4.45 a.m. at the airfield and a 5.55 take-off, with Hurricane II Cs, which had twelve machine guns, six in each wing. There's always a first time!

So, on 19 October, at 4.45 a.m., I had drunk a huge mug of hot cocoa, as had Squadron Leader Butch Barton. We were driven to the airfield and checked in with a night duty pilot. Then we inspected carefully the Hurricane II C, with Butch muttering about twelve 'B' machine guns instead of four 20mm cannons and some words from both of us about long-range 44-gallon wing tanks. Then we were ready. We were airborne at 5.55 a.m. and in loose formation we headed south-west, cruising at 250 mph, levelling off at 12,000 feet. We checked our map: we would commence our patrol south of Lampedusa, an island manned by the Italian air force. We would patrol at 6,000 feet, an area between the island and the African coast. We reached our position at about 6.40 a.m. and circled in a radius of approximately 10 miles, and with the aircraft hoods open and goggles on our foreheads, eyes like organ stops, we flew around and circled about three times, after which we had no sighting of any aircraft. The visibility was excellent, with some giant white fluffy cumulus clouds here and there. We could not miss anything.

At last Butch made a sign to me that meant we were to head for Malta. We had just turned on a north-east course, at altitude 6,000 feet, and I had closed up to Butch, who was now looking ahead, when I saw a huge tri-motor bomber emerge from one of these cumulus clouds, about 1,000 feet below us. Butch had not seen it because it was at right angles to his vision, whereas I was closing in on his starboard side and I was looking directly across. I moved my wings gently and Butch quickly looked at me, pointing over his left shoulder. Butch signalled a steep turn to port and, as soon as we turned, the pilot must have seen us, because he immediately commenced a turn to fly back into the cloud. With full boost, the Mark II engine had us in firing range very quickly. Butch fired a burst in a quarter attack, and the tracer field of twelve guns was something to see. I followed close to Butch, but diving under him, coming up under a lower target, and gave two 3-second bursts, hitting the middle engine and the belly of what was a Savoia tri-motor bomber, or possibly a cargo plane. The sight of twenty-four lines of tracer bullets was awesome, and the aircraft caught fire and in no time at all it was a blazing mess in the sea.

We turned for base at full speed, as it was certain that the fighters on Lampedusa would have been alerted. We were halfway to Malta when the excitement made me aware my bladder was bursting. Butch had at one time told me that he had this problem sometimes and watered the floor of his aircraft, so with the fight of my life I fought to find my organ, through lots of harness and flying overall. As my hood was open, Butch was looking at me and the antics of my Hurricane. Eventually, and just in time, I produced the offending gadget and with a breath of relief, let go. What a hell of a shock I suffered when the urine stream curved nicely towards the floor of my aircraft, but, for some reason, did not hit the floor but did a beautiful curve and floated right into the middle of my face! Hence the antics of my aircraft! When the stream stopped, I flew close to Butch and raised my hands and shook my head, and Butch shook his head. When we landed, he laughed like hell and congratulated me on the performance – not the action, but my antics. I said to him, 'You told me it was no trouble', and he said, 'That's right. But you did not close the hood!' We were congratulated for the deed, and my friends asked me to repeat the technical performance! Later, we were cursed somewhat, as the Air Vice Marshal's words were, 'Well done, we have proved the action. We will repeat the patrols.' The pilots were not amused. It meant the patrols would continue!

There was a bombing raid on 24 October. This time with three twin-engine Blenheim bombers, which carried heavy bombs. The attack target was on an important town of Gela, with the railway junction and oil tanks, and a significant railway bridge. Unfortunately, we were expected, and quite a number of the new Macchi 202s were waiting for us. After a fierce dogfight, we started returning to Malta. One Blenheim was lost, the crew taken prisoner. The rest of us received different damage to our aircraft, but no injuries.

On 2 November, on duty with my five pilots waiting for news from fighter operations, I was sitting in our sandstone ops building discussing tactics with some of the new pilots. A ground staff airman came into the room and advised me that a priest had pitched up; would I talk to him? I went outside and was shocked indeed to see a full-blooded elderly priest in perfect raiment, black on white and red – a complete picture. He was about 60 years of age, big and worldly, beautiful grey beard and powerful approach. He asked us to engage in a short prayer and hymn; we would sing to a small organ he had on a donkey cart. I was completely stunned – nothing like this had manifested itself since I had joined the air force. I tried to explain that we were at 'readiness', and at any time we could receive a scramble order that would have us running to our Hurricanes, which would have their engines running, and a take-off would damage his equipment, including the small organ. I phoned operations and explained my predicament. I was advised, 'No plots on the table yet, carry on.'

Our six Hurricanes were reasonably close together, and the priest had parked the organ about 6 feet from the tail of my aircraft. I asked him to place it in another spot, but he pleaded it was all right. I warned him, if we were attacked, to run for a split trench about 30 feet behind our ops building and to keep his donkey under control. 'Great, great,' said this big man in the flowing robes, and the service commenced. We were halfway into the first hymn when the scramble alarm sounded and hell broke loose as the ground staff started the engines. The six of us ran for our aircraft and, as I ran, the priest was standing near the side of my aircraft, a big man with his regalia streaming behind him from the draught of the running engine. He was bending forward in the strong blast and waving his arms as if to help me to run, and he was screaming something that the engine noise was too high for me to understand. So, at full throttle, off we flew down the airfield. I was truly worried as to what had happened to the priest and his organ and donkey as we gained height for the patrol.

The scramble was a false alarm, and we were ordered to return. About 20 minutes had elapsed as we taxied in and walked to our new ops building. One of the senior ground crew was ready to talk to me and said, 'We have never seen anything like it, Sir. As you opened your throttle for take-off, the priest, who was bending forward to keep his balance, was yelling, "Get a bastard for me and a bastard for the Church!" It was something to behold as the organ and his young Maltese musician were hurled into the slit trench. As for the donkey, they were still looking for him, as it had hurtled off. The little cart was matchwood.' The small van or truck that carried the priest, music boy and the organ had been loaded, and they had left the airfield. We heard nothing more. However, the ground lads agreed they had witnessed a funny if not alarming experience.

Another long patrol was actioned on 9 November. However, the patrol saw nothing and on return one of our best experienced pilots, Sergeant Rex, suffered a burst oil pipe in his Hurricane. He crash-landed in the sea about 40 miles from the island. His partner in the second Hurricane wirelessed headquarters and remained circling, as Rex swam until a patrol boat picked him up. No more patrols were suggested.

I had been suffering an unpleasant attack on my sinuses, which was giving me a lot of trouble. So on 13 November arrangements were made for me to see the only doctor available, an officer in the Royal Navy, housed in the naval dockyards. He anaesthetised the antrum and then applied an instrument to press through the bone to release the pressure. He administered the operation to both antrums, which, after two days, eased the pain. I suffered this six times, and the improvement helped. This did not affect my flying duties.

Meanwhile, two more squadrons had arrived, Nos 242 and 605. The Luftwaffe was now filtering back to Sicily – which did not bode well for the Christmas season. However, with the latest two squadrons and other recent arrivals over the previous two months, it appeared that we could put together a good show. The *Ark Royal* brought these latest squadrons, and on her return to Gibraltar she was attacked by a concentrated number of German U-boats and sank.

Returning from a patrol on a nice sunny morning, I left my aircraft and made my way to our sandstone ops room. Ginger Neil was sitting on a chair with what looked like a sheet of cardboard on his lap. Another seat beside him held a tray of watercolour paints and Ginger waved to me. I asked him, 'At peace then Ginger?' He answered, 'Get a chair. I want to ask you something.' This I did, and Ginger said, 'I have been reading your combat report on the Lampedusa patrol and as we have had some rest time I want to paint the action carried out by Butch and yourself.' He had outlined a rough sketch that looked very professional and I commented on his work. He then asked me if I minded. I answered, 'You are the acting Squadron Leader. Why should I mind? I would like to see the finished job.' He also said, 'I saw the picture that Flying Officer Anderson painted of yours and Sergeant Sheppard's fight with a Macchi 200 fighter, which you shared, confirmed, and gave to you as a friend. I thought I would do the same.' I could not express my feelings at such generosity. Both pictures hung in my room in Torri Combo and were complimented by Flying Officer Harrington every time he passed through my room. His interest waned when he offered to buy the picture, to which I replied, 'Like hell!'

No. 249 was on standby on 21 November when No. 185 Squadron was scrambled to intercept an Italian fighter sweep of Macchi 200s and Macchi 202s. It was a low-level strike on Hal Far at the south end of the island. Both attacker and attacked claimed damaged aircraft. However, there were no losses.

Someone must have booted the Italian backside, for the next day the Luftwaffe arrived, and Ju87s assaulted with the Macchi 200s. Squadron Leader Barton was leading us at 18,000 feet when we intercepted twelve Macchi 202s. The fight lasted as usual around 5 minutes before the Macchis turned for home. Squadron Leader Barton claimed one victory, two of our pilots claimed possibles. I only managed to damage two of the Macchis. However, I made no claims.

The Maltese aviation group technicians had been working hard to assemble one Gladiator from the badly damaged *Faith*, *Hope* and *Charity*, the three British Gladiator biplane fighters, which had achieved a remarkable fight in 1940 and had been virtually destroyed. RAF Headquarters had been asked if they could have this one Gladiator, which had been named '*Faith*', tested in flight before it became a historic monument for Malta. Sir Hugh Pugh Lloyd approved. So on 27 November it was transported to the airfield. Butch Barton and Flying Officer Beazley helped me to check the plane carefully; then I was ready to test it, before any enemy movement was anticipated.

I had read the technical papers on it for a number of hours the previous day. I climbed into the cockpit, double checked the controls while the engine ran smoothly, taxied into position and took off. I was airborne more quickly than in a Hurricane and, with my fingers crossed and silent prayers, the test commenced. When I levelled off at 4,000 feet, I turned slowly over Valletta and dived, climbed and dived once more and completed a slow roll, left and right. Then I returned and landed at Ta'Qali, very excited with the experience. '*Faith*' is still a major display in the Malta Military Museum, to this day.

A patrol was ordered for 'B' Flight – six Hurricanes were to share the escort to a fast, large ship, *Clan Ferguson*, bringing a varied cargo for Malta relief. This ship could maintain a speed of 25 knots and could out-distance enemy surface and submarine attack. However, the concern was that Macchi fighters and bombers might have knowledge of this ship and stage an attack. However, the distance from Sicily was a deterrent, as to intercept, assault and return to Sicily scared the hell out of pilots. Three Hurricanes would rendezvous when the ship reached 40 miles from Malta. The other three Hurricanes would relieve the first three, maintaining cover until the ship reached Valletta. No. 126 Squadron would be scrambled if the Italians headed an attack over Malta. The ship had to be protected.

Five miles from approach around the south of the island, enemy aircraft were reported passing over Gozo, the small island next to the main island of Malta. No. 126 Squadron was scrambled, while we, 'B' Flight, gained height for attack. Six 202 bombers were sighted with a number of Macchi 200s as escorts, at a height of 15,000 feet. We gained an altitude of 18,000 feet. We attacked head-on and broke the formation. This was successful, upsetting the bombers, which dropped their bombs before reaching Valletta Harbour, and then turned away. A good dogfight ensued. Two Macchi fighters were shot down and at least three Macchi bombers were damaged or shot down by No. 126 Squadron, which was in position. *Clan Ferguson* sailed into Valletta Harbour free of damage. A letter of congratulations and thanks was sent by the captain of the ship to RAF Headquarters. Two days later we were informed by the captain that the English company, Worthington, had donated 1,000 cases of Worthington Ale for the fighter pilots on Malta. All three squadrons allowed a number of pilots to visit the ship for a party arranged by the ship's crew.

22. 'Promises, Promises'

The first two weeks of December 1941 were full of surprises. Squadron Leader Barton quietly left the island, with no notice to his squadron, flown by flying boat to Gibraltar and on to the UK. Squadron Leader Mortimer Rose DFC arrived to lead No. 249.

On 21 December No. 249 was awaiting the arrival of a formation of British Wellington bombers, one carrying a replacement for Flight Lieutenant Sydney Brandt. The Wellingtons were attacked by CR 42 bi-plane fighters based on Pantelleria. We were scrambled to go to their aid, but we were too late to intercept. Two Wellingtons were shot down. The one in which Brandt was a passenger was damaged, and we escorted it to Malta. The Luftwaffe returned, and the German reconnaissance aircraft started to make their presence felt all over and around Malta, as they had done before they left for Russia. God help us! We still had many Hurricanes Is and a few Hurricane IIs. The promised Spitfires had not yet arrived.

The real challenge to the Hurricanes were four Ju88s, which returned during the morning of 20 December to attack shipping in the Grand Harbour, with a strong fighter escort of Bf109Fs together with a number of Macchi 202s. Twelve Hurricanes of No. 249 were scrambled to challenge the incoming formation, which was assessed to be forty strong. I had managed to fly a Hurricane IIC, armed with four 20mm cannons. I attacked the leading Ju88, which was protected from rear assault with armour plate behind the engine. I opened fire with a 2-second burst, closing so fast I nearly collided with the thing. I dived and twisted a very tight turn, coming towards the starboard side. I fired a 3-second burst, which hit the fuselage under the rear gunner position and then the root of the engine and the area of the wing root. Climbing away, I saw the engine blown from the fuselage and from above I saw the starboard wing collapse. Other pilots reported the 88 went straight down and crashed in the sea. I was attacked by 109s and I returned fire, and the tail area of my Hurricane was damaged, but I still had control. These Hurricane IIs had been borrowed from the MNFU, and naturally the aircraft were painted black. In a clear blue sky I had no place to hide. However, at least five Hurricanes covered me as I broke away.

In the next few days, Flight Lieutenant Neil and Flying Officer Harrington left the island, and then Flight Lieutenant Cassidy left by ship for Egypt. I began to wonder when my name would come out of the bag. I returned to my room miserably, when the Maltese batman pointed to the wall where I had hung my two pictures and noticed the Lampedusa one was not there. I turned to the Maltese and said, 'What happened?' The poor lad, ringing his hands, told me he had seen the 'Big fellow, very English, gone away. He took your picture.' Just as I was about to blow up, Terry Crossey came into the room and said, 'Hell, I thought you valued your picture. Now you sold it to Harrington.' I exploded and told Terry that no way had I sold it. And, as Harrington was always begging me to give it to him, he had actually stolen it. Terry, who was a good friend by now, advised me to phone the Military Police, and Ginger Neil and Harrington were to leave by ship that night. Later the police advised me that the ship had been cleared for sailing when they arrived at the dock and was already moving to join the naval escort. Words failed me as I sat on my bed and realised my loss.

I had a day off duty on 21 December and I joined two or three of the other pilots taking the squadron car to Valletta. We enjoyed the quiet mood of the Valletta Military Club, where we could sit in comfortable surroundings, play some snooker or join in with a poker school, and then on to the nightclub – a full day away from the misery developing. While we were quietly enjoying a break, Nos 249 and 126 Squadrons were scrambled to intercept a further Luftwaffe attack. Another new wing commander, Rabagliati, was now leading No. 249; he was quite famous as one of the Battle of Britain leaders. They were unable to reach the bombers and became embroiled with Bf109s and Macchi 202s. Dave Davies, Flight Lieutenant Beazley and Sergeant Etchells all claimed damaged or victories. Flying Officer Leggett, a new lad, was shot down and had to bale out over Grand Harbour, unharmed. There would be no rest for any of us from now on! We had also received news from headquarters that the new German onslaught was in the hands of the Nazi High Command, which had headed the Luftwaffe during the Battle of Britain.

Before we could get our breath back, we were scrambled the next afternoon – Nos 249 and 126 with reduced numbers to attack a number of Bf109s that were strafing the fishing boats off the Grand Harbour. Wing Commander Rabagliati led No. 126 and a new CO, Squadron Leader Mortimer Rose, led No. 249. We decided we would climb in pairs to give the impression that we were more Hurricanes than the Germans thought. We turned and dived into the 109s, and now it was low flying, which gave us a better entry into the fight. We could dogfight now, and the Germans did not like that, as we could out-turn them under these conditions. I damaged two, as one tried to close up on the other and nearly collided, but flew out of the fight, to the north. One of my long-time friends, Bob Matthews, who had joined us in Malta, dived to attack a 109. He chased it for about a quarter of a mile with me screaming, 'Twist and turn!' Another 109 dived on Bob's tail and shot him down. Another pilot of 126 Squadron saw the end result, as Bob's Hurricane crashed into the sea wall at Valletta. Pilot Officer Bob Matthews's body was recovered, and he was buried in Cappuccini Naval Cemetery.

The previous month Bob's and my friend 'Ham' Munro had also been killed by a 109. 'Ham', as he was known to all of us, was a Rhodesian – a tall, quiet, softly spoken lad who would always be ready to do his best, a quiet achiever. When Bob and 'Ham' joined the squadron straight from OTU, Squadron Leader Barton asked me to talk to them about combat and how to fly in a battle etc. Another pilot, Sergeant Rist, was added to my responsibility. For many hours I tried to explain what a Hurricane could do without falling apart. 'Flick rolls', 'diving turns', tight turns to just above a stall, and, as I had been taught, you fly the aircraft; the aircraft does not fly you. It certainly will not fall to pieces. Never chase a 109 without violent turns right and left. This involved a great deal of talk and hand movements.

I could not understand the butchering of these great young lads. Why could we not have new aircraft? Promises, promises! We all knew the poor old Hurricane had been and still was a wonderful aircraft. However, we did not have a chance against the Bf109s. Malta was becoming another Battle of Britain, only this time there was no place to hide. Like most pilots in the Battle of Britain, we had the feeling each day of 'Is this my turn?'

Christmas Eve brought four scrambles, but only one interception. Wing Commander Rabagliati led seventeen Hurricanes from Nos 249 and 126 after four Ju88s dived on ships in the Grand Harbour. This was the twenty-fifth raid in seven days, an indication of what the Luftwaffe had in store for us. The CO joined me as I attacked a Ju88. These German aircraft were the pride of the Luftwaffe, powerful, fast and well armed. I fired three 2-second bursts. I was so angry I nearly flew into the thing, which burst into flames and crashed into the sea. The second Ju88 was attacked by three of us, Crossey, Etchells and myself, and, although we did not see it crash, we certainly saw it covered in black and white smoke pouring from both engines, and losing height fast. Pilot Officer Moon, our Irish colleague, shot a third 88 down.

Entering the New Year of 1942 was no thrill to me. However, as fate would have it, Squadron Leader Mortimer Rose had been shot in the legs as his aircraft had been attacked by a Bf109F and he was hospitalised. No. 249 Squadron received good fortune, as Squadron Leader John Beazley was given command. John, a very good friend of those left in the original squadron from 1940, would now lead a virtually new squadron.

On 3 January 1942 I was promoted to acting flight lieutenant to lead 'A' Flight, which allowed John Beazley to take my hand in a teary gesture as he said, 'Tich [my squadron name acquired in the Battle of Britain], you and Terry Crossey are the only pilots left out of the original pilots in 1940.' I was thrilled to fight on with him. However, it was not to be!

January continued. In the previous two or three months, more squadrons had arrived on the island, one being No. 605 County of Warwick, another ex-Battle of Britain squadron. I was posted to No. 605 as 'A' Flight commander, based at Hal Far Airfield. And I was presented with what was announced as a 'well-earned' DFC. Dave Davies joined John Beazley as 'A' Flight commander. Terry Crossey was transferred to No. 126 Squadron. As this time we three were angry, praying to leave Malta. We had been in action, continual, from August 1940 until now, 17 January 1942, and still there was no relief.

During January I was introduced to No. 605 Squadron pilots. Their squadron leader was killed on his first scramble. The pilots were mostly new to combat conditions. It was explained to me by the RAF Officer Commanding Malta Group that, as I now had seen, the squadron had only five Hurricane Is, so I would spend some time flying with the new pilots and teaching them operational fighting in quiet periods. At this time the weather was really bad and stormy, and visibility could allow only two aircraft at a time for patrols. I was ordered to attend meetings at Luqa Airfield with other squadron leaders and flight commanders, to be addressed by Wing Commander Satchell and Sir Hugh Pugh Lloyd,

Air Vice Marshal, Mediterranean. A huge groan was heard when, for the umpteenth time, we were told that Spitfires had been approved for Malta and would arrive any day. In the meantime we would have to carry on with the mixture of Hurricane Is and IIs, and very few IIs. One of our greatest problems was the lack of serviceable aircraft. The last two months of deadly strafing by Bf109Fs fitted with bombs and cannons had decimated our fighters as they stood on the ground with no protection. Returning to Hal Far, Wing Commander Satchell assisted me with talks and pictures on fighter tactics and allowing patrols of pairs of Hurricanes around the island on a 20-mile radius over it, protecting the many fishing boats.

During my first week with No. 605 Squadron at Hal Far I enjoyed the first break from fighting. Terry Crossey, who had become a long-time friend, contacted me and asked me if I would be his best man, as he was going to marry the Maltese girl he had been associating with for the previous seven months. She was a lovely girl and I was not surprised. I was given a day off and used the squadron car to take me to the city of Rabat, which was on a hilly area overlooking Ta'Qali Airfield. Terry, being a Catholic, was accepted into his new family with great pleasure. His fiancée's father was a senior person in the Maltese government and, when I arrived at their home, I was impressed with the interest, beauty and obvious wealth of his lovely fiancée's parents. I had managed to keep my blue uniform tidy and was ready for the ceremony in the stunning cathedral. The wedding was 'dress' personified, and the service was quite long. However, the reception was wonderful. I managed to present a satisfactory introduction for Terry, including some nice remarks for his wife. The other squadrons managed to send representative pilots, who certainly contributed to the merriment. The miracle of the day was that there were no reports of attacks. Everything went off remarkably well. Driving back to Hal Far was like enjoying a wonderful dream. No battles, no bombs, no scrambles, the day was like walking into another beautiful world – until I got to the airfield gate, where, with the shouting and cursing of the guards, I 'woke up'.

Hal Far was principally a naval Fleet Air Arm station, where they had flown Fairey Swordfish aircraft (string bags) and Fairey Fulmars, both two-cockpit aircraft, before No. 605 Squadron arrived, and the only Hurricanes around were unserviceable. However, what with Nos 249, 126 and the initial 185 Squadron, No. 605 had to use Hal Far. An old sandstone house, similar to Torri Combo in Ta'Qali, catered as our 'mess' and living quarters, and I was given a room on the second floor with an outlook straight down the airfield and the Mediterranean Sea, the best quarters I had experienced. I opened my old parachute bag, hung out my meagre garments, and placed my 'lucky charm', my Lupino Lane rag doll which my fiancée had insisted on my taking. Lupino Lane was a wonderful comedian in one of the London variety shows. So far it was still with me.

23. 'Farewell to Malta'

The weather on 18 January 1942 was really grim; with rain and total (10/10ths) cumulus cloud, it was a test for flying. I was ordered to scramble three Hurricanes as well as mine (two pairs) and cover a convoy of three large and fast merchant ships, 40 miles west of the island, and escort them to as near to Malta as our fuel would allow. The total cloud cover, with a base of around 1,000 feet, should have kept the Luftwaffe away. However, Hurricanes from No. 249 would patrol about the cloud layer in case the enemy might try to locate the ships. I led the four in a 'two-two' formation, flying roughly parallel and at a distance to allow comfortable visibility. We flew at 1,000 feet at 180 mph, with reasonable visibility. We reached the convoy in about 15 minutes, waggling our wings, trusting the captains would recognise the RAF. We then circled the ships, two of us each side, and escorted them for 1 hour, when a second flight of four relieved us and brought the ships into Valletta's Grand Harbour. As far as we were aware, No. 249 had not seen any enemy in their patrol above the cloud layer. Thank God! For once!

On 24 January we were advised that Air Marshal Tedder had arrived from the UK on his way to Egypt, and would visit No. 605 that morning. This officer was a member of Marshal of the Royal Air Force, Dowding's operations team. No. 605 was placed on standby, and we waited with fingers crossed as to what would be discussed. We had been bombed, strafed and had lost a number of our Hurricanes, so we were altogether sadly depleted. Air Marshal Tedder arrived with his entourage and gave us a pep talk and a speech on what was happening in other theatres of war. All I could contribute, with the help of Wing Commander Satchell, was our sorry state of operation, with shattered aircraft in view, only three Hurricanes serviceable and half the squadron with little or no experience.

While we talked, there were two Luftwaffe fighters flying very low about a mile from the airfield, beyond the cliff overlooking the sea. Air

Marshal Tedder asked what they were. I explained that they were Bf109Fs. He looked at me in surprise and said, 'Why the hell haven't you scrambled and attacked them?' Now I was shaken and shocked, as I advised him that we had only three clapped-out Hurricanes, which could fly 100 mph more slowly than the new Fs and it would be suicidal for me to order a scramble and I would not do this. I explained to him that as soon as a Hurricane was scrambled, this pair of the latest fighters would make fools of them. Three Hurricanes had already been lost, and their pilots killed because, as they approached land, they were blasted by these Bf109Fs. Wing Commander Satchell led him away, fully explaining the problem. Air Marshal Tedder turned to me and said, 'I understand the problem.' And he said, so we all could hear, 'Well you won't have to wait much longer. You will have Spitfires soon.' Someone behind me said, 'Some chance.' And I silently agreed.

Some two weeks later, on 9 February, I was advised that the Senior Air Staff Officer (SASO) to the Air Vice Marshal, together with Wing Commander Satchell, were to visit Hal Far, mid-morning. On their arrival, we discussed the situation of the lack of serviceable Hurricanes, which now numbered three, and which were old aircraft as far as operations were concerned. Over the previous two weeks we had lost five aircraft, badly damaged, to the Bf109F fighters. Wing Commander Satchell was asked to take a phone call from headquarters, after which he quickly approached us, informing us there was a force of Luftwaffe Bf109Fs and Junkers 88 bombers approaching the island. This we expected, as the arrival of the latest convoy would be their target. Nos 249 and 126 were scrambled. We were unable to scramble a section.

We were walking in the vicinity of the underground air-raid shelter that the Navy had built a year or two earlier. The shelter was approximately 20 feet underground, and entry was a standard series of steps leading at an angle of 50 degrees to a 25-foot-long cave with an extended table and stools to cater for a heavy bombardment, which meant lengthy waiting times in the shelter. As we were talking at the entrance, there was a shout from a naval officer, who was running along with other personnel, 'Get into the shelter, they are sure to include Hal Far.' I stood at the entrance – the others had descended – to see and hear any approach, when there was a heavy burst of anti-aircraft fire and I saw a single Junkers 88 at about 5,000 feet, obviously aiming to dive on us. In what appeared to be a few seconds, I realised he would bomb the naval building as well as our few aircraft, including naval aircraft. I turned and hurtled down the steps, and three-quarters into my very speedy descent there was an awful explosion, and a blast of air picked me up, and I landed on the edge of the table. The shelter was secure and nobody was injured except myself – I had received some nasty bruises on my midriff and a strained wrist.

After about 15 minutes there was a shout at the top of the stairs, 'All clear, raid over.' Wing Commander Satchell led the SASO out of the shelter to see the damage. The bomber had hit about 20 yards from our shelter, two naval aircraft were badly damaged, and one of our three Hurricanes would be lucky to fly again. The rest of the damage was the corner of the old building in which my room was situated. There was nothing left of half of the old building. There was much discussion for about an hour. The wing commander and the SASO left after advising me to sort out my room disaster, and telling me I should attend a meeting in Valletta the next day. 'That was close,' I muttered to myself. 'Where do I live now? And how much of my meagre clothing is left? And what about my mascot, lucky charm, Lupino Lane?' I collected my bits and pieces, stuffed them in my parachute bag and pulled Lupino Lane, squashed and flattened, from under a chunk of sandstone. I was advised, as were the 605 pilots, to go to the naval quarters, where there was spare accommodation.

I was told on 13 February that a building had been secured in the fishing village Kalafrana in the southernmost bay of the island, Marse Scirocco. This bay was a seaplane bay in peacetime and now catered for RAF flying boats, flying between Alexandria (Egypt), Malta and Gibraltar. This building was about $1^1/_2$ miles from the airfield. This was rather funny, because it was where I had been visiting the only dentist on the island, a naval officer. For some weeks I had been seeing this dentist, as I had picked up a problem called 'trench mouth', which was blamed on dirty cups and glasses, probably in the various bars we frequented when off duty. Quite a number of the pilots suffered from this lousy problem. My gums were affected, and had to be treated with an awful liquid, which was supposed to cauterise the infection. It made me as sick as hell with the taste, as you swallowed when the dentist scrubbed the gums with cotton-wool strips soaked in the liquid.

The last time I had been for treatment was two weeks before this latest development, and then the dentist had told me I would probably have to be hospitalised, as my gums were in a bad state, bleeding every time I ate something. On this particular visit, I entered the surgery and a sailor asked me what I wanted. I said, 'The dentist.' He said, 'That's sad, Sir. He's dead.' I looked at the sailor and said, 'Don't be funny. I'm serious.' He said, 'I'm not being funny. The fool, during his break yesterday he went for a walk to the sea wall to watch some Bf109s attacking a huge four-engine flying boat which had landed in the bay the previous evening and had missed the "before dawn" take-off. One of the 109s must have noticed him in his white coat, and simply blew him off the sea wall, to be picked up by a naval team, riddled with bullets.'

So I returned to No. 249 then and worried, as there was no other military dentist on the island. I was thinking of being allowed to visit a hospital, when the move to No. 605 Squadron changed my mind. And now we had new quarters in this naval area. What next? Together with an adjutant from Air Force Headquarters, we were shown over the building that would be our living accommodation for the time being. As we walked round, making notes of rooms, toilets, washrooms and general requirements to billet 605 pilots and ground crews, I asked the Maltese representative why all the rooms were small for what was a peacetime holiday hotel. He looked at both of us and answered, 'Not a hotel. The holiday hotel further down the road facing the bay. This was very good peacetime brothel. Very good, very popular.' The adjutant looked at me and for a change we both had a good laugh, ending with, 'We had better not tell the 605 lads!'

For the moment we remained living under sparse conditions in the naval quarters, while the powers that be made the 'hotel' ready for occupation by No. 605 Squadron. One good thing about this situation was that, as it was about a mile and a half from the airfield, we would not suffer strafing raids, or casual bombing attacks when off duty. A small bus would take the pilots to and from the airfield and also cater for off-duty trips to Valletta. The squadron car would also always be available.

For the next eleven days we carried out routine patrols, as our fighter strength was down to five old Hurricane Is. We organised patrols of two Hurricanes at a time, with changes of pilots, maintaining watch at low levels, protecting the many fishing boats working round the south end of the island. These boats brought in many loads of fish for the islanders, as all our rations were very low. For many weeks now, our main meals had been spaghetti boiled, nice and white, with no sauces of any kind, accompanied by copious helpings of boiled pumpkin. Also, if you wanted it, there were small boiled fish, as bony as a skeleton, and dry bread.

Once a week the Salvation Army offered one slice of thick white bread with one fried egg, until it ran out of supplies. I made a blunder one day, talking to some chap who worked with a local newspaper, of which I was not aware. I happened to say, as we were discussing rations, that we were sick of bland spaghetti and pumpkin, which was brought to our kitchen on a donkey cart because of its size – at least a metre across. I ended by saying that we were 'looking' at the rats, which of course were all over the island. The next day the local paper announced, 'The pilots are eating rats.' Did I bury my head!

On the morning of 25 February I was called to Valletta Headquarters to the office of SASO and invited to sit down and listen to what he had been instructed to say by Air Vice Marshal Hugh Pugh Lloyd. 'Palliser, you have done a worthy operation with No. 249 Squadron without a break since September 1940, having been transferred from No. 43 Squadron which was pulled out of 11 Group to rest and reorganise after many casualties. He has advised HQ Cairo that you will be relieved of duties with No. 605 Squadron (not your rank of Acting Flight Lieutenant).' I remarked, 'Good God Sir, I can't believe it, I thought this would never happen.' He laughed and said, 'The Air Vice Marshal is in touch with all the activities of his pilots, which are recorded at all times. Now, you must gather your luggage etc. and expect to fly to Cairo in one of the Wellington Bombers due to arrive from Gibraltar tonight. You must report to the adjutant at Luqa, who will see to you boarding the Wellington allocated; your luggage will accompany you.' Luggage! My old parachute bag, which held a minimum of belongings. However, my Lupino Lane mascot was in it.

I had used the squadron car, so I reported back to Hal Far, and explained to the wing commander what I had discussed in Valletta, which he apparently knew. He gave me a smack on the back and said, 'Good show!', and then suggested I should not waste time but pack my belongings and return there for the night. They had a spare room I could use. I could then say my goodbyes to No. 605, which would also be leaving the island shortly, then they would organise a lift for me to Luqa. I walked out of the wing commander's office not knowing what to do or say. I felt like yelling to the four winds of fortune. However, the Wellington had to get me to Cairo, where I would report to the SASO.

With these thoughts going through my brain, I nearly knocked an old No. 249 Squadron friend off his feet. It was Harry Moon, a great Irish lad who had joined No. 249 as we left for Malta. He now was a flight lieutenant and had been posted to No. 126 Squadron for the time being. We walked over to the canteen for some coffee and I burst my lungs on telling him about my move. When we had both congratulated each other on our promotion, I asked him why he was at Hal Far. He told me he had been driven over by car to pick up a Hurricane from our small number, as the aircraft was to be allocated to No. 126 Squadron. He asked me what I was doing as the moment and I started to tell him. Then I suggested I could tell him the whole story if he could come with me to Kalafrana to pack my belongings and return to stay the night at Hal Far and be taken to Luqa the next day. He was pleased to have a drive with me, and off we went. I managed to tell him about my change. It was great being able to talk with an old friend.

Suddenly, I heard the old rasping howl of a Bf109F. I shouted to Harry, who was already craning his neck out of the window of the car. I pulled the car across the road, as a rasp of machine-gun fire ploughed into the field behind us. We had only 200 yards to turn into the village, with a large house on the corner. Knowing that the 109 had a fair radius to turn, I simply pushed the car accelerator to the floor just as bullets chewed up the road behind us, and, in turning, I rammed a fishing boat that was being repaired. Harry was out of the car as I joined him at the side of the sandstone house. Suddenly there was a burst of gun-fire from a battery, which was mounted on the roof and had fired at the 109 as it passed over the house. The 109 did not return, so we walked to the fishing boat, which, thank the Lord, was a small one, used only in the harbour. The fishermen were laughing at our contortion as we hit the boat and were more worried about us than the boat. However, I explained I would report this to the military and the damage would be fixed. The car, an old Humber, had no serious damage, so Harry accompanied me into our new quarters, where he laughed until he choked. Typically Irish, he said, 'That bastard 109 knew we were going to a brothel. Wait until I get back to 126 – what a tale to tell!' Harry and I, with my belongings, returned to Hal Far, where I bid him goodbye and good luck and watched him fly out in the Hurricane. When I told the wing commander of our experience, he said, 'My God we heard that 109 and realised he was heading down the road you had taken. Thank God he missed you.'

The next day, 26 February 1942, was the longest I had suffered for a considerable time. The Wellingtons, five of them, had arrived the previous night and had been landed far away from each other, as the

Bf109s and Ju88s were aware of their arrival and would try to destroy them. The Wellingtons would be attacked, as would the airfield.

I had been driven to Luqa Airport in the morning and reported to the commanding officer. I was invited to attend the briefing for the Wellington crews and was introduced to the pilot of the aircraft in which I would be a passenger, and to the reserve pilot, Pilot Officer O'Donnell. I sat beside him during the briefing and listened carefully to the instructions. We would be the first to leave the airfield at 11.30 p.m. Our flight time would be approximately $4^1/_2$ hours. Our landing airfield would be Kilo 26, on the west side of Cairo. The weather report was for 8/10ths cumulus cloud and misty conditions around midnight, at which time we calculated we would be airborne and praying the German night fighters would find it difficult to locate us after take-off.

The briefing ended at 1600 hours, and it was suggested that the Wellington crews and passengers proceed to where their aircraft were positioned and begin a first check by the crew, and make sure the passengers' luggage was stored and where we would sit. There were two RAF officers who were ground staff and myself. I was pleased I had dressed in my blue uniform, which sported my DFC below my wings. My bomber jacket was in my parachute bag, keeping Lupino Lane warm – some mascot!

After an hour in the aircraft we met the crew and returned to the mess to rest and talk and wait. When I had reported to the commanding officer in the morning, he had suggested I visit their mess and meet his pilots and enjoy their hospitality. This I really enjoyed, as Luqa was the home of Blenheims and Beaufighter aircraft. It was from this airfield that Adrian Warburton flew and became one of the greatest pilots in the Mediterranean.

In this rest period, I asked O'Donnell if I could make a suggestion to him about his navigation. We moved to another sofa and I explained how the Luftwaffe night fighters operated and how clever they were. They watched for flare path lights to be switched on and endeavoured to plan their attack, while a pilot settled down on course. They positioned themselves at approximately 5,000 feet and about 3 miles from the coast. Fortunately, tonight we had a good cloud cover, about 7/10s, and a slight haze. We would be taking off on the north–south runway. The flare path would be minimal, but the runway itself would be seen in the residual light from the cumulus cloud. So the course after take-off would be southerly. However, I suggested he kept that course at maximum speed and maintained an altitude of no more than 500 feet. The cloud and the haze would assist him. I suggested he maintain his course for not less than 45 minutes, then gradually gain operational height and true course. The Ju88s did not seem to venture further than 50 miles south of Malta, as it was such a long flight back to Sicily. We had a three-corner discussion, questions and answers. The other crew members, rear gunner, wireless operator and second air gunner, were invited into the final discussion.

At 11.45 p.m. we taxied to the runway. The control tower was quick in ordering our departure. Pilot Officer O'Donnell was down the runway at full throttle and, as we did not carry a bomb load, we were airborne and over Malta cliffs and away with no interference from the Germans. After we had reached our flight altitude and after 2 hours' flying, one could sense the relaxation of passengers and crew. I was as stiff as a poker, having crouched behind the navigator. I suddenly noticed O'Donnell talking into his radio mask. He nodded his head as if to give the OK to someone, when there was an enormous roar at the tail of the Wellington. I yelled to O'Donnell. It was impossible to be being attacked now. There was another burst of gunfire from the tail gunner's four Browning .303s before I could shout again. O'Donnell quickly lowered his oxygen mask and yelled, 'We are out of range of any enemy attack. The rear gunner wanted to clear his four machine guns.' My throat was dry with shock. The two passengers in the rear were clinging to their seats and as white as sheets, as the navigator went back to speak to them and explain the drill. The rest of the flight was smooth, and after $4^1/_2$ hours we lined up in the circuit of Kilo 26 and waited our turn to land. We were in Egypt! Farewell to Malta and thank God! Only as we taxied to our parking bay did I believe I had left the island.

24. Third Phase of My Destiny

Having been welcomed at Kilo 26, I was briefed and then offered a bed until the morning, after which I enjoyed a hearty breakfast. Offered eggs and bacon, I accepted a small helping, knowing I would be sick if I gourmandised. I was then taken in the air force car to the RAF Headquarters in Cairo. It was mid-morning on 27 February 1942.

The Senior Air Staff Officer greeted me and invited me to sit at his desk, and commenced to debrief me. He had before him my report from Headquarters, Malta. He talked to me, referring to the report, recognising my record, including my short experience with No. 43 Squadron and then my history through No. 249 Squadron, and congratulated me on my DFC. He mentioned he had interviewed Neil, Beazley and Harrington, who had been posted back to England. He noted my reaction to this news and immediately said, 'Sorry Palliser, I see you thought of returning to England.' He told me this was not possible, as the Middle East Headquarters had now signalled that, as from mid-February, all flying personnel must relate to the 'Pre-war Service', which meant I would, as would many others, have to finish three years of service before possibly returning to England. He certainly saw the disappointment in my face and, in his own way, apologised for the news he had given me. After about an hour of discussion, he advised that I was to take two weeks' leave of duty and collect a warrant for pay. 'Oh,' he said, 'you are to remain with your Acting Flight Lieutenant rank'. I thanked him for this. He ended my interview with saying, 'I want to tell you that Air Vice Marshal Hugh Pugh Lloyd would have awarded you the rank of full Squadron Leader. However, because of your continuous Service in Action from August 1940 until this present time, including ten months on Malta, you deserve a change.' He then introduced me to the headquarters' adjutant, who discussed with me what was to be my next move. I was booked into Sheppard's Hotel for two weeks, I was to make contact by phone each day, and he gave me a warrant for money owed to me and advised the bank, which I would visit. He suggested I catch a taxi to go to the hotel, and enjoy the leave.

I arrived at the hotel, wondering whether to laugh or cry. What a disappointment, with the news of the three years' service. But my destiny was holding out. What next? A squadron in the desert? That would be worse than Malta. A posting to the Far East, or maybe a nice job at headquarters? Sheppard's Hotel was brilliant – four or five star. The first thing I did was hang up my meagre clothes and Lupino Lane, battered and scruffy. Then, as it was midday, I visited one of the restaurants in the hotel and shocked the waiter when I ordered a twelve-egg omelette. The waiter, I suppose, could not keep his voice quiet, and said, 'A twelve-egg omelette! Not possible!' People at other tables looked in my direction. However, I braved it out a little louder and said, 'I have been fed rubbish for the last ten months on Malta and twelve eggs is what I wish to devour in your great hotel.' The next thing, he brought a senior waiter, who explained that I was either under the influence, or sick, or joking. I tried to explain to him, and in the end I asked him if a six-egg omelette would be possible. He gave in and, after a short time, a silver tureen was deposited on my table, the lid was raised, and there was my six-egg omelette. It looked like something from heaven – a huge mound of yellowy gold, hot and ready.

I ate slowly and steadily, not noticing the interest of the other diners. I finished, rose from the table, thanked the waiter and ambled out of the restaurant, listening to the clapping of the diners around me. I slowly walked to the lift and returned to my room. I looked in the mirror and retired to the toilet, where I was so sick I thought I would die. What a damned fool I had made of myself. I crawled into bed and surfaced at dinner, full of remorse. Thank God I had made it to the toilet and not damaged my uniform. I made myself respectable and walked warily into the restaurant, and made for a table. Close to me was a family with friends whom I had noticed at lunchtime. Two of the men left their table and, after some discussion with the ladies, walked to my table, and introduced themselves. One chap was Egyptian, the other French. They made quite a fuss of me and congratulated my demand for the large omelette. They had heard my remark about Malta and the food. The Frenchman in-formed me he was a naval officer on leave and had a tough time escorting tankers, laden with fuel, to Malta. The Egyptian man was a government official. They asked me if they could join me for a few minutes, and congratulated me on having been a fighter pilot on Malta.

They smiled when I apologised for my lunchtime demand. Again, I was relieved I had saved my uniform and recovered, having slept it off from midday. They invited me to the Egyptian's home, their invitation helped by waves from the ladies. I accepted and had a lovely time the next day, when a car picked me up and returned me to the hotel in the evening. After two years of fighting, the day was like a midsummer dream.

When I returned to my room, I received a note from a fellow Battle of Britain pilot, one who had been in Bader's squadron, Flight Lieutenant Bob Grassick, a Canadian I had met when No. 242 joined the wing with Stanford Tuck's No. 257 Squadron. He was staying at the same hotel and had offered to meet me the next day. From 28 February, Bob, joined by one of his pals from the squadron he was now in, and I had a ball. We visited many nightclubs and Groppi's restaurant, a large one-storey building with glass windows everywhere, where we could watch the passing show. We spent two days exploring the famous museum. Then we visited the pyramids, riding camels and joking with their owners. Apparently Bob was based in Cairo and was friendly with one of the camel drivers, as he visited the pyramids often. We enjoyed the new Badia nightclub, which was famous for its belly dancers. I also had the daily phone calls to the SASO office, waiting for the call to end my leave.

It was 2 March when I received a call to attend a meeting with SASO. I arrived at RAF Headquarters mid-morning, and was seated in the office of the Senior Air Staff Officer, a group captain whose name I cannot remember. With my papers in front of him, he remarked on my leave so far and asked if I had enjoyed the break, which I assured him I had. He then asked the first question, 'Palliser, with your experience, would you accept a Squadron Leader posting to No. 73 Squadron in the desert?' I choked and blanched and said, 'Sir, I have been on operations in the thick of everything since August 1940. And with ten months on Malta, I feel as sick as a dog. I have developed trench mouth, very bad sinuses, and there was only a naval doctor on the island who advised me I should have the attention of a good doctor when I reported to your office. Sir, I am a wreck.' He looked at me for a long time without speaking. I thought, here goes, a court martial. He then ruffled some papers and asked me if I would like a spell as a test pilot at Heliopolis, Cairo, or I could take charge of the fighter aircraft deliveries from the African West Coast to Cairo. My face registered my feelings. He left the office for about 10 minutes and on returning, he said, 'Palliser, there are some movements being discussed. I would like you to return tomorrow, same time, and we will renew this meeting.'

The next morning I entered the SASO office, stood to snappy attention, and was asked to sit down. He shuffled my papers and looked steadily at me. I was praying. Surely not the Far East – although it would have been better than the desert. Then he asked me, 'How would you like to go to South Africa?' I must have looked like a stunned mullet. Then I could not help myself saying, 'South Africa! Sir, just point your finger and I will walk there.' He burst out laughing, saying, 'Whoa there! That hit the bell!' Now this is what manifested itself. They had received orders from the Air Ministry to fulfil a request from South Africa to help their air force to train a fighter wing, with the assistance of three experienced squadron leader fighter pilots and six flight lieutenants with similar experience. An emergency had arisen in the shape of a Japanese battle fleet with large aircraft carriers in the Indian Ocean, possibly to attack the east coast of Natal, South Africa. The RAF would assist South African pilots to form a three-squadron fighter wing, which would be of great assistance to the defence of the east coast. They had chosen the pilots whom they would send. Only they were not sure of the third squadron leader. With my experience and with the Air Vice Marshal's approval, I would be number 3. I could not believe what I was hearing. Talk about destiny. I have to believe in it.

On 7 March I received an order to pack my luggage (my parachute bag), and at midday an RAF car would take me to Almaza, an enormous transit camp, situated on the north-west edge of Cairo. There I would spend the night, ready to be taken to the military airfield on 8 March. There would be a number of different personnel accompanying me, also heading for South Africa in a South African Air Force (SAAF) Lockheed Lodestar, a twin-engine personnel carrier.

When I passed through the gates of Almaza all I could see was plenty of desert and dozens and dozens of marquees and bell tents. An RAF sergeant approached me with the biggest smile possible and said, 'Bit of a shock, Sir. This shakes the hell out of new arrivals. However, your tent for the night is in a reasonable spot and comfortable for one night if you can stand the noise of the various regiments, RAF, various army and naval groups numbering many hundreds all in transit, relating to desert and naval movements.'

My final night, and what a send-off! The eight people who were also to board the flight were standing next to two or three bell tents, looking like lost souls in a prison camp. We were offered comfortable beds, and a night meal was brought to us with some tins of beer, after which we all had a good laugh and were ready to board a vehicle the next morning to be taken to the military airfield, where we were offered a decent breakfast. We were then taken to a flight office, where we were briefed for the journey to South Africa.

25. 'And Am I Glad To Be Here!'

After being introduced to a SAAF pilot, Captain Male, we boarded the Lodestar and commenced our journey from Cairo to Pretoria in the Transvaal, the northern capital of South Africa. It was 8 March 1942. The flight was most eventful and exciting for me, as I was very interested in the changes in the many African countries we passed over and where we touched down for refuelling and stopovers.

We landed at Luxor, a most important city on the River Nile, and the historical area of the ancient pharaohs of Egypt, on 9 March. We stayed overnight at a very old and notable hotel. In fact, we stayed until 10 March, which enabled us to visit the Valley of the Kings for a full day. The excitement was high, as guides accompanied visitors down many steps in the wall of a mountain, showing us the tomb of Tutankhamen in all its glory, and pointing to holes in the walls of other tombs, through which one could see the artwork and beautiful colours of paintwork on the inner walls, colours that looked as if they had been painted the day before. Thereafter we walked around the enormous columns and huge carvings of Egyptian statues. It was a stunning visit.

In the morning of 10 March the flight commenced over the desert to Wadi Sidna in the Egyptian Sudan, then on to Juba, just slightly north of the equator. We maintained a flying height of 8,000 feet, which allowed us to maintain a fantastic view of the terrain, as well as closer views of the River Nile, the desert and the oases, which stood out like green emeralds.

Juba was in the green density of the tropics and held the area of a British commissioner. We landed there to refuel the Lodestar. Our stay was about 3 hours, and I watched with a smile as the sturdy black Africans lifted dozens of 5-gallon tins of fuel, passing them through a material filter held over the valves of the aircraft tanks, thereafter kicking the empty light metal containers as far as possible into a quickly growing heap. It was most amusing watching these people laughing and criticising their mates as to who could kick the tins the furthest. At last the aircraft fuel tanks were filled, and we were ready to continue on our journey to Teroro, where we had to land to avoid a severe thunderstorm, which forced us to remain overnight, having had to land on a short airstrip.

An amazing surprise greeted us in the shape of a small English-style hotel, operated by a very eccentric British owner. We made our way from the aircraft to the hotel in a blast of tropical rain and high winds, where we were greeted by the hotel owner, who was dressed as if he was in Soho in London. He was a character and a sort of renegade offspring of British colonial times. He advised us there were rooms for the night and what the tariff was, plus a bath facility for a nominal price. However, if you did not have a bath, the tariff was 50 per cent more. He did not like dirty people. He was the talk of the Central African people.

We left Teroro the next morning. The next stop, still in Uganda, was Kasuma. Thereafter we flew on to Nairobi, where we refuelled at the first international airport since leaving Cairo. A number of our passengers left the flight, and we were once again airborne, flying over Kasama. Still maintaining a height of 8,000 feet, we flew along one side of a lake leading into Lake Victoria. Captain Male drew our attention to the breeding lake for flamingo birds. Disturbed by our engine noise, literally hundreds of these beautiful birds left the lake in a dazzling array of crimson and white – a marvellous picture! We then left Uganda and landed for fuel in Lusaka, northern Rhodesia. After a short stop, we entered into the northern Transvaal, South Africa, landing at Swartkop, Pretoria. It was the beginning of a new adventure for me. In particular, it was a marvellous relief to be away from a war zone.

At this point I must remark on a tragedy that took place later in the year. Captain Male, who was the SAAF's oldest pilot, was killed, flying the same route in the same aircraft. The engines failed, and the aircraft crashed into Lake Victoria after take-off. All on board were killed.

Pretoria is one of the capital cities of South Africa. The other is Cape Town, 1,000 miles to the southern limit of the country, facing the conjoined oceans of Atlantic and Indian. I was greeted by a number of SAAF officials and a wing commander representative of the Royal Air Force office, and taken to the headquarters of the SAAF at the military airfield, close to the city. I met a number of both RAF and SAAF pilots. There were general greetings and friendly talks on topics relating particularly to questions of our experiences in Egypt and Malta and the fighting generally. I had a shock to meet once more Dennis Steadman, whose car I had run into a pile of turnips in North Weald. That was good for much back slapping and exciting exchanges. The first was a natural, 'What are you doing here?' Thereafter there was a lot of chatting with other RAF pilots, who were here to assist the SAAF pilots. After some talking with the senior officers, we were handed over to the senior adjutant, who was responsible for our settling in. Our quarters were ready on the airfield and, after preliminary settling in, we were allowed to be shown around and mix with a number of the South African pilots and ground staff.

So, on 12 March, at 0930 hours we were assembled in the briefing room. There must have been at least eighteen men, with ten RAF officers, including the resident RAF wing commander, and eight senior SAAF officers. After a rather noisy few minutes of people greeting each other, we were brought to attention by the senior South African officer presenting his senior pilots to the RAF pilots. We had been introduced to the South African officer by our wing commander.

We were welcomed and then settled down to the briefing. To say we were surprised and shocked is putting it mildly. We were advised that, during the previous three months, South African forces had been informed that information had been gathered that reversed the possibility of an attack by Japanese naval and carrier forces on the east coast of South Africa (Natal). There had been an error of judgement by South African Intelligence, and it was accepted that the three-squadron 'wing' was shelved for future consideration. The shock held us dumbstruck for some minutes, when we burst into a tirade of 'What happens now?' The next discussions were of no consequence, as our wing commander was left to explain what would now be considered for us nine fighter pilots. This awful turnaround eased off when we were invited to lunch, after which we were briefed on what would be arranged for us.

I was summoned for another meeting with the RAF wing commander the next day, 13 March. At 10.00 a.m. he sat me down at his desk, and looked for a few minutes at various papers. He advised that my acting squadron leader rank was now cancelled. However, the Air Ministry had allowed me 'Substantive Flight Lieutenant' rank from this day on.

As my history file showed my war service so far, I was advised to take leave until my future was decided, as there were a number of plans being formed in relation to pilot training in South Africa. This related to Empire training maximisation, which included Canada. That afternoon I found myself with my parachute bag in a government car being taken to Johannesburg, and being introduced to accommodation in the

Officers' Club in Bree Street in this wonderful city. This was a large building that you entered through a double glass door into a very large room filled with tables, chairs and settees, catering for at least 50–100 guests. I was escorted to the office at the rear of this area, being watched by many varied officers with their wives and girlfriends, eating, drinking and communicating as if the war was not a problem. Arrangements had been made for a room for me, with the delicate suggestion that I must share a room with another officer, as the club was well occupied. As far as I was concerned, this was not a problem. This was certainly not Malta, and more and more I really believed in destiny. This was paradise. I was shown the room on the second floor of the club and, clutching my parachute bag, I entered a very acceptable room. I do not know who gasped or shouted first, but who was sitting on the other bed but Steadman. Talk about luck! After the back slapping, hand shaking and all the rude remarks had been exhausted, we both agreed that we were two lucky pilots so far.

After a nice breakfast the next morning, I approached the business desk to verify my stay until I had to move and was passed a note advising me that the Johannesburg *Daily Mail* would be pleased to interview me at 12 noon. At the same time the young lady passed a message she had written down after receiving a phone call from a gentleman who wished to speak to me at the number given. Naturally I thought it must be the air force office, so I phoned immediately from the desk. The call was not from the air force but from a man whose name I have forgotten, asking me if my name was spelt 'PALLISER'. If it was, would I please phone a number left with the message and speak to a Mr Palliser, who would be pleased to arrange a meeting with me. Miracles never cease! However, I rang and talked to Mr Palliser for some time – I am afraid I cannot remember his Christian name. He advised me that a friend of his in the SAAF had told him that a pilot from the RAF had arrived in Johannesburg, whose name was Palliser. I enjoyed his questions and his explanation as to who he was and accepted his invitation to join him on St Patrick's Day, 17 March, at the Rand Club, for an Irish lunch. In our conversation I had mentioned my friend Steadman and he was invited too.

The following day, 15 March, who should arrive at the club but Terry Crossey. More juvenile excitement! He had been posted back to his home town for some extended leave and he had been told that both Steadman and I had arrived in Johannesburg. That was three of us still alive and kicking! We picked up Steadman, found a corner in the club, and talked ourselves silly.

I told Crossey about the newspaper request and also the invitation for St Patrick's Day on the 17th. He then mentioned that he and his mother had been invited to a friendly party at his mother's friend's apartment in the city centre on 24 March. His mother's long-time friend, Mrs Loftus, was giving a party for two of her nieces and other guests. Mrs Loftus had been advised by Terry of my arrival, and she insisted that both Dennis and I come to the party and meet her nieces.

As we talked, the newspaper reporters from the *Daily Mail* arrived. So, excusing myself and promising to keep in touch, I joined the reporters at another part of the club. The discussion was in depth. I was asked many questions about the Battle of Britain and my experiences. They were amazed at my explanations. They said they did not always get told all the gory details and they mentioned how lucky they were to be so far away.

The lady asked me if I was pleased to leave England and the European war and come to South Africa, which is so far from England. I answered her with, 'I haven't come from England. I have been posted here from Malta.' The male reporter remarked, 'Don't tell me you were on Malta as well.' I answered, 'Yes, for ten months. And am I glad to be here!' He then explained that the paper had asked for the interview as I was the first RAF Battle of Britain fighter pilot with a DFC to arrive in South Africa, and my experiences were what people were wanting to read about. I must admit, I gave them plenty to print. The lady was wide eyed and gave me her thanks for the interview.

I could not believe the peace and carefree attitude around me. No scrambles, no air-raid alarms. There was laughter and a wonderful feeling of peace.

The next day I joined Steadman again and spent a number of hours sightseeing and shopping, particularly for new underclothes, socks and shoes, and also managing to have some buttons sewn on my two uniform shirts. I also invested in a sports jacket and civilian trousers, as we were allowed civilian dress for some hours while we were on leave. That was a comfort, as my uniform, including my battledress, was shabby and fairly dirty. All this created a wonderful change.

I was still thinking that at any moment there could be a possible posting to the Far East. The last two years had taught me the agony of fear and worry. I had to keep in touch with headquarters each day, or else

I would receive a message in the Officers' Club. This was certainly like civilian life again. Looking back, I realised I had not enjoyed a main break since I had joined No. 43 Squadron in August 1940.

On 17 March Steadman and I were prepared for luncheon in the Rand Club. I was so grateful I had been able to have my blue uniform cleaned and pressed. We asked the attendant at our club if she could explain how to get to the Rand Club. She raised her eyebrows and said, 'How lucky you are! That is our finest club.' We mentioned a taxi, but she suggested walking and seeing all the fine and interesting shops on the way. She drew a sketch of the walk, and when we arrived at 12 noon, we had enjoyed the walk around Johannesburg.

Mr Palliser met us at the entrance and escorted us inside, introducing us to the President and Secretary before we joined a number of Mr Palliser's friends. Seated comfortably in the lounge, we experienced many questions about the Battle of Britain and the many actions that had taken place, as well as details of the Hurricane and Spitfire capabilities. They were also interested in the Luftwaffe aircraft and aircrews. I found the discussion exciting, with the depth of interest these gentlemen pursued. We eventually proceeded to the dining room and enjoyed a very good lunch.

Mr Palliser questioned me in depth as to where I had been born and where I had lived and what work I had done before joining the Volunteer Reserve. When I explained my work as a student engineer, he passed me a company visiting card, which advised that he was a director of one of the large engineering firms in the Transvaal, by the name of Dowson and Dobson. He told me that if, like his father, I chose to come back to South Africa after the war had ended, he would offer me the chance of employment. I thanked him for the gesture. A car had been arranged to take us back to the Officers' Club. It had been an exciting few hours.

We were introduced to a number of SAAF officers, who invited us for outings in and around the great gold-mining city and its suburbs. This meant we had interesting days leading up to my invitation with Steadman to the party on 24 March.

That day, Terry Crossey arrived at the club to escort us to the party. We were pleased to be going to meet some local families. As we stepped out of the lift to enter this sumptuous apartment, I had no idea that I was on the verge of the most wonderful part of my future destiny that God could have given to me.

We entered a huge room full of people. At the far end of the room there was a large balcony overlooking a tremendous view of the city. However, I had no eyes for the view because, standing in the doorway leading to the balcony, was the loveliest girl I had seen in years, dressed in a very attractive cream suit, looking right at me. There she was, a redhead with a few freckles, standing as tall as myself, like someone out of a fashion book.

Everyone at the party was having a good time and gave us a great welcome, especially Crossey, a local lad who was now home after his experiences in the Battle of Britain and Malta. I was so glad we were wearing our uniforms and I for one felt as if I was about to meet a miracle. Nothing could stop me. I ploughed through the crowded room of guests until I stopped, opposite this lovely girl. For once in my life I was short of words and breath! As she faced me, she gave me a peck on the cheek and introduced herself as Ruth Smith. As I found my breath, Crossey came and pulled me away to meet our hostess, his mother and other guests. The noise was like a circus. I turned and looked back at Ruth, and Crossey yelled, 'Don't worry she won't run away.'

We all, but particularly I, enjoyed the best day I could remember. However, I was rude enough to circle around until I could talk to Ruth, although there were quite a few already seeking her attention. It was a remarkable day during which I paid homage to a charming hostess and Crossey's mother, both around the same age, engaging and full of life. As we left to return to the club, the hostess, Mrs Loftus, a widow, gave me a hug and said, 'We will see you men again. And call me Aunty Peg.'

Returning to the club I was walking on air, and it was not the stuff I had been flying through for the previous two years! I had made a date with Ruth, who worked in the city. She was to give me a call at the Officers' Club in Bree Street and have lunch the next day. Ruth indeed phoned me the next day, and we had lunch at a good restaurant, which she chose, not far from the club and from where she worked as a secretary at the Stock Exchange.

The next day, 26 March, there was a message to appear at air force office for a meeting that would determine our next move (panic!!). I arrived at the office at 9.30 a.m. hoping there would be a long and explanative talk. Without any delay, the wing commander waved me to the chair at his desk. His first question was, 'Are you enjoying the change and the Officers' Club?' To which I remarked on the tremendous reception I had received in just a few days. I also mentioned the newspaper interview, about which I asked, 'Did I break any military rules?'

He answered, 'No, not at all and I was very interested in your description of Europe and the Middle East.'

He then approached the subject of my continuity at the moment, in South Africa. I was to be posted to an advanced training school No. 25, the largest unit in the country, which trained all South African pupils passing through Intermediate and Advanced Training to the award of their wings. A new flight, which I would command, would have possibly two or three more experienced pilots. Our duty would be to lecture the new cadets, who had received their wings and needed to be taught fighter tactics. This was a new approach, as many young pilots had to be kept busy while waiting for postings to squadrons.

The worst news was that I was to go to a town called Standerton, where No. 25 Air School was located. Railway tickets and a description of the school would be delivered for me to the Officers' Club on the morning of 30 March, and someone would take me to the station and see me on the train. Standerton was approximately 140 miles from Johannesburg. I had only three days to earn Ruth's interest.

I phoned Ruth at her office and told her of my ill luck, and was promised she would meet me again for lunch and a chat. So, on the first day of three, Ruth phoned me, mid-morning, at the club, and arranged to meet me for lunch; then we would see something of Johannesburg and have dinner, after which she would go to her home in a town called Krugersdorp, some 18–20 miles from the city. There was a very efficient rail facility, which she used every working day.

At 11.00 a.m. Ruth arrived at the club, had a coffee with me and said, 'Let's go.' We had a great walk and talk and for a while sat in the grounds of the City Library and chatted, which included her explaining to me that she had told her boss that an air force friend had arrived from the Egyptian theatre of war and could she have three days' leave, which had been approved. In the evenings she would stay with one of her four sisters, who lived in the city.

Until the evening before leaving for Standerton, I had two and a half full days of wonderful relationship with Ruth. I told her of my deep interest in a friendship, to which she agreed. I said nothing about my failed tie with Jean, who had found another chap. That was over twelve months before and forgotten. I left with Ruth's phone number and home address.

26. No. 25 Air School, Standerton

It was 31 March 1942 when I arrived at Standerton, a small country farming town on the South African veld, after about a 4-hour journey. A car picked me up and carried me and my new suitcase and Lupino Lane to No. 25 Air School. As we drove through the entrance, I had quite a surprise to realise that this place was 'BIG'. In fact it looked a bit like Rissington in the Cotswolds, where I had finished my secondary and final training, and which gave me my wings, early in 1940 – only two years before but it felt like a lifetime.

Well – here we go! I reported to the adjutant and had a long talk, as he described the school and all that was in it. He was a very charming major (SAAF), about 40 years old. He questioned me in depth as to my experiences in RAF Fighter Command, showing deep interest. He arranged a junior officer to escort me to the chief instructor's office in the tarmac area, where I was introduced to Squadron Leader Headley and Lieutenant Wayburn, one of the flight commanders, both of whom greeted me in lighter vein. This was a pleasure for me after some leg pulling and friendly questions. Lieutenant Wayburn (Ellis) helped me to find my allocated room and assisted me to get organised. This did not take long, and it was close to lunchtime. Ellis accompanied me to the mess and introduced me to a great group of pilots (instructors) and ground staff, whose names I now cannot remember.

After lunch Squadron Leader Headley introduced me to Wing Commander (RAF) Snelling, the chief instructor of the school, who, I assumed after a fairly long interview, was a damn good person and a very experienced instructor with top Category A1, the highest category in the Royal Air Force. Wing Commander Snelling handed me over to Squadron Leader Headley, who placed me in the hands of two of the many instructors, Lieutenant Ellis Wayburn and Lieutenant Tilly, with instructions to explain the activities of Air School's Training Flight.

I exclaimed to my guides that I was not an instructor, having been a fighter pilot on Hurricanes and Spitfires from August 1940 until March 1942, and that I had been fortunate in being posted from Malta and the Middle East to South Africa. They were not over-surprised, as Wayburn suddenly remarked, 'You must be one of the RAF fighter pilots who were supposed to help us form a fighter wing. There was talk of Japan bombing Natal from carriers some time ago, which disappeared as wrong information.' I confirmed that and mentioned, 'I am here as a lost soul awaiting whatever is in store for me.' In the meantime I was to talk about fighter tactics and fighter experience to some of the young pilots who had gained their wings and were awaiting postings. The rest of the day was meeting more instructors, examining aircraft, regulations and personal friendly discussions, which I really enjoyed, until evening dinner and bed, ready for the next day and duties. It was all very interesting.

The next morning was 1 April. I enjoyed breakfast – bacon, egg, and sausages – with a warning, 'Don't delay on helping yourself to bacon as Ellis, a Jewish chap, is desperate for bacon.' It was the first laugh of the morning.

Issued with flying kit and parachute, I was introduced to the advanced trainer. I was surprised, as when 'Miles Master' had been mentioned to me the day before, I had expected to see the 'Miles Master I', which I had flown a few times in the UK. This Mark I was a beautiful aircraft, smart, fitted out like a good motor car, with well-designed controls, a very satisfactory instrument layout and a throttle that was designed for a comfortable hand, not just a strip of metal. The engine was a Rolls-Royce Kestrel, with in-line cylinders. It was as sleek as a show plane, except that it killed people, because the aileron design had serious problems and shed the ailerons during aerobatics. When this Miles aircraft was wheeled out of the hangar, the aircraft that I was faced with looked larger and uglier, with a huge Bristol Mercury XX engine. It was capable of 245 mph, with a climb capacity of 2,000 feet per minute – quite an aircraft. It was a two-seater, with the instructor in the rear cockpit and the pupil in front. The rear seat was fitted with the facility for the instructor to pivot a Perspex cover in conjunction with raising his seat slightly so as to see the pupil's head and shoulders; this was generally used when taking 'blind flying'.

As there were three of us from different squadrons in the Middle East, arrangements had been made to satisfy the station commander and the operations' commander. The three of us with no flying training quali-fications would be responsible for the student pilots who, after receiving their wings, would be taught operation fighter tactics, until their postings to regular units. I was given responsibility for the activities and warned of sensible instruction and 'no irresponsible activities'. The warning came from Wing Commander Snelling, at the request of the flying school commander. Group Captain Barling, who had never been connected with 'action' experience, made it known to us that we fighter pilots were reckless and inclined to forget rules and regulations. Wing Commander Snelling was as friendly as possible in telling the three of us that he could understand the concern of the school commander in this very large training school. Giving me a pat on the shoulder, he walked with us to the Master II, which we would take turns in flying for initial flying and handling, as was necessary when flying different types of aircraft.

So we commenced our small operation, which was only to fill our time until permanent postings were organised. Once more I shuddered, as I knew this type of responsibility would not last. I completed a close external check on the Master II, accompanied by a senior mechanic, then a thorough check of the instruments and controls. I started the engine, which reminded me that I had flown many hours on Harvards with a radial engine. This caused no worry. Taxiing out for the take-off, I was thrilled to start flying once more after such a long rest. I taxied and felt the movement so easily with the wide wheelbase, similar to the Hurricane, and felt plenty of power in the engine. I reached the runway and obtained permission for take-off, opened the throttle and suddenly the thing was hurtling down the runway like a Spitfire! In no time at all I was away and climbing.

The purpose of this flight was not only to experience a different aircraft, but to test this with altitude during aerobatics and general handling. It included some time learning the district, as this school was in the Transvaal, which did not have too many landmarks on which to navigate, except a lonely but main railway line, which could always be useful. The controls were smooth and the aircraft was wonderfully nimble, handling like a fighter. Reaching 12,000 feet (no oxygen), I commenced a series of aerobatics – namely, slow and fast rolls, both left and right, a number of times, one flick roll with my fingers crossed, steep dives and 'escape dives'. When being attacked from behind, you closed the throttle and quickly pushed the control column in the port or starboard quarter of the cockpit. Then, you moved the rudder the same way to create a vicious fall to the side while turning. This would help to escape a stern attack from enemy aircraft. When attacking bombers, you performed tail, quarter, half or underneath attacks. Head-on attacks were ruled out after Squadron Leader Bader, having had two or three tries during the Battle of Britain, had not been aware in one attack that the Luftwaffe had placed a number of Messerschmitt 110s in the front of the bombers. The 110s sported four 20mm cannons in the nose, and Bader lost a few pilots.

I finished a very interesting flight and returned after landing and taxiing in. The aircraft was refuelled and made ready for the next two trips, which would complete the first day. Tomorrow there would be pupils to meet.

For odd discussions, we were in touch with Captain Tillburn and Lieutenant Wayburn, two flight commanders who were very friendly and always ready to help to entertain us in the mess. They also arranged assistance for us to be driven, with other instructors, to and from Johannesburg for weekends, which helped me greatly.

On 2 April we were offered a list of what we would teach our pupils – namely high dive-bombing, formation flying, instrument flying, blind flying (ZZ approaches to night flying), fighter attacks (variation), air to ground (front gun), low flying, low-level bombing. We three pilots were Flying Officer Dennis Steadman, Flying Officer Jack Kay and myself. We had all flown on operations in the Battle of Britain and Malta, from August 1940 until March 1942. The allocation of pupils each day would be related to the length of time of each flight. We commenced the new operation, mid-morning, with a break for lunch, and completed each day at 16.30 p.m. If the pupils wished to ask further questions, we would be available in the evenings.

The operation commenced satisfactorily, with approximately six or eight flights a day, depending on unforeseen problems, although the weather was consistent as far as our plans were concerned. In the month of April 1942 we flew twenty-one flights with most of the variations re-corded. Most flights were approximately 40 minutes, with some 1 hour long. The pupils were excited and very interested with these lessons and were always keen for explanations on the ground.

Under the same conditions we flew twenty-nine flights in May. One or two of the flying instructors joined us, particularly when we were teaching formation flying. During the weekends we were taken to Johannesburg with various instructors. Some had families, and others had girlfriends, as I had. I was mad keen on visiting Ruth, whom Terry

Crossey had introduced to me. I booked a room at the Officers' Club for the weekend, and Ruth arranged to stay with one of her sisters. Life was wonderful.

Flying continued into the next month, and the three of us were really satisfied with our success with this training. However, in the first week of June we had a sad crash. Steadman took off with a pupil, and onlookers and the duty tower people viewed a clean take-off and climb towards the railway line, when suddenly the Master II nosedived into the railway embankment. I had just finished a flight and together with another instructor we managed to reach the crash scene. The aircraft had split in two. The engine and front seat had landed over the other side of the embankment and the rear half had rested on the airfield side. The pupil was badly hurt and died before he was removed from the front cockpit. Steadman was conscious, dazed and in shock. However, he mumbled 'engine quit dead'. This was as bad an accident as any I have witnessed on operations. Steadman was taken to the local small hospital and later transferred to Johannesburg for full examination.

That evening the accident was discussed for hours and after a while I thought I heard one of the pilots say 'sabotage'. I turned to Lieutenant Tilly and asked if he had heard the remark. He agreed about the remark. Then the senior officer in the mess called for silence and advised us to cease discussing the accident until further notice. The experts would carry out a massive check on the wreckage. To lose a pupil was terribly sad, and I was informed that this was the first tragedy with a loss of life, although there were always minor accidents to be expected in such a large flying school. The flying continued with reduced numbers. However, we managed to fly twenty-five flights.

There was no news concerning the crash into July. However, we knew the wreckage was undergoing careful examination. There were five flights, of which ours was the fifth. The four main training flights would have approximately six or seven qualified flying instructors. This was a busy school. Pilots and mechanics were ordered to increase engine checks before take-off.

Flying Officer Kay and I continued with our duties and carried on with fewer pupils for our 'flight' record. I called my pupil and walked to the Master II scheduled for me, which looked like an absolutely new aircraft. Fresh yellow paint and very trim. I addressed the mechanic, who was assisting my inspection, and I was informed it was a machine that had just left the hangar, after a timed complete overhaul. It certainly showed up against all the grubby ones on the tarmac. I helped the pupil into the front cockpit and climbed into the rear. I started the engine, and carried out the necessary engine and other checks. Satisfied, I tightened my harness and waved away the 'chocks'. We commenced taxiing for the take-off. We had gone about 50 yards when the pupil in front shouted and waved his hands, and as I reached for my communication tube I realised that there were none fitted in his cockpit, as he was trying to tell me. No wonder I couldn't contact him when we taxied. I immediately turned the aircraft around and taxied back to the parking line. The mechanic ran out as I parked and I yelled to him about the speaking tubes and told my pupil to leave the aircraft while I waited for another.

As I waited, I saw an aircraft with two pupils climbing in. It was allowed for pupils who had been awarded their wings to carry on flying as they waited for posting. I waved to them and suggested that we took their Miles Master II, and that they took the newish one, which had no communication tubes. They accepted my request, being happy, as I had been, to fly a clean aircraft just out of the maintenance hangar. While I, with my pupil, walked to the aircraft that they had left, the aircraft we had vacated taxied out ahead of us. By the time we had reached halfway to the runway, we saw the two lads who had swapped with us take off. As I was looking at the instruments and settling in the cockpit, I heard my pupil scream 'No, no, no!' I whipped my head up and looked where the pupil was pointing to see the aircraft I had just vacated in a ball of fire and tumbling to the ground about 1,000 yards beyond the airfield.

I stopped the aircraft and taxied quickly back to the parking line, jumped down and joined a number of instructors who had witnessed another terrible tragedy. I was later told I had run to the group shouting, 'It should have been me, it should have been me!' They grabbed me and calmed me down, as I finally told them of the lead-up to the accident. I can never forget to this day those two young lads, Weeks and Walker, killed by sabotage, which was confirmed at a later date by aircraft accident officials.

Flying continued after lunch. We managed to make seven flights, after which I was told to proceed to Wing Commander Snelling's office to report on the accident. The next day I attended an interview to explain my knowledge leading up to the horrible accident. I had barely slept that night and could not get rid of the image of that massive ball of fire and the Master II falling in pieces, with those two happy young lads, proudly sporting their new wings, ending their lives like this. The wing commander kept me to attention as I told him of my experience concerning the change of aircraft. I told him all, as I had already written in my report. Once again I said that it was my fault, to which the wing commander said, 'Don't be a fool, you did the right thing in changing aircraft. How the hell did you know what was to happen?' I mentioned how I heard an instructor say, 'More sabotage.' What did that mean? He gave me a queer look, saying, 'You have been here nearly four months and have never been told of our worst problem, Ossewabrandwag – operations of sabotage.' I told him no, I did not understand. The interview finished with an order to visit the adjutant, who would fill me in on the saboteurs.

I contacted the adjutant, and was invited to visit him immediately. He walked me to a table on which were two very thick and large record books. He opened the first and pointed to many photos of head and shoulders ground staff in khaki uniforms. He explained that both record books were photos of known Ossewabrandwag saboteurs, who were photographed so they could be referred to, so a suspect anywhere in the school could be subjected to a check by the Military Police. Record books like this existed in every office on all stations in South Africa, as those types of Boers were German sympathisers and trained to do any damage to any object anywhere. The adjutant advised me that naturally nobody could remember all these faces. However, it was vital always to check the aircraft as much as possible and to report the smallest defect. I left his office thinking, 'Do we ever get rid of warfare?' I was to learn much more as time moved on.

The training progressed, with only two of us teaching operation tactics. Halfway through 9 July, we were joined by a South African captain who had been in action in Ethiopia, fighting the Italians, early in the war. This was a great help, and there were no hold-ups, which allowed us to fly a heavy day's mix of various tactics. The day's total tally was nineteen flights, excluding aircraft testing. The month contained twenty days of flying and five days of lectures and explanations.

On 23 July I was called to report to RAF Headquarters in Pretoria. This, to me, could only mean another segment of my destiny. The wait had been just on four months of exciting life without bullets and bombs, although the accidents had been horrible experiences. I had been able to enjoy many weekends in the company of my girlfriend Ruth. These meetings were becoming more exciting, as I was told she was now waiting for me and had not carried on with her parties and other dates.

She accepted that our friendship was now serious.

I arrived at headquarters, being welcomed by the wing commander, who asked me to be seated and then spent a few minutes congratulating me on my work at Standerton. I had received a very good report from Wing Commander Snelling. Then he sat back, placing a folder with reports on his desk. He looked at me for what seemed several minutes and then said, 'Palliser, the board has studied your time in the RAF and you have done well in operations and apparently earned your DFC. I have been allowed to offer you one of two postings. You were posted here as Acting Squadron Leader. You led No. 605 Squadron on Malta. The board would offer you a squadron in the Far East.' My guts went mad, and I was nearly sick with the shock of what I had dreaded. He offered me a glass of water, as he noticed the awful effect that I could not control. Then he said, 'However, you can remain in South Africa if you will consider becoming a qualified Flying Instructor.' I nearly choked with this further offer. And, trying to be calm, my answer was, 'I would be pleased to attend a course for Flying Instruction, Sir.' The wing commander leaned forward and said, 'Very good, Palliser, I feel that is what you will be good at. You never know, you may really like this country as I have. You might meet one of our lovely South African girls.' I could not hold back the great smile as I said, 'Thank you Sir.' I was advised to return to Standerton, which would be arranged immediately, pack my kit and return to the Officers' Club, where I would receive further orders. I would have to leave for No. 62 Air School Central Flying School (CFS), to be there on 28 July. If this was not destiny, what was? Four days with Ruth.

27. A Miracle to Stay in South Africa

I could not reach the Officers' Club in Johannesburg quickly enough. I was on the phone to Ruth immediately and asking her to see me after her work, which she managed in the late afternoon.. It was 23 July. Over a cup of tea I tried to blurt out what had happened. However, I was so excited I had to wait to get my breath back. Ruth told me she had phoned her sister and would sleep there and organise some leave until the evening of the 27th, when I would catch a late night train that would get me into Bloemfontein in the early morning of 28 July.

The four days were marvellous. I was lost in a new world of happiness, which had not happened since the late 1930s. First Ruth asked me to meet her mother in Krugersdorp, and possibly her second sister. Her family consisted of one son and five daughters.

We arrived in Krugersdorp around lunchtime on the first day, where I met Ruth's mother, a most charming elderly lady who had lost her husband when Ruth was born in 1922. Mrs Smith told me that her husband was a red-headed Scotsman with a good position in the prosperous gold and diamond business. She laughed when she advised me that all her daughters were lovely redheads and full of mischief. They showed me around the district. The town and the surroundings were so pretty. It felt like a scenic country and a laid-back area on the high escarpment of the Gold Reef, stretching 30–40 miles east and west at altitudes between 4,000 and 6,000 feet above sea level. The Reef, as it is called, enjoys a lovely climate in both winter and summer: 0–17 degrees in winter and a maximum in summer of 29 degrees

The next three days were the happiest I had enjoyed for many years back to my teens. The time passed like lightning and, before I expected, I was on the train to Bloemfontein in the Orange Free State. I had fallen in love in a big way with Ruth, and she reciprocated my feelings in a sincere manner.

I had met all her sisters, aged from 19 to 55 years. Ruth's brother was

an engineer on one of the gold mines about 50 miles from the Reef, so
was too far away to be introduced. The fourth sister, who was married,
appeared to be the 'captain on the bridge', being of much assistance to
the total family – a great lady.

My final visit to Krugersdorp was for a family discussion concerning
Ruth and myself, with this fourth sister, who wasted no time in questioning me as to my relationship with Ruth. She explained that the fifth sister,
who was also married, had also been in touch and supported the
questioning. Helped by nods from Ruth, I explained my background,
family, engineering qualifications and life from 1939. I firmly stated my
positive feeling for South Africa and mentioned my talk with Mr Palliser
of Dowson and Dobson. This created a raising of eyebrows. I also
stressed that I was now proceeding to Bloemfontein on a flying instructors' course, which, unless I lost my life, guaranteed me at least two and
a half years in South Africa. After my return to the UK for demob, I
would definitely return to South Africa. In conclusion, I remarked, I was
determined to show my love for Ruth, if Ruth and the family accepted
my feelings. The answer from the sister was: 'The family have discussed
this with Ruth. However, I understand that your flying course is in
Bloemfontein, 200 miles away, and will be for three months. This will
give Ruth and yourself time to consider the strength of your relationship.' I replied, '200 miles, that is about 1 hour by air, and military
aircraft are constantly flying to and fro, which means I will be able to
have a few weekends until my course is completed.' I would apply to
instruct on elementary flying, and the training schools for this category
were all on the Reef. I would apply for instructing at either Baragwanath
or Randfontein, both in the Johannesburg area. I ended the meeting by
telling them that I was a poor-attending Anglican, but that I said my
prayers and sincerely believed in God. My maritime captain grandfather,
who, with his school principal wife, had both shared my education,
explained, 'Church is one thing but no matter where you are, believe in
God who controls your destiny.' And as I had explained, after the previous
two and a half years, 'I believed'.

Now I was in the train to Bloemfontein, going to CFS, heading for
another niche in my life.

No. 62 Air School, Central Flying School

I arrived at the air school on 28 July, after a night journey from
Johannesburg. I had managed enough sleep to be ready for the escort to

the welcoming breakfast and a visit to the recreation building for the introduction to the flying course. There were three courses: Elementary, Intermediate and Advanced. The latter was split into single-engine and multi-engine aircraft. The air school was very large, having commenced before the war, and now assisting the Empire Training Unit.

The introductory welcome was very noisy because of the gathering of South African and UK pilots who had, like myself, been operational pilots in many areas of the fighting. Quite a number were SA pilots who, as a matter of necessity, were also included in the course.

I must mention there were two categories of South African army and air force people. Those who were willing to fight outside the country were distinguished by a red tab on each shoulder. Those who wished to remain for home duties did not show the red flash. As our meeting ended, we approached the noticeboard that allocated the dwellings – decent wooden structures, which would allow for a bed, pedestal and cupboards for eight people. The names of who would live in which hut were posted on the noticeboard in the main building for our information. The main notice board would inform everyone on each course as to the training flight, the names of the pupils in each flight, and the name or names of the instructor to report to. As luck would have it, Steadman and Crossey were here too. And the three of us were in the same hut; the only other name I can remember was Bobby Locke.

The next morning we reported to our flight area to be introduced to one Flight Lieutenant Morrison from the UK. He would be the responsible instructor throughout the course. I was called to my first flight with Flight Lieutenant Morrison, who was waiting beside a Tiger Moth. He greeted me with a handshake and advised me to fasten myself into the rear cockpit. I gave him a big grin, as I remembered my very first flight. Oh, how destiny had shaped my life.

We were airborne without any fuss and, as we flew to a reasonable area, Morrison commenced the 'patter', going over the very beginning and then handing over to me to voice the explanation to him as a pupil. We had already run through the 'preparation of flight' before I started to talk about controls. Morrison gave me his first criticism. 'You speak too fast, showing no feeling, just a stream of words, forgetting to place feeling into a slower and forceful explanation.' I was not delivering the information correctly. Morrison said, 'Remember how you listened to your instructor, when he might have used words that you didn't understand. Slow down your talk and speak clearly with short phrases, not a bundle of words. And you might add in your experiences.' I soon realised I was not in the room talking over a pint of ale. I had to remember the pupils knew nothing.

The first trip lasted an hour and I landed feeling this was not 'pie in the sky'. I had quickly to learn how to speak to someone who did not know anything about the subject. The challenge was certainly there! I had been issued with literature. Now to listen to Morrison, and then to study the books. Morrison explained his remarks and I really understood. He then approached another would-be instructor. There was no rest for me, as he pointed to another Tiger Moth and requested another of our team to try initial teaching – for 45 minutes.

During July I flew training flights with Morrison. One flight was in the Avro Tutor, a fine aircraft a little larger than the Tiger Moth and with a radial engine, which was quite exciting. It was new to us, however. It was probably flown before the Tiger Moth, in the early 1930s. Five flights with different pupils in our team launched the method of flight training with exchange of instructing patter. Total flying time the first day was 5 hours 20 minutes, with time for changes, refuelling and discussing our flights. We reported to Flight Lieutenant Morrison at the end of the week's flying and for the month's results.

The month found us testing each other with ground training from the flying books supplied at the beginning. These books were like Holy Grails, displaying diagrams and describing the patter and aircraft controls in careful English language. Naturally we had time for eating, sleeping and evening visits to the city. It was amazing that none of us ventured forth for the first week – we were enthralled once we understood what had been offered to us. Teaching other would-be pilots strengthened our efforts to the limit and also gave us huge responsibility, especially the few ex-fighter pilots who happened to be lucky like myself.

I was able to keep in touch with my girlfriend Ruth, advising her that I could catch a night express train to Johannesburg and return on the Sunday night. I was able to catch some sleep each way.

One great surprise I received on my first trip to Johannesburg was to see Steadman walking towards me on Bloemfontein Station. I said, 'What the hell, are you going to Johannesburg?' I knew that he had left hospital after the crash at Standerton, but did not know he stayed at the Officers' Club to recover. He said to me, 'Remember our visit to the apartment of Mrs Loftus with Crossey?' 'Yes,' I said. He said, 'You were making eyes at the one called Ruth. Well, when I recovered from the crash, I received a call at the club from Ruth's sister, Joyce, who had heard from Ruth of the crash at Standerton and that I had been resting in the Officers' Club before going to Bloemfontein. So I asked her if she would like to visit me, which she did, and now we are a foursome.'

The course continued into August. Now we were as keen as mustard. I flew with Flight Lieutenant Morrison, and he was extremely active, judging our flying actions and also our explanations, as we carried out the flights with our pupils. I had flown nearly 1,000 hours since 1939 and learned much on a variety of aircraft. However, I knew nothing with regards to this responsibility of teaching. Morrison explained that he was satisfied with me. However, there was still much to learn. The month's tally of flights was six with Morrison, plus one flight test with the chief flying instructor, Captain Budd, and fifteen flights learning with different team pupils, two of whom were Steadman and Crossey.

On one particular afternoon during lunch, Steadman talked to me about his crash and told me that it was found that a fuel valve had been damaged. No sabotage. However, the accident that I had seen, the one that caused the death of the two young pilots, had been proved to be sabotage. The fuel tank of the aircraft was in the starboard wing root. Small damage had occurred in this area, like a fine drilled hole, which had caused leaking fuel. The Miles aircraft radial engine is inclined, during take-off with full power, and after levelling and reduced revolutions, to create a long flame flash for a few seconds. This flash had hit the leaking fuel, and the aircraft simply blew up. Clever sabotage!

The flights as usual consisted of teaching with Flight Lieutenant Morrison and random checks of our ability. This amounted to one flight, a cross-country check flight with Lieutenant Southy (SA) and another check with Lieutenant Sumner (SA). The second flight ended with a forced landing because of an engine problem. We returned – no damage. There was a further check with Lieutenant Sumner for night flying. The day flights amounted to sixteen instruction flights. There were also one progressive, one night flight and thirty-nine team flights, which were about 50–50 in Tiger Moth and Tutor aircraft. It was quite a month and, with the patter learning on many nights, there was really much competitive interest. The month was signed off by Flight Lieutenant Morrison and Captain Budd (SA).

September 1942 was the penultimate month of the training course. I had worked hard, as I was really keen on the responsibility of both the verbal teaching and the flying lessons. I had requested the initial training course, as I never forgot the teaching I had received in Perth, Scotland, from two of my instructors, Flight Lieutenant Sammy Trout and Flight Lieutenant Lawson. Flight Lieutenant Trout in particular, one of the pre-war RAF pilots, was very skilled in aerobatics in the 'Hendon' Aerobatic Air Shows in the UK during the 1930s.

I had joined the RAFVR in July 1939, too late to enjoy any flying. However, I received six months' ground training before September. My two main instructors gave me every encouragement, as I took to flying like a duck to water. Flight Lieutenant Lawson gave me the lessons in navigation and Flight Lieutenant Trout soon had me learning aerobatics, as well as giving me tips on manœuvring when being attacked by enemy aircraft. The hours spent with these two 'gods' helped me to have good marks at the end of my courses. They taught me to fly in Tiger Moths and, as they said, 'In the next flying course, Advanced, you have the passport for complete understanding, as this is just a larger aircraft with more instruments.'

Tragedy was always around the corner. News for us three RAF friends was that two of our other RAF friends who had joined the multi-engine programme had been killed when the twin-engine Oxford they were flying exploded in mid-air as they reduced height to practise in the low-flying area. They had completed upper-air lessons and carried on to the low-flying area to complete their low-flying programme. A local farmer watched as the starboard wing exploded as the aircraft reduced height. The aircraft crashed, killing both men. It was found to be blatant, proven sabotage by experts examining the remains of the aircraft. The leading edge of the starboard wing, laminate wood, had been cut through by some sharp tool. Pieces of the destroyed wing, 2–3 feet long, betrayed the fine cuts. On the Sunday, the CFS pupils and we three friends formed the largest funeral procession ever seen in Bloemfontein. It stretched for three blocks, with many local citizens joining in. These two British pilots, like ourselves, had fought in Europe and the Middle East for the last two and a half years, only to be murdered in a supposedly free country. However, the Ossewabrandwag had struck once more.

The lessons continued, and we experienced the heaviest month in the full programme during September. Training flights for the month totalled seventy-two. These included:

Night flying
Forced landings

Cross-wind take-off and landing
Powered approach and landing
Precautionary landings
Medium turns
Climbing and gliding turns
Low flying
Side slipping – not for monoplanes
Spinning
Steep turns
Instrument flying
Stopping engine and starting in flight

October 1942 marked the final month of the course. The details below are from Official Log Book entries.

Sequence of Instruction, Elementary Course

1. Familiarity with cockpit layout
2. Preparation for flight
3. Effect of controls
4. Taxiing
5. Straight and level flight
6. Climbing
7. Descending
8. Stalling
9. Medium turns
10. Gliding and climbing turns
11. Approach landing
12. Spinning
13. Side slipping
14. Steep turns
15. Instrument flying
16. Low flying
17. Taking off and landing out of wind
18. Precaution landings
19. Forced landing
20. Restarting engines in flight
21. Aerobatics
22. Night flying

23. Pilot navigation

24. Formation flying

Aircraft flown

Tiger Moth

Hawker Hart

Avro Tutor

Instructors

Flight Lieutenant Morrison (RAF)

Captain Ellis (SAAF)

Captain Cross (SAAF)

Flying Officer Grandy (RAF)

Flight Lieutenant Rea (RAF)

Flight Lieutenant Lister – CFT Test – (RAF)

The last day of the course was 19 October. Crossey, Steadman and I, after enjoying the last day, caught the train to Johannesburg, where, for the first time since 1940, we would be separated. Crossey was going to the East Rand Airfield in Nigel, east of Johannesburg. Steadman was going to Johannesburg Airfield, Baragwanath. I was going to the airfield at Randfontein, west of Johannesburg.

28. Randfontein

I arrived there on 20 October, after catching a local Reef train, which deposited me in 40 minutes, enabling me to catch a taxi and arrive at my destination, No. 2 Air School. Reporting to the adjutant, I was welcomed and introduced to the chief flying instructor, Squadron Leader Winton, another RAF officer. He invited me to sit, while he explained my duties and assured me I had come to a well-organised school. I was allocated to No. 3 Flight to commence my duties.

I will now relate some of the extraneous experiences of my continued life in the RAF, encompassing the years until I rejoined civilian life.

In November 1942, returning to the airfield from a training flight, I observed a Tiger Moth ahead of me, being flown solo. The aircraft was flying two red strips of streamers attached to the flying wires, one at the end of the lower wings. This indicated a pupil on his first solo circuit and landing. This was to warn other pilots to 'give way'. I ordered my pupil, who had advanced experience, to widen our approach until the solo pupil had finished landing. The pupil entered the down-wind leg nicely, and flew to a mark above some buildings on the ground, where he commenced his turn to 'cross-wind', prior to his approach for landing. As he turned I noticed he was maintaining quite a flat turn – even my pupil shouted. There was nothing I could do, as I saw the pupil was aware that something was wrong, and he crossed the controls, which caused the aircraft to enter a spin, ending in a bad crash among the buildings below.

In the meantime, I broke away, flying low over the ground crews, pointing to the direction of the crash. They acknowledged and I made a quick circuit, landing to join a car going to the crash. Unfortunately and tragically, the pupil was dead. We could do no more. However, the teaching continued. I was ordered to attend the local police court, where the accident was reviewed and a verdict passed as to the cause of the crash. Having witnessed the accident, my evidence was accepted by the judge. This young pupil was a member of the RAF. His family was notified by headquarters. The training resumed.

In the same month I was teaching a pupil aerobatics and after a number of demonstrations I requested the pupil to complete a 'loop'. He entered the loop correctly and proceeded nicely over the top of the loop with perfect control, to complete, when there was a loud cracking sound. I took over and looked around and above the centre, under the fuel tank, and noticed one cross wire had snapped and another looked as if it was damaged. I was about 10 kilometres from the airfield and not able to assess the wing damage. I described to the pupil the possibility of the upper wing being weakened, which might cause a crash. I gave him the option, as we were at an altitude of 4,000 feet, to take to his parachute. I intended to try to coast back to the airfield, of which I had a clear view, and I certainly wished to be able to know what had caused the damage. I also knew that the Tiger Moth was a very strong aircraft. The pupil told me he preferred to risk it and stayed in the aircraft. I made a safe landing, as I used a semi-gliding approach and made an easy landing. I was able to taxi to the hangar area, where an inspection was eventually carried out, revealing sabotage by heavy metal pliers: the one flying wire had been cut and the other partially severed. We were lucky!

By January 1943 I had made many friends in the flying school and had also been given an excellent chance of following my destiny with my sweetheart, Ruth. The airfield was only 15 kilometres from the town of Krugersdorp, where the family lived, and I had been able, with the help of free weekends, to visit Ruth and her family, to a point where everyone of Ruth's family had accepted that we could be engaged in November 1942.

Now we were to be married. And the greatest surprise on this occasion was that Dennis Steadman, my long-time friend, had pursued Ruth's sister Joyce, and the four of us were to have a double wedding. The wedding would be in Johannesburg cathedral in the morning of 23 January.

After the agony of two years of shocking air fighting, we were truly happy with so many friends in South Africa. What we did not expect were the wonderful friends who appeared from Standerton, the Central Flying School, Bloemfontein, Baragwanath and Randfontein. We had two weeks' honeymoon and then returned to duties. Ruth and I lived in a hotel in Randfontein. I continued instructing at Randfontein until

September 1943. I was recategorised from 'C' to 'BE' in July 1943, and on 5 August I was authorised to test and send pupils for their first solo flights.

On 13 September 1943 I was operating from an advanced secondary airfield, teaching the art of flying in formation of three aircraft in 'Vic' formation. We flew off the airfield independently and, gradually, as I led the arrowhead, I brought them closer to an inverted 'V' formation, flying straight and level and then climbing to 4,000 feet and commencing turns to port and starboard. The two pupils were performing magnificently as I led them into steeper turns, turning as we lost and gained height. Suddenly I felt my seat move, which I thought was imagination. However, as I went to turn to port descending, my seat lurched and dropped to the cockpit floor. I immediately tried to straighten the turn and decrease the descending speed. I could not move the controls at all. I was sure the pupils sensed something wrong as I managed to hold the stick with my left hand and furiously waved them away with my right arm. The upper aircraft cleared nicely. However, the lower aircraft missed my wing by inches.

By now I was spiralling in descent and could not move the stick. However, in desperation I forced my feet from the rudder bar and pulled as hard as I could, which moved the seat up far enough to allow me to straighten the aircraft. The pupils closed on me and I signalled return to the airfield, which they obeyed. All I could do was to line up on the airfield, which was approximately 3 kilometres away, and control an emergency approach straight, using the engine, as I descended, and judging my descent to make a decent landing, which might not be a three pointer. I landed safely and was able to taxi to the parking area.

One of the flight commanders spoke to me as I stood by the aircraft. 'What happened? I thought you were going to crash.' I suggested we get in touch with our main airfield and have some riggers sent over to look at my seat. In the meantime he had noticed that my bucket seat was loose. The aircraft was trucked back to base and placed in the hangar for inspection by the responsible people. I was issued with a report later. The finding was that the seat screws had been loosened to allow the seat, after some amount of flying, to collapse on the turntable, which operated the ailerons, so, with the weight of the pilot, the ailerons could not move. More sabotage.

Between September 1943 and January 1944 Ruth and I experienced our first venture in our married life when I moved to No. 4 Air School,

Benoni, and we moved into a hotel in Benoni. Arrangements to travel to and from the air school were covered by an air force vehicle, which did a round journey, picking up a number of married instructors who lived in various parts of the city. My first lesson relating to marriage commenced when I realised that it is one thing to enjoy a friendship with a lovely girl you hope to marry but quite another when marriage begins and immediately you leave the family environment and jump straight into wartime military responsibilities in a strange place. This big change hits you with a great shock! I had to leave the hotel to carry out my flying duties. My wife was alone for the first time in her life. What could I do? Luckily the question was answered in the first week when the chief flying instructor explained that a number of wives and girlfriends of the officers had formed a club. This made my wife very happy and was a great relief to me.

So, on 28 September 1943, I was welcomed by Captain Eden, SA Chief Flying Instructor, to command 'B' Flight. I was also advised that I would be required to assist him with testing of various pupils from all four flights when required. When I was introduced to the 'B' Flight instructors, I was made aware that most of them were experienced pilots. As they had not yet been selected for operational duties in the Middle East, they were remaining very active as first-class instructors. The instruction programme was exactly the same as at Randfontein and Baragwanath, and we were still flying Tiger Moths. Some of the instructors were a little cool towards me on my arrival, as some of them were three or four years older than me. However, over a period of time, I made sure I accepted their capabilities and age and held their respect. Over time, when I was approached over the months to explain my experiences in action, they all stated they were keen to face action outside South Africa.

I gave them all a laugh when, one day, I walked out of the crew room to carry out my flight test of a pupil. I noticed that none of my instructors had moved to their own aircraft, but were watching me! I assisted the pupil, who was halfway through his course, to climb into his seat, then proceeded to climb into the cockpit. I connected the communicating tubes and suggested the pupil should start the engine. As he waved to the airman who would turn the propeller, I relaxed, commenced checking the instruments, and gripped the throttle lever, which seemed large and soft. I looked down at my hand and found I was holding a multi-coloured snake wrapped around the throttle with its tail hanging below. I ripped my harness off and leapt out of the cockpit as well as any

Olympic hurdler and shouted, 'There's a snake in my aircraft!' In the meantime I was trying to get the pupil out of the cockpit, as he just sat there smiling. I turned to see the instructors and ground crew laughing their heads off. I had forgotten a previous conversation about snakes, when I had let them know I was not attracted to such creatures. So their plan had worked. Walking back to the edge of the tarmac, I put on the worst face I could muster and, as I reached them, I joined them in their laughter. I turned to the senior instructor and said, 'Thank you for the welcome. I would rather have had a Messerschmitt 109 up my arse.' This caused more laughter and broke the barriers.

The total elementary flying training was the responsibility of the three air schools, all based on the Transvaal Reef, accepted as the Gold Reef of South Africa. Johannesburg was the major city in the length of the Reef, comprising many towns and villages. The Gold Reef lying east and west was at an altitude of 4,000–6,000 feet, stretching between 50 and 60 miles each side of Johannesburg. It was accepted as a wonderful area for flying training.

Outside of the fixed training programmes I experienced a couple of unexpected, flying-related actions.

When a pupil exceeded 8 hours' training leading to his first solo, he was to be tested by another senior pilot in the flight to find the value of his training on all aspects of the initial 8 hours. If his general flying, including take-off, was acceptable, he was allowed an extra $1^1/_2$ hours to concentrate on acceptable landing capabilities. If this extra time did not produce positive improvement, he had to be tested by the flight commander or the chief flying instructor, working in a mainframe of 18 hours. This applied if the pupil had upper-air, general good flying characteristics.

Towards the end of the course, a pupil had been flying a solo programme on a Friday afternoon. As we were closing for the weekend, a message was taken by the duty pilot that the pupil had made a forced landing in a field 20 miles north of the air school. The time was 5.00 p.m. and most of the instructors had left for home. The CFI and the ground engineer approached me and asked if I could handle it the next day, Saturday. I accepted.

The farmer in whose field the pupil had managed to land explained exactly where he was and how to reach his farm, which was situated on a byroad from the main road. It appeared that the pupil had flown beyond his time and had run out of fuel. However, he had had enough to land. The aircraft was in a newly ploughed field, and the farmer would assist us if we brought fuel and a mechanic to make sure there was no damage. The school mechanic was ordered to take a 'ute', which was a small truck, tools and fuel. The CFI apologised to me for this inconvenience, saying that I should be back by lunchtime if I could fly it out.

We managed to find the farmer after a few wrong turns on country roads. He guided us to the aircraft, which was about a mile from his home. We had to leave the truck, as we were unable to drive because of the fences and growth in the fields. The pupil hung his head and apologised. I told him he must return with the mechanic, while I tried to fly the aircraft out. The pupil had mentioned that the field was ploughed and, landing down the rows of the field, the aircraft had landed safely; however, the tail might be damaged. The farmer and the pupil helped to carry petrol cans plus a few tools, and we plodded over the other field until we arrived at the Tiger Moth and the furrows running down the field. Whatever next?

The mechanic turned to me and said, 'The aircraft looks OK. It's covered in soil and the tail has a few tears and clods of soil on it, but everything could be made ready. However, how are you going to take off with these ruts of fresh soil?' It was a miracle the pupil had held the stick back and had managed to keep the plane in the ruts. I looked at the line of ruts running way down the field and spoke to the farmer. 'Sir, I can't get the aircraft off this. The soil is soft and it would be a miracle if I could avoid scraping the sides of the ruts.' I was about to say 'Mission impossible', when the farmer turned and spoke in Afrikaans to one of the dozen black workers who had congregated around us. Then he asked me how long a run I would need to take off. I said, 'In soil like this, on a flat surface, 800 metres.' The farmer then said, 'I have spoken to my black foreman, and he will have all of his men tramp up and down, and flatten the width necessary for your aircraft.'

The mechanic had put fuel in the tank and checked the undercarriage and propeller, giving the OK. I suggested he take the pupil and return to the airfield and report to the duty pilot and the CFI. I also asked him to have the duty pilot phone my wife and advise her I should return about 4.00 p.m., the time now being 11.00 a.m. The farmworkers measured the area and, starting their wonderful tribal singing, started to walk, stamping the ground with the farmer guiding them. The farmer offered me some beer and apologised for the absence of food. I watched the area slowly flatten out. The black foreman spoke to the farmer and looked at me. The farmer laughed and spoke in Afrikaans, then said to me, 'My lad asked if you would join them for a while as that would bring them luck.' I didn't hesitate. I shook hands with the black lad and spent half an hour walking with them. At about 4.00 p.m. I managed a reasonable take-off and returned to the airfield, where a volunteer gave me a lift to my hotel and a very worried new wife.

Another notable experience was when I had to test a pupil in a 'forced landing' procedure. We arrived at the area for this test and proceeded to attempt two forced landings, flying to the field area from 1,500 feet to an actual landing. The pupil managed very good approach landings and I was very satisfied. I flew the aircraft to return to the airfield and, flying at 1,000 feet, I looked ahead and saw a peculiar dark cloud. I spoke to the pupil and pointed to this cloud, which looked like a giant dark grey ball. The pupil was unable to reply and as I turned to proceed, there was a massive bang on the windshield at the front of the aircraft and we were in a swarm of locusts. I could not see a damned thing. There were squashed and crawling locusts all over us. I looked over the edge of the cockpit, trying to see ahead, and suddenly I was hit in the side of my face with locusts. At that time the engine choked, and I had to look for a forced landing.

I turned to port and I noticed the mass was like a huge ball. Luckily I flew out of the mass and noticed a field – there were many in the open country. I landed and then had to wait until we could get help, which came quickly, as the field was next to the main road and a motorist who had stopped to watch the locusts drove us to the village, where I could phone the airfield. The mechanics arrived and cleared the engine mess. Fortunately the ground was hard enough to allow me to take off and return to the airfield. 'A frightening experience,' I said to the doctor, as he stitched a severe cut in my cheek where the locusts had hit me hard. I carried on with instructing and testing until 20 January 1944. Then, on 21 January I received a shocking blow to my future.

29. Serious Illness

In January 1944 I had developed a cold that quickly got worse. During the morning of 21 January I experienced a coughing fit that I could not control and, as my wife ran to phone the doctor, I had a shocking haemorrhage. My bed looked like a butcher's chopping block. My wife did not panic and made sure the doctor understood what was happening, and, as the bleeding ceased, she made every effort to change my clothing. She helped me to an armchair and held me until the doctor arrived, which, I am glad to say, was very quick. The doctor insisted that I would have to be transferred to the military hospital at Baragwanath, as my condition was serious.

In the meantime, although I was completely exhausted, I managed to tell my wife and the doctor of my similar experience in December 1940, when I had finished my testing on the Merlin 20 engines, which had been a new development for the launch of the Hurricane Mark II and the Spitfire Mark II. Unfortunately, at that time I was placed in a local sick bay for a few days until there was no sign of blood in my sputum. Within a week I was returned to operations. Although I still had a heavy cough at times, I was able to carry on without further incident.

Ruth, my wonderful wife, was a strong lady indeed and immediately, despite our short marriage, set into motion our future. Ruth packed up at the hotel and moved back into her mother's apartment in Krugersdorp to live. I contacted the RAF Headquarters for assistance and continuous advice. Ruth was supported all the way, visiting me as often as was possible. For her to reach the hospital was a half-hour train ride to Johannesburg and then a long bus ride through the native territory to the hospital, about 5 miles south of Johannesburg City. I am sure Ruth's journeys to see me were a nightmare that only residents of Johannesburg could know.

After three months of treatment and medication, I left the hospital, never to return to flying in South Africa. Because I was English and in the RAF, I was advised I should live with Ruth and her family until I received notice to return to England for further examination as to my future. Many nights I dug my face in my pillow and screamed with the agony of this dreadful situation. We had been informed that Ruth would follow me to the UK under the Wives Repatriation Rules. The last few years had made a man of me, but the prospect of a change in my lifestyle was enormous as I considered the forthcoming separation.

The powers that be had no mercy, and on 24 May 1944 I was advised to report to headquarters, with my luggage, to be transported to Durban, where I would board a huge Dutch liner, which had been converted to a hospital ship. The hospital ship, HS *Oranje*, left Durban for the UK via Egypt and the Suez Canal. We reached the Suez in June, where we received a huge shock when we were told to disembark and proceed to a huge air force transit camp. British and American armies had reached Anzio in Italy and there were many casualties. We would have to wait to continue our journey to the UK in other transport; no more reasons were given. 'There was a war on.' The huge camp was already filled with Australian aircrew who had been held there for a number of weeks, waiting for transport to take them home to Australia. With the awful heat and conditions, the Aussies were very unhappy and wasted no time in passing on their situation to us sickies waiting to leave for the UK.

On 17 June we joined a number of walking wounded and boarded the British liner TS *Ormonde*, which sailed through the Suez Canal into the Mediterranean, passing Malta and Gibraltar, arriving in the UK on 6 July 1944. I proceeded to London and made arrangements for a short stay during which I reported to the Air Ministry to find out what my movements would be.

I had to report on 10 July 1944 to a medical RAF officer, who, after a two-hour discussion, decided I must have a thorough examination at the RAF hospital, after my medical papers had been read. I spent two days in hospital, being checked upside down and inside out, answering many questions about my flying and the whole description of the haemorrhage and I was also asked for more details of what happened in December 1940. At the end of two days, I sat facing a senior RAF doctor, who explained that I had developed bilateral bronchitis, which must have been there in a dormant fashion before I joined the air force. I explained to him about a similar statement that had been put to me by a Major Phillips, who had looked after me in South Africa and who was a top specialist over there. I told him that in my teen years I played soccer, which had made him wince, and that I had represented my school at 15 years old, playing in the country juvenile finals. I also was a good long-distance swimmer and had played tech college water polo in 1939. Also, when I was examined in the Royal Air Force Volunteer Reserve in June 1939, I could hold the mercury for 1 minute 40 seconds, which surprised the doctor at the time. This doctor was truly astonished and he explained to me as I finished my history, 'Well, you seem to have a good lung capacity now for someone with your present condition. Also, although you show the result of your problem, you seem to be a chap who looks after yourself.' He then advised that he had in his possession my VR medical test and also the results of my medical when I had been commissioned. He also said, 'And I see here your award of the DFC. Now this is what I have decided. Your operational flying is finished. There is no more 30,000 feet for you.' I was given a medical reference which allowed me to carry on flying. 'However, you must never fly beyond 15,000 feet.' I was allowed leave until 2 September, when I had to report to No. 15 EFTS, Carlisle. This allowed me to visit my family and have a quiet period with them in Bournemouth.

30. No. 15 EFTS, Carlisle, NW England

I arrived at No. 15 EFTS on 8 September 1944 and reported to the adjutant, who immediately arranged an introduction to the commanding officer, Wing Commander Homersham. I sat in a chair opposite him and did not enjoy the piercing look of this elderly CO with plenty of medals on his chest. I thought he would never speak, until he said, 'So you are a Battle of Britain pilot' – to which I agreed. He then said, 'Do you understand, you will not think you know everything and you will obey my requirements at all times?' I nearly fell out of my chair. I said, 'Yes Sir', and thought, 'What the hell is all this about?' I stood up after a quick talk on the qualities of 15 EFTS. He dismissed me to return to the adjutant, whose name I have forgotten. He led me to the chief flying instructor, Flight Lieutenant Stevenson, who greeted me like a long-lost brother. It was a day of shocks!

Flight Lieutenant Stevenson introduced me to Flight Lieutenant Galbraith, an old-timer who had missed operations. However, he had been an instructor for quite a few years. He greeted me with a firm handshake and bellowed in broad Scots, 'It's great to have you. I understand since your Battle of Britain days you have completed a good long period in instructing.' I confirmed that it was so. He said, 'We need experience badly, as too many of the instructors here are very new.' I learned it was a large school and had now to accept, not only new pupils, but young lads who had been awarded their wings. However, as the war in Europe was showing signs of ending, there was very little demand for replacements. Consequently the school had to cater for full-time training and also for qualified pilots, who must remain interested in continual flying and, in some cases, might wish to remain in the RAF. So Carlisle was a very crowded school, with a tough CO. Galbraith had been informed that, if he agreed, I was to be his deputy.

There was a senior pilot reporting to Homersham, named Squadron Leader Lash. I believe he reported to the CO as a supernumerary. He was a great chap! He summoned me to his office on 9 September and suggested I took him for a flight. Carlisle was on the border of Scotland, to the north, and of the beautiful north-west Lake District. Lash pointed out the lovely scenery, in which he was very interested. He asked me to carry out a number of manœuvres in the Tiger Moth we were flying, which I did, as I would have done if I were a pupil, after which, as an hour had passed, we headed for the airfield and his office.

He was interested in a quick run through of my background and said, 'When the CO is not around and we are talking together, call me Robert and I might call you Tich.' What a shock! I was quick to thank him and ask, 'How do you know my squadron nickname?' He said, 'My friend John Beazley, whom I have known for many years, kept me in touch with some 249 pilots.' I was pleased and surprised as we ended our talk. From then on I had three friends, Robert, Stevenson and Galbraith.

As with my entry into flying training, I will add together the actual training flights I completed from 8 September 1944 until 21 September 1945, when I was promoted to an FIS – Flying Instructors' School. However, I will describe some interesting events I experienced in this period at Carlisle.

The local air force cadets based in the Carlisle area had been allowed to receive glider training from pilots of our air school. The gliders arrived on a large vehicle followed by a small truck carrying a winch equipped with a small-diameter cable on a drum, with a length of approximately 300 yards, for launching the glider. Oh, for a camera! The glider looked as if it had arrived from a prehistoric era. It looked like an aircraft's wooden skeleton, with all the required fittings and one upper wing, ready to fly. It was fitted with a wooden seat and strap, a moveable foot rest, a control column for all flying movements, and a hook and lever arrangement for the pilot to release the hook after a given height, worked by being pulled quickly by the motorised drum. When the cable was released, the pilot with a similar control as in a Tiger Moth might gain height by ground 'thermals', reaching a maximum height of 500 feet. The pilot would then fly a simple half circuit, turning left or right and entering another turn downwind, a crosswind turn for the landing approach, and landing. The flying time was no more than 10 minutes. We all checked the glider, gently touching the covering of the flying membrane surfaces and last of all the heavy-duty shaped skid for landing and take-off. To cut a long story short, a visiting instructor spent two days teaching us the glider actions, especially the initial 'rope pull'. Three of us instructors spent the last three days of the week lecturing the cadets and then showed them how to fly. At the week's end the cadet instructor returned and thanked us for commencing the flying. However, he explained to the CO that we were enjoying the flying while the cadets watched. It was forgotten that we had taught the cadets quite a deal of airmanship! We were ordered to return to our flights after the most amusing week for years.

Another memorable incident occurred when I was still in 'F' Flight and extremely busy with the new arrivals of pilots who had been withdrawn from operations as squadrons reduced their requirements relating to the way the war was heading. There was an increase in flight duties, which included officers of flying officer and flight lieutenant ranks. I was informed of a new development that was high in the opinion of the wing commander, which was a reintroduction of a competition called 'The Bennett Bags Cup'. This was a competition for shooting, held by all the teaching units of the three military groups, Navy, Army and Air Force, in the north of England commands. The competition was made up of teams using .303 army rifles, shooting at targets ranging from 1,000 yards to 100 yards, advancing, and shooting single shots, five shots and rapid, under running and walking conditions. Our wing commander was anxious for his air school to win the trophy at all costs. It was left to me to choose seven men from the flying ranks to be picked for a responsible team to win! I had three weeks to raise a team, which would practise on the local range, which was to be the final venue for the competition. The wing commander stressed it should be easy, as there were so many officers and men available. We practised with quite a number of men over three weeks, being driven to and from the range, supplied with rifles and ammunition. In the end we had chosen the seven best shots in our opinion and entered the competition. And we won the 'Bennett Bags' silver cup.

The presentation was organised, to be held in one of our hangars. The whole school of possibly 100 men were to parade in a smart march past the attending visitors, including the Air Vice Marshal of Northern RAF Training and also the senior officers of the armed forces, with wives and families. Also present were the local mayor and quite a few Carlisle residents. I led the parade, band playing, visitors shouting and clapping, and we halted at the mark for the presentation. Wing Commander Homersham was beaming and looking every inch the winner. The parade halted, turned left, facing the crowd and I, feeling awful at facing the wing commander, strode from my position and, with a smart 'right turn' and salute, looked straight ahead and accepted the silver, well-worn cup. The wooden base was loose. I tucked the cup against my left breast, trying to steady the base with my fingers, made a smart step backwards, saluted, and turned right as if a Messerschmitt 109 was on my arse. And I watched the cup do a beautiful climbing turn over my shoulder, with me holding the base nicely. The sound from the crowd was the 'Song of Silence' for 10 seconds, which allowed Wing Commander Homersham to turn to the Air Vice Marshal and mutter those famous words he had in store for me, 'There you are. He's a Battle of Britain pilot. I knew he would do that!' I stood, faced the crowd and said, 'Sorry', walked ten steps to where the cup lay, not damaged, picked it up, fitted the loose base and returned with dignity to the head of the column and ordered the march to carry on. The next day I faced the wing commander, listened to what he had to say and suggested to him politely, 'Sir, you knew the cup was unstable as far as the base was concerned and the way you handed it to me, told me what to expect.' I was dismissed and never spoken to by him again. Squadron Leader Lash agreed with my fury.

The final incident for me was December 1944. I received a communication from the Air Ministry that my wife had obtained her clearance to join me in England, early in 1945. Nothing else mattered, and I proceeded with my flying under the command of Squadron Leader Lash.

By April 1945 I was now responsible for 'B' Flight, having received confirmation of my past test results, which meant my instruction grading was now 'A2' category. No. 15 EFTS was now receiving many more pilots who would be fortunate not to be hurled into the fighting line, although, as could be expected, quite a number were keen to see action. There were now six flight offices, 'A–F', each with complements of six instructors to handle the heavy intake of these pilots. Leave was granted to a number of them, which eased our commitment. However, our work was to maintain flying efficiency to the limit. So the work remained steady, with the pilots understanding and enjoying the instruction instead of a transit camp. The atmosphere was getting happier as the news every day, week in week out, was of the advances in all of Europe, until the news exploded, on 5 May 1945. Armistice was announced for the West. Japan was still fighting. We had anticipated the news, and for some weeks we had, with the help of many experienced volunteers from those we were instructing, been practising a huge flying formation of thirty-six

Tiger Moths flying over Carlisle and the district, as a salute to the Victory. We trained the pupils to fly in reasonable 'Vic' formation, in three squadrons, a 'wing' of Vics in line astern, led by Squadron Leader Lash. It was a great show, and a surprise to the civilians around the area. This was proved by the comments received that evening. No mishaps, a perfect formation.

Ruth, my wife, arrived in Liverpool on 10 July 1945, on the *Oranje*, a huge Dutch liner. I met her and, after much hugging, tears and kisses, packed her luggage in my car and headed for accommodation I had arranged in the city. After two weeks' leave we had settled down, with Ruth very happy and meeting other wives, and enjoying Carlisle entertainment.

Flying continued, and on 21 September I was posted to No. 10 Flying Instructors' School (FIS) in Woodley, close to Reading, west of London. My 'A2' grading had placed me as an instructor teaching the selected pilots to become the future peacetime instructors. It was a very responsible position. Ruth and I found accommodation in a quaint village called Hurst, about 4 miles from the airfield, which housed the factory base for the famous Miles aircraft manufacture.

I reported to the adjutant, who walked me over to the flight offices area and introduced me to my flight commander, Flight Lieutenant Parkin, a jolly 6-footer, who slapped me on the back and rocked my spine nicely. Looking at my uniform ribbons, he said, 'You are a Battle of Britain pilot!' Wing Commander Homersham flashed before my eyes. However, he told me he was one too. The next hour was all talk about squadrons and flights; then he suggested taking me to the wing commander's office and introducing me to 'Basil Rathbone' – or at least he was the spitting image of that gentleman. This was Wing Commander Noyes, a very smart, tall, efficient presence who shook hands and gave me a hearty welcome, ending with, 'Do you play bridge?' Fortunately I had played much bridge in South Africa and said, 'Yes,' Parkin gave me a dig in the back but my fate was sealed.

I commenced my duties as a flying instructor on 22 September 1945, and a new life experience was before me. My first flight was with Flight Lieutenant Parkin and in a Miles Magister, a type I had flown a few years before – a damn nice trainer, steady and capable for aerobatics. We returned to the airfield and Parkin asked to see my logbooks and looked at me with a big grin and said, 'Bugger me, you have instructed a hell of a lot longer than I have. You will enjoy your work here.' I really did enjoy this teaching, accepting work very seriously, and smiling at the response of these pilots I was training. I have included a page from my logbook to refer to some of those who were really interested in a serious future.

During April 1946 the wing commander discussed with me a request from the Air Marshal's office, to advise me of being selected to join the post-war Royal Air Force Flying School. He informed me that arrangements should be made for me to proceed to Hullavington, where senior pilots were commissioned to test instructors for advancing to the accolade of 'A1' category, classified as 'Exceptional'. After I had settled down from the shock, I explained to Wing Commander Noyes that it was my intention to return to civil life and to South Africa to take up engineering. Wing Commander Noyes did not mince words. He replied, 'Palliser, if the Air Marshal's office wants you to report to Hullavington, you will report there, even if you leave the air force next week. Now, I suggest we discuss this after you return to Woodley. You will report to Hullavington on 3 April, and do not fail!'

I arrived at Hullavington, having been authorised to fly one of the school's Magister aircraft, at 0800 hours and was greeted by one of the staff. I was escorted to the chief instructor's office. A number of instructors attended, and I was introduced all round, together with Squadron Leader Tew, who was presented as my test instructor for the day. I was escorted to another office, where Squadron Leader Tew could interview me and commence my examination. I was pleasantly offered coffee and toast, although I had enjoyed breakfast at Woodley. Tew presented, for my interest, records of my arrival in South Africa, my choice of becoming an instructor, my time at Bloemfontein CFS and subsequent flying at Standerton then Randfontein, Benoni, Carlisle and now Woodley. The day was exhausting, with theory and practical flying, in particular in the Tiger Moth, Magister and Harvard, and concentrating on the intense flying programme. I realised the importance of the depth of knowledge and experience that was expected of me. However, as I returned to Woodley, I felt happy about my capabilities and relaxed when I arrived and proceeded to my lodgings and my wife.

I continued instructing until 24 April 1946 and, after a period of leave, until 16 May, I was posted to the RAF Post War Central Flying School (Elementary). The school was based at South Cerney near Cirencester and close to the command centre at Little Rissington, all in the beautiful Cotswolds, and very close to Oxford. I had qualified for my 'A1' classification. I was introduced to so many instructors and ground staff that I have forgotten their names.

I was appointed as 'B' Flight commander and attended meetings as to responsibilities relating to pupils and their experiences. We flight commanders had to prepare lectures on flying characteristics, and remind pupils of the whole of the list of air force flying instructions. The would-be instructors were a mixture of nationalities: UK, Australian, Canadian, South African, Indians from the Punjab, Poles, Czechs, Dutch, and so on. Most of them had experienced air action, but at the tail end of the war. However, they all had many hours of flying, including experience in different types of aircraft. We worked hard to bring the flight units into full operation. It took many days before we were reporting to headquarters of the success of all procedures. The theory part was a huge success, and I can say what a thrill it was to renew the lectures, reminding me that theory was a serious addition to the aptitude of flying.

In this post-war recognition of training, it was a pleasure to have time for sport, as in previous years. Also, for the mixture of nations, arrangements were made to have occasional organised bus trips to show the pupils the lovely countryside the Cotswolds had to offer. These trips included the wives of instructors, who would offer explanations of Britain's countryside. I was able to take my wife, a South African girl, and she was thrilled. I had found accommodation on one of the local farms, which was a big change for us and a happy one.

Flying training settled down, and we were kept busy with different pupils, according to their flying experience. We used the Tiger Moth, Miles Magister, and Harvard, day and night, with two afternoons per week for theory of flight. Our training had depth, particularly as we had to study the characteristics of the four-engine aircraft, so as to be able to fly all aircraft if necessary. We did not include jet aircraft at this time.

While we were stationed at Woodley, Ruth and I discussed the idea of my remaining in the RAF. I explained to her that my length of service had allowed me to leave the air force at Christmas 1945. However, I had signed on for one more year in order to realise the final effort of obtaining the class of 'A1' instructor. It was my aim to leave the air force in the near future for us to return to South Africa and for me to finish my fifth year of my engineering diploma. When I had joined the RAFVR in 1939 I had finished my fourth year.

One day in August 1946 I was at a meeting discussing the progress in

South Cerney when I heard that, after the training school in Egypt had been lost, plans were being made to open an old pre-war flying school in Rhodesia. I immediately applied to speak to the commanding officer at Little Rissington, a request that was granted. I appealed to him to assist me in applying for a posting to Rhodesia, as I wished to return to South Africa at the end of my second extra year, to return to engineering and civil life. The CO listened and advised me that he held my records, as he must, after I had been posted to his command. He understood my wife was a South African and that we had been married there. After further discussion, he agreed to help me. I returned to South Cerney and explained the situation to the commanding officer, who advised me to report to Rissington. He agreed to the possibility of my application and I returned to my work.

It was 26 September when I was called to the CO's office to be told I had been accepted for a posting to southern Rhodesia, and would receive instructions from a Wing Commander Lunn, in a few days. I was advised to pack up and give notice to our landlady that we were to leave for yet another destiny. I said goodbye to my friends and I looked towards the airfield of Little Rissington, where, in April 1940, I had arrived from Perth, 11 EFTS, to commence my intermediate and advanced training for my wings. It was a 360-degree turn in my career. Destiny is nebulous, an unknown factor. However, it has looked after me in the utmost manner. I had time to remember those barmy days when we completed our courses and raced for the equipment store after reading the notice of those who had passed their wings exams. That meant we received two pairs of cloth wings for 4d each. Then the quickest thing I ever did was sew them on my uniform!

31. Royal Air Force, Southern Rhodesia

On 5 October 1946 I proceeded to the special train in London and boarded the SS *Orontes* at the London Tilbury Docks. The voyage was very interesting. We sailed past Gibraltar and through the Mediterranean, passing Malta, which brought back sad memories. We then went through the Suez Canal and down the African coast to Durban in South Africa, where we arrived on 27 October.

Our new commanding officer, Group Captain Judge, was an extremely hard officer, and he had made it clear to the officers and NCOs that he would not tolerate any nonsense during the voyage, nor the train journey to Rhodesia, from the hundred-plus airmen who would be the different working parties in running the flying school. It took little time for us to board the special troop train, which would carry us north through Natal, the Orange Free State and Johannesburg in the Transvaal, and then on to Bulawayo and Heany.

I had managed to phone my wife's mother and given her the approximate time when we would reach Johannesburg, where we would have an hour's rest while food, water, and supplies were obtained for the train. Group Captain Judge and Wing Commander Lunn called the officers and NCOs together and stressed that it was up to us to see that none of the airmen left the platform or misbehaved. The railway personnel would be there to assist us. We arrived in Johannesburg on time at approximately 11.00 a.m. I had been given permission to meet my wife's family, as I knew, as well as an exchange of greetings, they would want to know why Ruth was not with me. The agonies of military service! The family were there, and I spent half an hour with everyone talking at once, with tears, laughter and questions. I was sad, as Ruth's mother, whom I cherished, was ill and could not be there. However, she had sent a lovely letter for me to digest. I felt there and then that I was home at last and I would enjoy my final year in Rhodesia and return to study and enter civilian life. The order came for me to board the train. We continued our journey to Bulawayo, where we would have a fleet of cars and buses to take the contingent to Heany Airfield about 20 miles north-east of the city.

The RAF Heany Air School was a post-war airfield, but it had been partially used through the early 1940s, so all the necessities, living quarters, hangars, messes and so on were in good condition in this hot, dry climate. However, it would take some time to bring it to acceptable operation. So it was all hands to work, and let us be proud of success! While the CO and Administration commenced their duties, the flying personnel worked on the valuation of the many aircraft in the hangars. Aircraft of all makes had been parked there for a few years, which would mean hard work for the mechanics and officers with the cross section of trades necessary. The pilots had many tests to carry out, on the ground and in the air, to bring the training up to standard. The aircraft were Tiger Moth (DH82A), Harvard II, Anson, Miles Magister, Cornell and Miles Master I and II – the latter not for training. The whole air school was a hive of industry, from 31 October until 20 November, when the first flight was launched. At that time, I took Squadron Leader Buckley to Cranbourne, another training centre in Rhodesia.

Twelve flights were logged satisfactorily in November. I flew Wing Commander Lunn to Pietersburg, a large air force base in the northern Transvaal, South Africa, where he discussed the takeover of a number of Tiger Moth aircraft that could be released to Heany. Wing Commander Lunn was advised that several Tiger Moths were to be picked up from Pretoria. We returned to Heany the same day, after all arrangements had been completed.

On 30 November Wing Commander Lunn called me to his office with my logbook. After a long friendly chat, he looked through my logbook and explained that the confirmation of my 'A1' category had been received too late to catch our departure. The wing commander had received the details, which, he said, would allow him to place his stamp covering the Air Ministry item in the last record of my flying at Woodley, as that was my last FIS school. This accompanied my 'Leaving Certificate' assessment.

In December we experienced a short flying programme. We flew senior Rhodesian officers who had joined the new flying programme, from Pietersburg, where they had helped to arrange for some of the aircraft for delivery to Heany. We would be sent to fly them to Heany at a later date. We filled the second half of the month helping to complete ground and flying tests of the aircraft, which had been serviced. Christmas and New Year we were allowed a number of days to visit Bulawayo and see some of the historical places and enjoy the city's welcome.

January 1947 meant more flying, checking the new flying instructors and visiting the flying school in Salisbury, the headquarters of the Rhodesia air force. During the first week we received a request from the government, asking if we could use our aircraft to help them find a number of explorers who were missing in the rugged territory close to the Zambezi River. Group Captain Judge approved a search to Wing Commander Lunn, who suggested I use three Harvard aircraft to search the territory suggested. I would take Flying Officer Cant, our air force doctor, who would carry some medical supplies with him. I briefed the two pilots that we would fly in open formation about half a mile apart, flying at 1,000–2,000 feet. With a range time of $2\frac{1}{2}$ hours, we could cover a good area of the district suggested. We patrolled a vast area, sometimes coming down to 500 feet along the bank of the mighty river. We had calculated that, as we had a westerly wind, we might be drifting too far along the river. We returned to Heany for refuelling, when Squadron Leader Lunn walked across the tarmac and told us the explorers had been located along the river to the west of our search. The authorities had been informed of the news by tribal natives using 'tom toms' (tribal drums) to send a message to the commissioner and his men that they had located their camp approximately 50 miles west of where we had been advised to patrol.

In February I had to fly SAAF pilots to Pretoria to bring back to Heany a number of Tiger Moths. We used one of the Ansons that had been checked, and I piloted the plane to Swartkop Airfield in Pretoria. It was a fine sunny day and the pilots made themselves comfortable in this old aircraft. The map showed us our first sighting, the Limpopo River. I sighted a river that was completely dried up, with no signs of life, and thought that the Limpopo must be further south. This we all agreed. Just at that time we ran into a heavy rainstorm, which had suddenly developed. There was a 'bang' on the starboard wing as the fastener over the fuel tank flew off. The next thing, a large leak developed down the side of the windscreen. One of the pilots sitting beside me in the navigator seat yelled, 'What next?' As if in answer, there was a really heavy jolt, and the Perspex in the nose where the bomb aimer might be blew right off its fastening. Thank God we were in clear air now.

In all the banging, I checked the map and realised from the ridge of the low mountains we were crossing at that time that the Limpopo River was indeed very dry. With Pretoria on the horizon, the pilot next to me said, 'Hey, I didn't know the Anson could do 240 mph.' 'Don't be damned silly!' I said, as I looked at the gauge, which had been moving between 120 and 130 mph. Now it was moving around the dial like a drunken sailor. I could feel the Anson was on an even keel, but what was happening? The pitot head must have been damaged.

As we approached Pretoria, I had been flying at 4,000 feet. I gained height to 5,000 feet and warned the other pilots I was going to 'stall' the Anson to feel the reaction of the airframe. With no speedometer, the Anson created a slight vibration and waffled into the stall, which I corrected immediately. I tried it once more and calculated I was pretty sure of the landing. But the radio had died. I entered the circuit at, I estimated, 80 mph, and, as the main runway was north–south, I flew a little wide of the downwind leg on which we were flying, made a wide turn to port, and gave myself room for a fairly long approach. I was grateful for the wind direction. I had blipped the engines as I was on the downwind leg. I came off the boundary at 50 feet, experiencing good control, and held steady as the speed reduced to just over a third of the runway. I was about 2 feet from touching the runway. I closed the throttle and pulled the control back for a not so heavy three-point landing, and applied the brakes. They didn't work! However, the landing knocked some speed off, and I prayed quietly we would stop before the end of the runway. And we did! In no time at all a car and a truck were racing from the tarmac. The car pulled up and a SAAF major ran to the Anson, yelling blue murder, and swearing in English.

I managed to exit without falling out of the aircraft to apologise the best I could, when the swearing tapered away and a voice said, 'Tich Palliser. What the hell do you think you are doing with a landing like that?!' The mad major was an old friend of mine who had instructed with me in Randfontein back in 1942. I explained what had happened while we were driven to the duty pilot's quarters, and the Anson was towed to the end of the tarmac, near the hangars. We were escorted to the senior pilot's office, where I explained about our visit, that we had to fly Tiger Moths back to Heany. We were all officers, so we were invited to the mess, where I explained our problem to the chief flying instructor. He was aware that we were coming, and were meant to be taking the Tiger Moths to Heany while I flew the Anson back. It was great to talk to my old friend Baxter about our experiences over the past two years. It was suggested we should stay until the next day, and the Anson was being checked.

Late that afternoon I was informed that the Anson had been grounded for a long time. The brake system was weakened. The pitot head was completely stuffed with dead caterpillars. The South African mechanics declared 'It was a miracle the Anson lasted the trip.' A report would be sent to our headquarters. I could fly an extra Tiger Moth with the others.

The return flight had to refuel at Bite Bridge, on the border of South Africa and Rhodesia. A large field was used by local flyers at weekends. There were no facilities, so a local garage was alerted with cans of fuel for us to complete the journey to Heany. When it was my turn for fuel, I asked the man in charge what had happened to the 5-ton truck that was badly damaged near the entrance to the field. I asked how a vehicle of that size could have an accident on an open straight, miles long. 'Oh,' he said, 'that wasn't an accident. The driver had engine trouble and had opened the bonnet to try to repair it. As he pulled his body from under the retracted bonnet, there was a great bull elephant looking at him from the back of the lorry. It was wild animal country. However, the driver dropped his tools and ran like hell up the track of the flying field.' The elephant had stuck his trunk into the engine recess and wrapped it around the red hot engine. The result was a truck, wrecked by a 12-ton mad elephant, that would be left there for ever, as the area was miles from a town. Whatever next? The problem with the damaged Anson, which had had to stay at Pretoria, was accepted by the Group Captain. We six left the airfield with the Tiger Moths and a story to talk about.

We were still working on the Heany school in March 1947, but it was nearing readiness for accepting pupils. However, it was important to have the cross section of aircraft absolutely ready, which was proving difficult. Out of the blue, the adjutant called me to explain that my wife was halfway down the African coast, along with more air force staff and other wives. The ship should dock in Durban in early April. When I informed the CO, he gave me permission to have two weeks' leave, which would allow me to meet my wife and bring her to Rhodesia. The structure of the school would be Group Captain Judge, Wing Commander Lunn and Wing Commander Hyland Smith, an officer from the Rhodesian Air Force, to whom I would report, as senior flying instructor. It would be some time before pupils would arrive, which helped us make sure all the aircraft were serviceable. Wing Commander

Hyland Smith and I would test the instructors who would form the training flights.

On 9 April the adjutant called me with the news that the ship my wife was on would be docking in Durban on 11 or 12 April. He had notified the Group Captain, who had approved the travel voucher. And, on the evening of the 11th, I was biting my nails and walking up and down the wharf with dozens of other families waiting, not particularly patiently. The huge liner docked slowly and was positioned to complete the berth. Covered steps were lowered from quite a few positions, and I was tense and jittery. I was sure that waiting for a fourth action scramble on 15 September 1940 was child's play compared to this!

Eventually Ruth, together with other families, was running to me, tears pouring down her face, which I matched. It took a while to settle down. People came from the SAAF office, informing us they were there to help us through the authorities, and a hotel had been booked for the night, after which a train to Johannesburg, then Bulawayo, had been organised. Three other wives of our officers accompanied us to the hotel, where we cried, laughed, joked, and talked as much as possible. I had notified Ruth's family when we would be in Johannesburg, and we would be staying with her second sister. Ruth's mother was very ill. We had a wonderful four days with the family, and we spent plenty of time with Ruth's mother. Ruth being the baby of the five lovely redheads, there was much to discuss – more than time would allow. So we enjoyed the families, with more tears and hugs; even the husbands got into the act!

So, on 16 April 1947, two happy people were 'home' at last, and ready to finish our air force career and launch into living and working in Johannesburg. We agreed it was much better for me to finish my fifth year of engineering, having completed four years in the RAF Volunteer Reserve. I arranged accommodation in a comfortable residential hotel in a park area of Bulawayo. As it turned out, the others would join us, as would a number who had arrived in the first voyage. This was excellent for Ruth.

I reported for further duty on 19 April, thanking Group Captain Judge for the leave I had just had. The following day saw the first flight tests of three new pupils, after which I finished testing more aircraft.

In May and June we were absorbed ferrying around some of the commissioned ground people and administrative staff. The trips were fairly long: Pretoria, Salisbury, Thornhill, Kumalo – all overnight trips. Then there was the first air test with three pupils in an Anson, and one air test in a newly built Tiger Moth for aerobatic qualities, which was great fun. I finished the test by completing a 'falling leaf' manoeuvre, which made the CO grind his teeth. Also in late June I was asked to fly a Rhodesian army colonel, to give him a flight in one of the newly overhauled Harvards – however, steep turns only.

On 26 June Wing Commanders Lunn and Hyland Smith were asked to form a wing of five Harvards, in arrow formation, and perform a low-flying formation salute at a service being held at Bulawayo Airfield. We believed it was for a Rhodesian Memorial Battle Anniversary, and there would be quite a crowd in attendance. There was also a request for a short aerobatic display before we returned to Heany. After the double flypast, I was to break away and satisfy the crowd. I reached 5,000 feet and did a slow 'roll right and left'. Then I approached 6,000 feet and broke into a 'spin', recovering after four turns. Then, for the hell of it, I completed a 'flick roll' left and right and returned to Heany. The wing commander gave me a hard look and walked away. They were the last aerobatics I would do in my life.

The school came to life in July 1947, with young pupils and quite a number of officers and NCOs. There were instructors to be tested and final proof of readiness for teaching to be shown. Then August and September saw my last flights of my total service.

Then, on 1 October 1947, after a hot party in the evening, and a moment for us to clear our heads and complete our thank yous, we boarded the evening train in Bulawayo to Johannesburg. Ruth had been with me long enough in Heany, and we had been able to relive the memories of our separation, with tears in our eyes and heavy sobs. Now we thanked God and destiny for our chance to carve out a new life.

Epilogue

In November 1947 I was enrolled in Johannesburg Engineering College for two years, two nights a week, 7.00 p.m.–10.00 p.m. I accepted a position of junior draftsman from the engineer I had been introduced to in 1942. I would be learning a cross section of engineering work, with a very understanding employer who respected my civil life, with the interference of seven years of air force and war to recover from.

In January 1951 one of the largest engineering companies in South Africa, Fraser and Chalmers, offered me a position in one of its departments. My mentor, who had motivated me in grasping much knowledge, technical and general, and filled me with confidence, suggested I should accept, as he was ready to retire. I accepted, and added to my knowledge much information and confidence in the operational side of the gold and uranium mining business.

In July 1959 I was offered a position in a small company, West & Du Toit, which had obtained a franchise selling oil hydraulic equipment. It could not hold the business unless an engineer was employed to be responsible for the hydraulic equipment. The company in question was Sperry Vickers, a division of Sperry Rand Corporation of America, one of the world's largest firms, not to be confused with UK Vickers Armstrong. The business prospered, as oil hydraulics, coupled with pneumatics and 'electro tecs', was making big roads in engineering.

I was eventually appointed Sales Manager in August 1965. Eventually Sperry Vickers bought out West & Du Toit, and appointed me as General Manager of 'Sperry Vickers Hydraulics SA'. In July 1967 I was appointed Managing Director of the business covering all of South Africa, with agencies in Africa, up to Nigeria and all parts south of the Sahara Desert. Then in May 1970 I was appointed Managing Director of Sperry Corporation, covering Sperry Vickers, Univac Computers, New Holland Agricultural, Sperry Office Equipment and the shortly to be divested Remington Shaver.

In July 1973 I was interviewed by Head Office. During the interview I was requested to consider a transfer to the Far East with responsibility for Sperry Vickers Hydraulics, covering Australia, New Zealand, and all of Asia and with annual visits to Japan and India. I accepted the responsibility in July 1974, but only if I could operate from Melbourne, Australia, the reason being that I was 55 years old, married, with one daughter who was finishing college. Hong Kong and Singapore were impossible for my family to suffer the intense heat.

I finally retired in January 1982, after enjoying a wonderful career. I was supported in my retirement by my wife Ruth and my daughter Gill. Then I adopted another daughter, Marianne. After the loss of my dear wife, my two daughters have cared for me.

Acknowledgements

A big thank you to the following people: Wing Commander Tom Neil DFC*, AFC, AE, Bronze Star (USA) (RAF Retd) for use of photographs from his publications and use of his two wonderful paintings; Bob Yeoman and Chris Yeoman, for making the publishing of this book possible, and David Pritchard for the cover images; Nick Lawson, for extensive technical help; Robert Crossey for helping with terminology in the 'Malta' section of the book, and Brian Burton, for assistance with editing.

Index

Action involving Squadron Leader Barton and Pilot Officer Palliser. (*Courtesy of Tom Neil*)